SUBVERSION

Other Titles of Interest from Georgetown University Press

From Quills to Tweets: How America Communicates about War and Revolution
Andrea J. Dew, Marc A. Genest, and S. C. M. Paine, editors

Russian Cyber Operations: Coding the Boundaries of Conflict
Scott Jasper

The Russian Understanding of War: Blurring the Lines between War and Peace
Oscar Jonsson

Surrogate Warfare: The Transformation of War in the Twenty-First Century
Andreas Krieg and Jean-Marc Rickli

ANDREAS KRIEG

SUBVERSION

THE STRATEGIC
WEAPONIZATION
OF NARRATIVES

GEORGETOWN UNIVERSITY PRESS / WASHINGTON, DC

The publisher is not responsible for third-party websites or their content. URL links were active at time of publication.

Library of Congress Cataloging-in-Publication Data

Names: Krieg, Andreas, author.
Title: Subversion: the strategic weaponization of narratives / Andreas Krieg.
Description: Washington, DC: Georgetown University Press, 2023. | Includes
    bibliographical references and index.
Identifiers: LCCN 2022022616 (print) | LCCN 2022022617 (ebook) |
    ISBN 9781647123352 (hardcover) | ISBN 9781647123369 (paperback) |
    ISBN 9781647123376 (ebook)
Subjects: LCSH: Information warfare. | Narration (Rhetoric) | Subversive activities.
Classification: LCC U163.K75 2023 (print) | LCC U163 (ebook) |
    DDC 355.3/43—dc23/eng/20221221
LC record available at https://lccn.loc.gov/2022022616
LC ebook record available at https://lccn.loc.gov/2022022617

♾ This paper meets the requirements of ANSI/NISO Z39.48-1992 (Permanence of Paper).

24 23   9 8 7 6 5 4 3 2 First printing

Printed in the United States of America

Cover design by Jeremy John Parker
Interior design by BookComp, Inc.

CONTENTS

ACKNOWLEDGMENTS

The beginnings of this book take me back to early 2018 as I was putting together an idea for an edited volume on the Gulf Crisis that had divided the region since June 2017. For the first time a political crisis between neighboring Arab Gulf state regimes had spilled into the public sphere, polarizing and mobilizing the people of the region and beyond. At a diplomatic stalemate in 2018, the crisis appeared to have moved entirely into the information environment, where weaponized narratives kept fanning the flames, with tangible effects both on regional civil-societal mobilization as well as academic and policy-making discourse in the West. The research on the origins, motivations, and solutions to the Gulf Crisis, which was only formally solved in 2021, opened my eyes to the potency of information and influence operations. I am ever so grateful for the often-polarizing academic debate on this issue.

I would like to express a special thanks to the members and colleagues at the Royal College of Defence Studies, with whom I had the pleasure of testing my concepts and theories. Their practitioner's input has been extremely important in shaping the direction of this book. Likewise, my gratitude goes to the reviewers of the book, whose comments and recommendations have been instrumental in sharpening the focus of this book, which transcends a variety of different academic disciplines. Pushing the boundaries outside conventional thinking about warfare and conflict is particularly hard when the crux of the argument is fundamentally about the perception of truth. A special thanks goes also to the Royal Automobile Club and Royal Airforce Club in London, whose libraries and business centers have provided me with refuges in which to read and write over the past three years.

Above all, I would like to say thank you to my amazing family—my wife, Zohal; my daughter, Amalia; and my son, Issa—for their patience with me as I spent months with research and writing under the most difficult of circumstances during the COVID-19 pandemic. They provided the necessary balance in times of writer's block, tedious editing, and self-doubt.

ABBREVIATIONS

AfD	Alternative für Deutschland
AGSIW	Arab Gulf State Institute in Washington
AIPAC	American Israel Public Affairs Committee
ARD	Arbeitsgemeinschaft der Rundfunkanstalten Deutschlands
BBC	British Broadcasting Corporation
CBC	Canadian Broadcasting Corporation
CDU	Christlich Demokratische Union Deutschlands
CGTN	China Global Television Network
CIA	Central Intelligence Agency
CNN	Cable News Network
COVID-19	Coronavirus disease 2019
EU	European Union
FARA	Foreign Agents Registration Act
FBI	Federal Bureau of Investigation
FDD	Federation for the Defence of Democracies
FPÖ	Freiheitliche Partei Österreichs
IRA	Internet Research Agency
ISIS	Islamic State in Iraq and Syria
KGB	Komitet Gosudarstvennoy Bezopasnosti
MENA	Middle East and North Africa
MbR	Mohammad bin Rashid al Maktoum
MbS	Mohammed bin Salman al Saud
MbZ	Mohammad bin Zayed al Nahyan
MI6	Military Intelligence Section 6
NATO	North Atlantic Treaty Organization
NBC	National Broadcasting Company
PSYOPS	Psychological Operations
PR	Public Relations
PVV	Partij voor de Vrijheid
RT	Russia Today
SRMG	Saudi Research and Marketing Group

Stratcom   Strategic Communication
TbZ   Tahnoon bin Zayed Al Nahyan
UAE   United Arab Emirates
UKIP   United Kingdom Independence Party
UN   United Nations
USIA   US Information Agency
USSR   Union of Soviet Socialist Republics

Introduction

The Armed Forces . . . has been called by the Egyptian people
for help, not to hold the reins of power, yet to discharge its civil
responsibility and answer demands of responsibility.

—Wilson Center, "How Egypt Unraveled"

The words above are how then–chief of the Egyptian Armed Forces, General
Abdel Fattah el-Sisi, announced the ouster of President Mohamed Morsi by
the military on July 3, 2013. After months of growing protests across a country
that had not found calm and stability in the postrevolutionary context since
2011, the Egyptian military seemingly answered the call of the street for political change to expel the country's only ever freely elected head of state. Yet the
narrative of the Egyptian military selflessly stepping in on behalf of the Egyptian
people was part of a carefully planned subversion campaign. The military coup
that would constitute a watershed moment in the Arab Spring, turning the tide
in favor of the counterrevolutionaries, did not just feature the Egyptian armed
forces and intelligence community but had also received support from a rising
regional power: the United Arab Emirates (UAE).[1]

Obsessed with the threat of Arab civil society to regime security, the UAE, a
small state in the Gulf, had been waiting for an opening to fight back against its
self-proclaimed nemesis, the Muslim Brotherhood, which had won the first free
elections in Egypt in 2012. Amid widespread sociopolitical and socioeconomic
grievances in postrevolutionary Egypt, Abu Dhabi had found a receptive audience among secular liberals in the country alienated by the incompetence of
the Brotherhood government. Instead of relying on conventional hard power,
the UAE began to target the sociopolitical consensus in an already-polarized
information environment in Egypt in early 2013. While channeling funds to
a small group of disenfranchised secular liberals, the so-called Tamarod, to
build a protest movement against the ruling party,[2] Abu Dhabi simultaneously
reached out to the leading news networks in the country in an effort to change
discourse on the Brotherhood.[3] Weaponized narratives started to vilify the ruling party and president as "un-Egyptian," as a threat to national security and
responsible for domestic instability.[4] These narratives fell on fertile ground
with an aggrieved public whose expectations of political reform and economic

1

stability postrevolution were not met. Thereby, the UAE was able to ripen civil-societal mobilization against the political status quo, building up the Tamarod from a fringe grassroots group into a movement that would operate as a front group to translate weaponized narratives from the virtual domain to the streets of Egypt.[5] What looked like genuine civil-societal activism in June and July 2013, with millions of protesters on the street, had in fact been strategically ripened through a variety of information networks, to be exploited by the Egyptian armed forces as a pretext to overthrow the government.

This episode shows the potency of weaponized narratives used by an external actor to (de)mobilize civil-societal activism in the information environment in an effort to erode the sociopolitical consensus or the sociopolitical status quo. Weaponized narratives had been carefully orchestrated into a subversion campaign that would not just alter the dynamics of public discourse in Egypt but also mobilize parts of civil society to reject the political status quo in the country. Thereby, these narratives were not necessarily all built around dis- or misinformation—many were based on facts repackaged into palatable storylines that resonated with the biases, identities, and beliefs of targeted audiences. Thus, the issue of weaponized narratives is far greater than disinformation or the lack of factuality per se. Narratives are the stories that structure our realities, create and maintain identity, and provide meaning to people, institutions, and cultures.[6] Narratives are integral elements to build a societal consensus on "truth"—and whether this "truth" is then built on facts or false information becomes a secondary consideration. That is, even the "truth" can be subversive if orchestrated through weaponized narratives that subtly and gradually alter the building blocks that provide meaning to the world where we live.

However, not all weaponized narratives are necessarily subversive in their impact. To achieve subversion, weaponized narratives require a level of orchestration and strategic effect to undermine a sociopolitical consensus or status quo—as was the case in the UAE's subversion campaign in Egypt. In this book, *subversion is defined as the strategic exploitation of sociopsychological, infrastructural, and physical vulnerabilities in the information environment by an external adversary to erode a sociopolitical consensus or status quo.* As an attack on the integrity of the public sphere, weaponized narratives undermine the relationships between individual members of civil society as well as the relationship between civil society and the governing authority. It is here that weaponized narratives have the power to disrupt discourse in such a way that the public is first unable to reach a consensus among itself and then finds it even harder to translate it into consensual policy outcomes. Over time, weaponized narratives thereby do not just undermine the sociopolitical consensus but also ultimately alter the sociopolitical status quo—that is, how a community, a government, or a state defines itself and its core policies.

In so doing, this book explores how vulnerabilities in the sociopsycholog-ical, infrastructural, and physical domain of the information environment can be exploited by external actors trying to achieve strategic objectives through the subversive potential of weaponized narratives, below the threshold of war. Thus, subversion needs to be understood as a tool of twenty-first-century statecraft, expanding the information level of power and influence in an effort to achieve strategic ends without having to go to war. It is about the careful engineering of narratives to exploit an audience's sociopsychological and emotional state to "deliver information to the target to incline it to voluntarily make the predeter-mined decision desired by the initiator of the action"—a strategy built around cybernetic research by the Soviet mathematical psychologist Henri Lefebvre on how to control and potentially manipulate social systems in the gray zone between war and peace.[7]

STATECRAFT BELOW THE THRESHOLD OF WAR

Subversion has developed into a means and a way for states to compete in the twenty-first century in a geostrategic environment that is globalized, privatized, securitized, and mediatized. The digital revolution has transformed all aspects of human life, accelerating globalization and global interconnectedness. Con-cepts of geography and time become meaningless in a world where humans interact increasingly in a public sphere that is borderless and where informa-tion and ideas are shared rapidly around the globe.[8] All interactions, activities, and transactions between individuals, communities, states, and private sector organizations are either shaped or take place in the global commons where the regulatory power of states and governments is limited. In this globalized space, international norms are contested from the bottom up, challenging the interna-tional rules-based order that developed in the post–Cold War era.

The information environment, "constituted by all informational processes, services, and entities, thus including informational agents as well as their prop-erties, interactions, and mutual relations," is one such globalized space where information technology has allowed for new, open-ended communities to take shape that connect and integrate via heterarchically structured, decentralized networks.[9] Although states and governments become nodes in these networks, only a few digital authoritarians have found means and ways to subvert the indi-vidual's communication power—power that the individual in a liberal context can wield widely and while enjoying full autonomy from society and state.[10] Like the international system itself, the information environment is characterized by a degree of anarchy due to the absence of a higher regulatory authority.[11]

The perception of anarchy in the global information environment is further reinforced by relatively low barriers to entry for a variety of actors, of which state organizations are only a small minority. The information environment is truly privatized because, apart from the infrastructure being owned and operated by the private sector, norms and rules in this globalized space are subject to multistakeholder initiatives.[12] It is particularly in the information environment where the state's authority has been withdrawn as the state dispatches authority and control to private entities outside the state's command and control. Assemblages between the state and private sector are being created, whereby activities in the information environment are delegated by the state to the private sector—creating a level of dissociation between the state and the executing agent that provides the former with a degree of plausible deniability.

Another distinct feature of the geostrategic environment in the twenty-first century is the securitized way with which states in particular develop their strategies and policies. Faced with the intangible challenges arising from within an apolar or multipolar international order, policymakers, the media, and civil society find it ever harder to agree on tangible threats. Instead, risks are being securitized in a highly subjective discourse, which polarizes the information environment and—as in the case of the COVID-19 pandemic—make it ever more difficult for policymakers to adequately allocate resources. The process of framing challenges and prioritizing policy responses is severely undermined, particularly in liberal democracies, by how narratives can mobilize or demobilize first the public and then policymakers. In the postmodern "risk society," as Beck defines it, rationality and hysteria often coexist and overlap and can be manipulated through targeted narratives.[13] As this book intends to unpack, it is these loose ends of strategic discourse that are most vulnerable to the workings of weaponized narratives.

This leads to the last defining element of the twenty-first-century geostrategic environment: mediatization. Information is created and shared instantly, multidirectionally, and interactively with an almost unlimited reach, scope, and scale, leading to a process of mediatization where any attitude and behavior of any actor in the sociopolitical space is shaped by (social) media discourse. The information revolution sustains networked societies that transcend virtual and physical spaces and are held together merely by evolving channels of communication. Without traditional media acting as gatekeepers, the impact of social media on the information environment appears to be a double-edged sword: celebrated by some as "liberation technology,"[14] while criticized by others as mere "slacktivism,"[15] for the indignant pseudoactivist in the "age of anger."[16] The mobilization power of information, both online and offline, has created new vulnerabilities as narratives influence public discourse and potentially activate aggrieved audiences. Power has been effectively diluted from existing authorities to leaderless masses, whose aggregate power in both the virtual information space and on the street does more than just disrupt, as the 2021 storming of the Capitol Building in Washington demonstrates. The power of narratives to mobilize "activists" can be exploited to challenge existing authority structures in liberal and illiberal societies alike. Thereby, the hypermediatization of the twenty-first century has made information not just a source of power but also power in itself.[17]

It is against the backdrop of a globalized, privatized, securitized, and mediatized geostrategic environment that governments increasingly seek means and ways of competition to achieve strategic ends with plausible deniability, discretely, and at low political, human, and economic costs.[18] The reason is that conflict in the twenty-first century exists on a continuum with no clear beginning and no clear end. Competition is a constant and takes place in what Lucas Kello defines as a permanent "state of unpeace."[19] Hence, governments and states need to remain engaged in activities that are neither limited in geographic space nor limited in time—something that fundamentally challenges conventional statecraft and strategy making. Most of these activities do not fall within the conventional parameters of war but take place below the threshold of war in a space that some define as the gray zone.[20] As Nadia Schadlow writes, "the space between war and peace is not an empty one—but a landscape churning with political, economic, and security competitions that require constant attention."[21]

Although some of these activities might involve the military lever of power, competition becomes more efficient and sustainable when other activities outside this lever take precedence. The Russian notion of a full-spectrum war thereby draws on a whole range of activities that ultimately revolve around influence rather than brute force.[22] Widening the spectrum of conflict thereby means that all elements of a nation's power are being used to achieve influence—namely, affecting the attitudes, decisions, and ultimately behaviors of the competitor or adversary. In the case of Russia or China, for example, the levers of influence are not just institutions of the state but also influence networks that draw on the whole nation, comprising individuals, the private sector, and nongovernmental organizations. A defining characteristic of these influence activities in the gray zone is ambiguity about the influencer's intent, the participants, and the legality or normativity of these activities.[23] Most important, these networks of surrogates allow states to operate with plausible deniability because the attribution to the sponsor of an activity is nearly impossible.

The evolution of statecraft that goes along with this development has been well described by Daniel Ronfeldt and John Arquilla in their concept of *noopolitik* as an antithesis to conventional Realpolitik. Derived from the Greek word *noös*, the mind, *noopolitik* describes statecraft in the information age essentially as securing spheres of influence not through hard power but other activities that shape ideas, values, norms, and narratives.[24] The information environment becomes the most important sphere for statecraft, where states operate through heterarchical information networks that link state and nonstate actors to work conjointly. In many ways the conventional hierarchical setup of state-craft, whereby the government delegates intent to executive branches of the state, are unfit for the tasks of dominating spheres of influence. Conventional hard power, which today still consumes most resources in foreign and security policymaking, delivered by men and women in uniform, is incapable of provid-ing success when victory today is no longer about "whose army wins, but whose story wins."[25] Instead, statecraft in the age of influence requires states to develop networks outside the core institutions of government that allow the state to utilize the full spectrum of a nation's capabilities and assets.[26] Though the state remains a key dispatcher in these networks, the nodes of the network develop more organically and, unlike traditional institutions of statecraft, are not man-aged hierarchically but in a heterarchical, decentralized manner creating a level of dissociation between the sponsor of activities and the executive agent.

The overall objective of full-spectrum influence activities or *noopolitik* remains the contest of wills—to draw on Von Clausewitz's fundamental defi-nition of the nature of war—except that the means of warfare might be more sociopsychological and sociocultural than kinetic.[27] Taking place in the gray zone of a globalized, privatized, securitized, and mediatized geostrategic envi-ronment, the clash of wills in the twenty-first century is part of a global *Kultur-kampf*, though not necessarily between civilizations but belief systems. Unlike in Von Clausewitz's conceptualization of the clash of wills, coercion takes a back seat. The weaponization of narratives is rarely coercive; it is much more subver-sive, eroding an adversary's will gradually, subtly, and most often without the adversary noticing.

THE ARGUMENT

Subversion is thus a twenty-first century activity that exploits vulnerabilities in the information environment to achieve strategic objectives below the thresh-old of war with plausible deniability and discretion. It makes use of weaponized narratives to achieve influence on the strategic level, allowing an external adver-sary or competitor to undermine the sociopolitical consensus and ultimately the sociopolitical status quo. It is an attack on the sociopolitical center of gravity, with the intent to "undermine the military, economic, psychological, or politi-cal strength or morale of a governing authority."[28] Subversive activities target a community's information-psychological core that affects how individuals stand toward one another and how individuals interact with and trust authority, most notably those established authorities that produce, vet, and disseminate infor-mation and knowledge, ranging from the political establishment and the media to the scientific community.[29] The subversion of trust between community and authority eventually weakens the bonds that hold together society and can help mobilize unrest both in the virtual and physical spaces.[30] This subversive potential can work overtly and sometimes, as in the case of Russian meddling in Western election campaigns, more covertly. Thereby, "distinguishing subversion from legitimate expressions of political dissent is a problem only for democracies; for totalitarian regimes, all opposition is inherently subversive."[31] Nonetheless, while authoritarians might be better equipped to defend against weaponized narratives, the victims of subversion are not only liberal democracies, just as the perpetrators are not necessarily only authoritarians. Though this book focuses on how authoritarians have successfully employed subversion, it is conceivable and probable that liberal democracies learning how to compete in the information space against weaponized narratives are going to engineer their own subversion campaigns.

The ultimate goal of subversion is to control and manipulate civil-societal activism via weaponized narratives in order to undermine the integrity of the public sphere where the sociopolitical consensus is built. Weaponized narratives can undermine not just discourse but also the relationships of individuals with one another and toward the governing authority, which in extreme cases can cause a change in the sociopolitical status quo—that is, in how a community, a government, or a state defines itself and its core policies. Following the cybernetic concept of reflexive control, weaponized narratives are to incline target audiences, both collectively and individually in the case of key decision-makers, to voluntarily make the predetermined decision desired by the information warrior.[32] Thereby, weaponized narratives generate effects, measured in terms of mobilization, on an influence continuum that ranges from undermining social media discourse on one end of the spectrum to a strategic shift in policymaking on the other end (see figure I.1). These effects might occur sequentially, simultaneously, or coincidentally and are therefore difficult to attribute to a particular perpetrator or singular operation. As the case studies will show, weaponized narratives are usually inserted on various levels simultaneously to generate maximum effect. The cumulative effect of these activities is measured based on the level of mobilization achieved, which ranges from 1, a low level of mobilization, to 5, a high level. Only when levels of mobilization reach factors of 3 and above are weaponized narratives actually subversive—that is, they affect the relationship between the government and the governed and are therefore policy relevant. However, because influence develops its full potential over time and draws on a range of activities taking place simultaneously, an activity triggering tactical mobilization on the lower end of the spectrum might ultimately reinforce or support mobilization on the higher end. For example, Russia's erosion of public trust in the United States' electoral process after its meddling in the 2016 and 2020 US presidential elections required

[handwritten note: domains in the context of OJ's... PrESII]

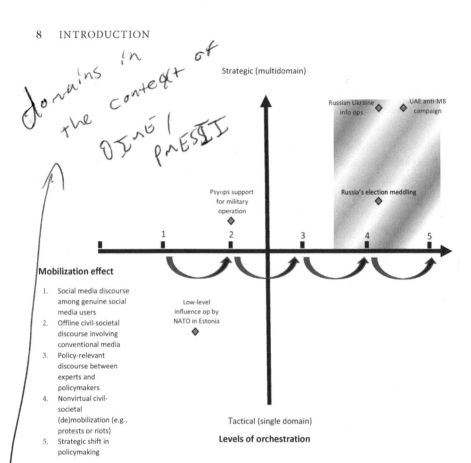

FIGURE I.1. Levels of Mobilization and Orchestration on the Subversion Continuum.

low-level social media mobilization to coincide with high-level mobilization on the policymaking level to generate the overall cumulative effect.

This is why the other axis in figure I.1 features the level of orchestration as another key indicator for the subversive effect of weaponized narratives. For weaponized narratives to be subversive, they need to be disseminated across a variety of different domains that activate multiple important nodes in the subverting power's information networks. A tactical influence operation by NATO trying to get Estonians to engage with an anti-Russia narrative on social media is therefore not subversive, even if it is shared or liked, unless it is plugged into other simultaneously ongoing activities. Likewise, a psychological operation by a military psyops unit managing to persuade an adversary force to withdraw from an objective might have a small subversive effect but is not tied into a strategically orchestrated subversion campaign and achieves only a low mobilization effect. Psyops as an operational support tool for a military campaign on its own does not undermine the sociopolitical discourse or consensus—that is, the discourse or consensus between the government and the governed. Subversion campaigns integrate a full spectrum of influence operations, releasing weaponized narratives across a variety of domains, and require tactical activities to be tied into a larger strategy. Only then can a tactical influence operation travel up the mobilization ladder, shaping attitudes and behaviors beyond the immediately targeted audience.

A MEANS OF WARFARE

Looking at subversion in the context of warfare, this book draws on concepts of hybrid warfare,[33] surrogate warfare,[34] and full-spectrum warfare[35] to illustrate that weaponized narratives are a malign tool that, albeit considered widely a measure short of war,[36] can be just as effective in achieving strategic effect as conventional, kinetic operations. At the same time, subversion operations are not the prerogative of the state, as they are delivered by information networks that are not state-centric and therefore make it a tool that should lie outside the scope of the conventional military. Because subversion takes a whole-of-nation approach, concepts such as psychological operations (psyops), executed predominantly by the military, are too narrow to grasp the complexity of these activities.[37] The weaponization of narratives in part falls within the parameters of information operations, but because the concept (at least in US military doctrine) is still very state- and military-centric, it is too narrow to grasp the full-spectrum element of it.[38]

Nonetheless, the argument in this book contends that the strategic orchestration of subversion by an external adversary to exploit an audience's sociopsychological, infrastructural, and physical vulnerabilities could be considered a means of warfare. Therefore, the metric of violence that is often considered to be a paramount threshold for the definition of war is considered in this book in a much wider context across the spectrum of conflict, which exceeds traditional boundaries of organized violence. Instead, subversion constitutes a means of warfare that, despite its primary effect not being kinetically or physically violent, can and does generate spillover effects that should be considered physically violent. When weaponized narratives mobilize people to take action in the physical domain through protest, sabotage, or riot, then the secondary or tertiary effect of changing peoples' will is violent. In this way, especially political violence, as an extreme form of civil-societal activism, can be triggered through subversion to ultimately disrupt the sociopolitical consensus or status quo. Thus, taking an outcome-oriented approach, this book agrees with the general observations of Thomas Rid that the effect of information operations "is less physical, because it is always indirect. It is less emotional, because it is less personal and intimate. The symbolic uses of force through cyberspace are limited. And, as a result, code-triggered violence is less instrumental than more conventional uses of force."[39]

However, this book argues that subversion campaigns of weaponized narratives can have cumulative effects that amount to an act of war—an idea Rid rejects. The reason is that when orchestrated strategically, subversion delivers death by a thousand cuts, whereby ripple effects of weaponized narratives are eventually violent.

For subversion to be a means of warfare, it needs to be attached to a *political end*, namely, linked to a political objective. A single troll or influencer, regardless of his or her followership, weaponizing narratives without being tied to a broader organizational and political agenda cannot be strategic. Further, subversion needs to affect the *wills* of actual human beings—something that is hard to measure. Disruptive discourse on social media that is maintained merely between trolls and bots with occasional human engagement is not strategic. This relates to the final attribute; subversion needs to have a spillover effect in the *physical world*. That is to say, subverted or subverting discourse can be strategic only if individuals as social or political actors transport narratives into the physical world. Subversion needs to draw on the power of discourse to mobilize or demobilize individuals both online and offline. Subversion cannot be strategic without physical action or inaction triggered directly or indirectly by the cumulative effect of weaponized narratives. This physical effect tends to develop into physical violence over time.

Subversion, so far, has been a means of warfare mastered by authoritarian countries that find it difficult to compete conventionally in the twenty-first-century geostrategic environment. The two main case studies in this book, Russia and the United Arab Emirates, have been purposefully selected because their cases demonstrate how weaponized narratives can be first orchestrated strategically and second achieve high mobilization effects. The ability of disruptive discourse polarized by Russian trolls during the 2016 and 2020 US presidential elections, to affect individual decisions to vote or abstain from voting, undermined public trust in the integrity of the US electoral process.[40] The same can be said about a campaign by the United Arab Emirates to affect the decision of British prime minister David Cameron to launch an investigation into the Muslim Brotherhood in 2014.[41] Though China, among others, is an equally important information warrior in the twenty-first century, so far, the physical effect of its subversive activities in the information environment could only be measured domestically and within the extended, Mandarin-speaking public sphere. However, the potential of China to transfer its lessons to subversion campaigns overseas, particularly against Taiwan, is high.[42] Russia's war against Ukraine for the first time showed how China as a fellow digital authoritarian could help amplify Russian narratives against a common ideological adversary in the West[43]—yet the physical and strategic effects of this alliance of disinformation still need to be seen.[44] What seems likely is that the Chinese information infrastructure developed around the globe will be used eventually to shift from strategic communications to subversion.

Having learned how to control and manipulate the civil-societal space at home, digital authoritarians have already applied their lessons of domestic subversion to the global public sphere to achieve strategic ends. Nonetheless, though liberal democracies are currently on the defensive in the information space, they are eager to close the gap. Although posturing as defensive information warriors, units such as the United Kingdom's Seventy-Seventh Brigade have capabilities that are used offensively and could become subversive if plugged into more strategically orchestrated whole-of-nation campaigns.[45]

OUTLINE OF THE BOOK

This book commences by posing the fundamental question "What is truth?" Chapter 1 introduces the reader to the sociopsychological and cognitive barriers to objectivity. Apart from the philosophical debate on the concept of truth, it is important to understand the cognitive realm of the information environment, which has become ever more vulnerable in the era of microtargeting through technology. Effective subversion campaigns rely on a sound understanding of the biases and potential heuristic shortcuts that a specific target audience employs to process information. Moreover, in chapter 1 we draw a connection between the individual cognition and the wider sociopsychological effects that shape the perception of "truth." The concept of "truth" as a social phenomenon explains the potential ripple effects of subversion on social cohesion and sociopolitical stability.

Chapter 2 looks at the informational or media domain as the "gatekeeper of truth." Building on the previous chapter, we show how vulnerabilities in the sociopsychological domain are being exacerbated by vulnerabilities in the twenty-first-century informational environment. Civil society as the public sphere, which is defined by the media environment, must be understood as the most important contender of political power and authority, and not just in liberal society. Consequently, the role and function of the media, both conventional and social media, as traditional gatekeepers of truth shapes the extent to which the public sphere acts as a stabilizing or destabilizing factor in sociopolitical affairs. The chapter looks at the various vulnerabilities arising from the expansion of the social media sphere, where trolls, bots, and big-data-fed algorithms create artificial echo chambers and media trends that frame objectivity and set agendas for public discourse. Finally, chapter 2 links the media sphere with academia, where "experts" do not just set agendas but more importantly also set the parameters and metrics for "truth."

Chapter 3 examines in greater depth the concept of subversion to show how the vulnerabilities in the sociopsychological and infrastructural domain can be exploited in the physical domain of the information environment. After outlining the history of information operations, we show how subversion can be more effective in the twenty-first century due to fundamental changes in the information environment. This chapter assesses the potential of subversion as a strategic instrument of power in an essential contest of wills. In a context of ambiguous warfare, the chapter shows that the weaponization of narratives follows a six-step process that can potentially deliver powerful strategic effects on a range of virtual and physical domains of the information environment.

Chapter 4 unpacks the dichotomous contest between "liberation technology" and "digital authoritarians," showcasing the (de)mobilizing potential of weaponized narratives in the domestic domain. Although the Arab Spring had initially been hailed as a success of liberation technology, the counterrevolutionaries have subsequently shown that the revolutions in information technology can be abused to enhance regime security over public security. Whereas the "Al Jazeera Effect" in 2010 and 2011 showcased the mobilizing power of new media in breaking the barrier of authoritarian monopoly of truth, the response by authoritarians, not just in the Arab world, has been one of usurping and subverting the public sphere. In so doing, regimes in China, Russia, and the UAE have put subversion to the test in a domestic environment, providing important lessons that could be applied to subversion operations overseas.

Chapter 5 sheds light on the dimensions of Russia's information network and on how the Kremlin has invested in subversive information operations as one of its most powerful tools in full-spectrum warfare. The Russian doctrine of *dezinformatsiya* builds on the KGB's experience during the Cold War but has found new means and ways via extensive on- and offline information networks to promote its disruptive narratives. We deconstruct the subversion strategy of President Vladimir Putin's Russia in the context of a contested information environment in which the strategic effect of information operations can be more far-reaching than in the past. This chapter goes beyond Russia's experience in Georgia, Estonia, and Ukraine to look at how its extensive lever of information power can in the future exploit fundamental vulnerabilities in liberal information environments, as in the case of the 2016 US presidential election.

Chapter 6 widens the debate on information and influence networks to focus on the UAE as an information warrior—a small Gulf state that in the past fifteen years has built an extensive network of media, expert, and policymaker surrogates across the Arab world and the West to strategically shape discourse and affect political decision-making. Threatened by the developments of the Arab Spring, the regime in Abu Dhabi embarked on a counterrevolutionary campaign to disrupt and suppress the public sphere across the region. Simultaneously, as this chapter shows, the UAE activated its extensive information and influence network to not just boost its own image in the West but also to change public discourse on regional developments and actors in Washington, London, and Brussels. Most remarkably has been the UAE's success in targeting influencers and policymakers in the United States, where its alliance with neoconservatives provided it with considerable political capital during Donald Trump's presidency. At the same time, the UAE has become a subverting power in the Middle East, shaping how millions of Arabs look at political Islam, the state, and civil society.

 Finally, in chapter 7, we look at how communities can become more resilient in the information environment, across the sociopsychological, infrastructural, and physical domain. Accepting the fact that weaponized narratives will become a constant within public discourse, liberal societies in particular need to find ways to withstand the onslaught of weaponized narratives more resolutely so as to limit their subversive impact. Because weaponized narratives cannot be contained entirely, resilience in the information environment means minimizing the effects they can have on target audiences. This chapter suggests potential countermeasures to weaponized narrative campaigns that could help liberal societies preserve their character while ensuring that individuals and communities are not falling prey to polarizing and disrupting content of weaponized narratives.

NOTES

1. Butter, "Sisi's Debt."
2. Kirkpatrick, "Recordings."
3. Holmes, *Coups*, 252.
4. Elmasry, "Unpacking Anti-Muslim Brotherhood Discourse."
5. Na'eem, "Egyptian Crisis," 51.
6. Allenby, "Age of Weaponized Narrative."
7. Vasara, *Theory of Reflexive Control*, 7.
8. Rosenau, *States*.
9. Floridi, *Information*, 9.
10. Castells, *Communication Power*, xxxix.
11. Krieg and Rickli, "Surrogate Warfare."
12. Krieg and Rickli, *Surrogate Warfare*, 44.
13. Beck, "Living in the Risk Society," 335.
14. Diamond, "Liberation Technology."
15. Morozov, *Net Delusion*, chap. 7.
16. See Mishra, *Age of Anger*.
17. Kello, *Virtual Weapon*, 5.
18. Krieg and Rickli, "Surrogate Warfare," 71.
19. Kello, *Virtual Weapon*, 74.
20. Hoffman, "Examining Complex Forms."
21. Schadlow, "Peace and War."
22. Galeotti, "Hybrid?" 291.

23. Barno and Bensahel, "Fighting."
24. Ronfeldt and Arquilla, *Whose Story Wins?* 23.
25. Nye, "Information Revolution," 7.
26. Jonsson and Seely, "Russian Full-Spectrum Conflict," 2.
27. Scales, "Clausewitz," 34.
28. US Department of Defense, *DOD Dictionary*, 224.
29. Moscovici, "Notes," 225.
30. Rosenau, *Subversion and Insurgency*, 6.
31. Rosenau, 16.
32. Thomas, "Russia's Reflexive Control Theory," 237.
33. See Hoffman, "Hybrid Warfare."
34. See Krieg and Rickli, *Surrogate Warfare.*
35. See Ryan, *Full Spectrum Dominance.*
36. Kennan, *Measures Short of War*, 4–14.
37. See Austin, "Psychological Operations."
38. Joint Publication 3-13, "Information Operations."
39. Rid, *Cyber War*, 37.
40. Jamieson, *Cyberwar*, 104.
41. Delmar-Morgan and Miller, *UAE Lobby*, 35–36.
42. Roberts, *China's Disinformation Strategy.*
43. FPC, "How the People's Republic of China Amplifies Russian Disinformation."
44. Bandurski, "China and Russia."
45. *Wired*, "Inside the British Army's Secret Information Warfare Machine."

ONE

·······

The Sociopsychology
of Truth

In 2017, Britain's BBC confronted people on the street with a riddle: "Father and son are driving in a car. They get into a car accident. The dad dies and the son gets rushed into A&E. The surgeon says 'I cannot operate. This is my son.' Who is the surgeon?"[1]

Most respondents came up with the most abstruse answers about who the surgeon could be. Only a handful stated the obvious: the surgeon was the boy's mother. The riddle was supposed to expose people's unconscious gender bias, triggering them to automatically assume that a surgeon was male.

This exercise highlights how we filter information to create our own reality, our "truth," consciously and subconsciously. Even when we consider ourselves "enlightened" thinkers prioritizing rationality over emotionality, and critical reflection over mindless pondering, our brain is wired in a way that our cognitive processes remain intact, despite the exposure to an overload of information. Many of these cognitive functions that help us stay sane and focused amid an unfolding infocalypse present vulnerabilities that can be manipulated so as to disrupt our age-old quest to find unmediated "truth."

This chapter commences by diving into the philosophical debate on what truth is—the fundamental question that, in the age of "alternative facts" and "fake news," needs to be addressed. The Greek *aletheia* and Latin *veritas* describes a concept that refers to the reliability in the construction of links and relations between observations. Thereby, the debate on how to derive knowledge and scientific truth (i.e., epistemology) lies at the heart of the modern sciences and is under constant attack by those trying to usurp the scientific method in the era of "alternative facts."

It is in the presentation of facts where the sociopsychological barriers to truth, which are discussed in the second section of this chapter, become essential. The question of who says what, in what way, to whom becomes a more important metric of the information value than the extent to which the information relies on facts. The source of the message, the content of the message wrapped in emotions and narratives, and the audience's susceptibility to how it is being said determine the extent to which the audience considers something as being truthful.[2] An audience's biases become the determining factor in how information is being received and evaluated. The constructivist dimension of truth is highlighted by Nietzsche, who described "truth" as "a movable host of metaphors, metonymies, and anthropomorphisms—in short, a sum of human relations that have been poetically and rhetorically intensified, transferred, and embellished, and that, after long usage, seem to a people to be fixed, canonical, and binding."[3]

From this point of view, truth and absolute knowledge do not exist per se but are always the product of a social consensus. And our cognitive functions are being shaped by our social context—something that can explain how the perception of what is truthful and what is not has become bent in the face of the infrastructural revolutions in the information environment. In the era of social media, the recognition of "truth," and even "fact," has been democratized to make "truth building" an inclusive exercise unconstrained by centuries-old norms of scientific inquiry—rendering the quest for "truth" entirely meaningless. More importantly, the democratization of "truth building," where each voice, whether learned or unlearned, is morally equivalent, leads to a gradual erosion of the societal consensus. This challenges sociopolitical discourse and thereby the stability of sociopolitical affairs.

We conclude this chapter by showing that the perception of truth originates in the individual's interaction with its social context, essentially making the point that while truth is subject to social construction, facts are not. However, our sociopsychological vulnerabilities become barriers to how we use facts to build narratives to make sense of the world around us.

THE PHILOSOPHICAL QUEST FOR TRUE KNOWLEDGE

Without getting bogged down in the philosophical debate about whether "objective truth" is actually achievable, it is important to start the discussion on the weaponization of narratives with an inquiry into the norms and standards that have been developed over centuries in the arts and sciences to arrive at a consensus of truth and fact. Although the philosophical debate on "truth" is infinite, it should not be used as a caveat to any attempt to separate facts from fiction. That is, while appreciating the sociopsychological process underlying "truth finding," scientific tradition has laid down means and ways to arrive at facts—something that is often disregarded by those who try to establish a moral equivalent between scientific fact and opinion. Whereas there are opinions and alternative opinions, there cannot be facts and alternative facts.

In liberal thought, the journey to discovering the objective truth began in ancient Greece. Living in an oral society, the classical philosophers Plato and Aristotle were confronted with an information environment where information was communicated by the means of recitation. The memorization of Homer meant, for example, that students would internalize poetry and relive history through their own eyes, thereby losing the objective detachment from the information. Plato, possibly the first "scientific man," therefore advocated the written word, arguing that information transported in text would allow for an abstraction of the object observed, creating a more objective detachment between the observer and the observed.[4]

Plato most famously illustrates this point in the *Allegory of the Cave*, where he describes prisoners having lived all their lives being chained to the wall of a cave having to experience the world behind them in reference to shadows on the wall. Their reality or truth is based solely on the shadows being projected by objects passing by a fire behind them. Only after one of the prisoners breaks his chains and is able to slowly ascend from the cave does he realize that his senses had misled him: He discovers that reality is quite different from how he thought it would be.[5] He realizes not only that the shadows he accepted as reality were mere reflections of objects but also that these objects were effigies of reality. The prisoner's journey out of the cave toward the sun is used by Plato metaphorically as the individual's intellectual evolution through education, namely, the rejection and overcoming of the sensible world. At the end of this journey, the discovery of the sun symbolizes the individual's true emancipation from sense-experience to see reality objectively through reason.[6]

Aristotle appears to be somewhat less purist in his observations on rhetorical proof. He argues that persuasion through dialogue might never be based just on logos, or reasoned logic, but also depends on ethos and pathos. That is to say that we accept being persuaded when a logical line of argument is conveyed by ethos (the way the speaker's character is being perceived as being truthful) and pathos (the extent to which the speech grasps the emotions of the audience).[7] Aristotle's idea of a golden mean of truthfulness lies in finding the balance between falsehood and brutal honesty, with the latter potentially antagonizing the audience.[8]

For Aristotle, truth is about how statements correspond to observations of reality or facts and concepts that have already been proven to be true. Yet correspondence theory, to which Plato subscribes as well with caveats, still relies on a circular argument, because we as humans have no means of establishing facts other than through our senses.[9] The fact that our senses can deceive us, as Plato contends, again calls into question whether any observation of reality can ever be the same as reality—or whether reality as such actually exists. Take a look at the statement "the Australian viper is the most poisonous." Most of us cannot verify this statement just using our own senses. So the perception of the truthfulness of this proposition depends on how this proposition corresponds to other facts that we have become to accept as true. As Christian Unkelbach and Sarah Rom show, the proposition that "the Australian viper is the most poisonous" is more readily accepted as truthful by an audience than the proposition that "the Swedish viper is most poisonous," simply because we associate Australia more with dangerous animals than Sweden.[10]

Fast-forward to the seventeenth century, and the debate on objective truth still revolves around how observations can be verified without being distorted by human senses and sensation. Emerging from the era of religion, where belief was the predominant metric for truth, the philosophers of the Enlightenment reclaimed the philosophical tenets of antiquity: reason, rationality, and logic. Descartes's famous maxim of "cogito ergo sum" reduces the debate about truth to only one certainty: that nothing exists beyond a doubt but oneself and thoughts.[11] Nonetheless, for Descartes, interrogation following rules such as problem deconstruction, skepticism, and critical reflection could help the philosopher with the establishment of true knowledge.[12]

It is in the constitution of liberal epistemology—namely, the method of generating knowledge—that the Enlightenment, by returning to the premises of ancient Greece, laid the foundation for what we as scientists today consider to be factual and objective knowledge. The "scientific" approach to generating knowledge based on either the ancient tradition of deduction or Francis Bacon's revolutionary method of induction might be the most important legacy of "enlightened" philosophers. Though deduction derives conclusions from a set of proven premises, Bacon contends that induction can derive probable conclusions from generalizing repeatedly observed phenomena.[13]

Bacon's method of inductive reasoning challenging the Aristotelian method of deductive reason was not without criticism. David Hume argued against it, stating that making generalizing conclusions on the basis of causality defies rationality.[14] For example, the famous causal inference "All swans must be white" from the observation that "All swans I have seen are white" shows the limitations of induction. The truthfulness of the conclusions that can be drawn from induction depend on seriality and sequence and can therefore not provide certainty but only probability. Hume argues that in induction, a single observed fact is inflated to build an entire belief—something that makes induction particularly vulnerable to abuse in support for conspiracy or pseudoscientific theories, as is discussed below.[15]

Immanuel Kant objects to Plato's purist thinking of truth as well, arguing that our mind can only experience reality as a system that is bounded by certain rules and laws. Consequently, no scientific or theoretical knowledge would be possible that is inconsistent with the boundaries of our cognitive abilities—something with which Hegel largely agrees.[16] For Hegel, direct apprehension or unmediated knowledge detached from beliefs and assumption is logically absurd.[17] Therefore, the quest for "objective truth" is a circular one, if only unmediated knowledge counts as such.

Hence, in their critique of pure reason, Kant and Hegel provide a legitimization for empiricism as the foundation of the modern sciences. The method of empirical observation, the experimental method, albeit sense-based, constitutes the foundation for the institutionalization of knowledge and truth. It allowed for the sciences to no longer appear just as "natural philosophy" but to develop into a system of knowledge generation based on general truths and laws obtained and tested in a peer review process. For the empiricists, true knowledge had to be dynamic, exposed to constant testing, review, and reflection, to allow one's own and other's findings to be both verified and falsified. Nothing was meant to be excluded from critical examination, interrogation, and potential falsification. As John Locke, one of the main English empiricists of the seventeenth century, writes about his own research, "As soon as I discover it not to be true, my hand shall be the forwardest to throw it into the fire."[18]

Nowhere was the institutionalization of the sciences so apparent as with the foundation of the Royal Society in London in 1660, providing a platform for the sciences to develop their own system of scientific discourse. Scientific truth became a product of a social institution that would remain open for public scrutiny to build trust between the authority of science and the wider public.[19] The idea of the gentlemen philosophers who developed their own conventions and codes (those of trust, civility, honor, and integrity) might sound antiquated.[20] But it shows the standards that scientists at the time were expected to meet in order to become reliable authorities on truth. The institutionalization of knowledge laid the foundation for a "regime of truth," as Foucault calls it, or "a system of ordered procedures for the production, regulation, distribution, circulation and operation of statements."[21]

From these standards and practices evolved a set of norms that ought to guide scientific inquiry in the pursuit of knowledge. According to Robert Merton, who outlined the normative foundation of science in a 1942 article titled "A Note on Science and Democracy," the sciences ought to be guided by four norms: communism, universalism, disinterestedness, and organized skepticism.[22] The first norm relates to collective ownership, whereby all scientific research should be open and accessible to the scientific community, allowing for testing and falsification of new theories and findings. The second norm, universalism, refers to the ambition to make science universal in its applicability and testability, regardless of the status of the researcher. Third, disinterestedness is what should guide scientific research rather than personal gain or particular interests. Finally, organized skepticism refers to both methodology and institutional codes of conduct that ought to facilitate critical and reflective scrutiny on any finding or theory.[23]

Thus, though these norms and standards of scientific inquiry might not provide a silver bullet to do away with the philosophical concerns over the existence of "objective truth," they nonetheless provide a handrail to follow to establish or test facts. Although facts and scientific findings will hardly ever be unmediated, critical scrutiny, healthy skepticism, triangulation, and constant peer review can minimize some of the effects of sense distortion—while accepting that peer review and scientific inquiry are themselves processes subject to human bias.[24]

The closest we might be able to come to depicting an objective reality is a responsibly epistemic evaluation of sense data. The closer scientists can come to identifying constant, individual-independent, lawlike patterns amid a stream of sense data, the closer they come to "objectivity."[25] The epistemic responsibility of the scientist remains to build arguments on substantiated evidence and facts in keeping with the norms and traditions of the scientific method.[26] In fact, for the scientist and the layperson, as well as the journalist and the media consumer, the human mind (as the processor of sense data) might be the biggest barrier to the idealist concept of "pure reason" and "objective truth."

COGNITIVE BARRIERS TO TRUTH

The greatest vulnerability in any information environment remains the human brain. The way we process information sets us up individually and collectively for manipulative exploitation, causing us to create our own "truth" and "reality" that might be dissociated from the complexity of the real world around us. Sociopsychology distinguishes here between two main types of biases, cognitive biases and motivational biases—the former are biases based on unconscious cognitive processes, while the latter are biases that are motivated by preferred outcomes. For example, our tendency to seek out information that confirms existing beliefs is a cognitive bias. Our tendency to accept information from a source we trust as credible or like-minded is a motivational bias. Another distinction is between "hot" and "cold" cognition, where the former is cognition colored by feeling and the latter is cognition not mediated by emotion.[27] This section commences by discussing cold cognitive barriers before looking at social and emotional dimensions—that is, hotter dimensions of cognition that shape the reality in which we live. As Dacher Keltner and Robert Robinson write, "There is perhaps no more dangerous force in social relations than the human mind."[28] Its manipulation can trigger, escalate, and entrench group conflict. Understanding the extent to which our cognition erects barriers that distort our created image of reality and truth is important.

One of our brain's most characteristic features is its efficiency and practicability, triggering our perception of truth to always take the path of least resistance.[29] Confronted with information and sensory overload, our brain has developed ways and means to remain operational, both in the processing of information and in information-based decision-making. In his theory of "bounded rationality," Herbert Simon makes the case that humans are satisficers seeking *optimized* rational solutions rather than *optimal* rational solutions due to cognitive and temporal constraints.[30] As the riddle in the introduction to this chapter shows, our brains unconsciously process information via heuristic shortcuts to come up with a solution that is practical but often suboptimal, illogical, or irrational. The unconscious bias that surgeons are male is a heuristic shortcut that allows us to solve problems quickly but, as in this case, not always optimally. We humans, as Fiske and Taylor highlight, are cognitive misers, adopting strategies to simplify complex problems—strategies that prioritize efficiency over effort in the cognitive processes of generating a decision or solution.[31] That is to say, heuristics provide us with good enough answers, not necessarily with accurate answers.

Thus, heuristics are responsible for many of our biases as our brains try to cope with their information-processing limitations relating to selection, decision-making, and information storage as well as emotional and moral motivations.[32] In particular, when thinking under uncertainty, in an ever more contested information space, where categories of true and false are more indistinct than ever, we tend to resort to cognitive shortcuts that rely on past experience or perceived probabilities. They help us make decisions, solve problems, or provide answers. The case of the surgeon who cannot operate on his son illustrates such a so-called representativeness heuristic, namely, the tendency to judge the likelihood of the surgeon being female by the extent to which it resembles the typical case[33]—and the typical case expected here is that most surgeons are male.[34]

Cognitive biases are therefore integral parts of our brain's information processing and often operate unconsciously. Despite the fact that these cognitive barriers to objectivity are inherent features of human cognition, we all tend to believe that others are more biased than we are. Part of our need to maintain an overall self-image of being moral and therefore truthful is our naive realism to assume that biases are the other side's problem. Ego defensiveness and the need for self-enhancement means that we approach "truth" individually from a standpoint of seeing our own biases as the norm.[35] Further, there appears to be a pervasive belief that one can dissociate oneself from biases to see the "objective truth" and that anyone would make the same judgment if provided with the same information as oneself. Consequently, following naive realism, a person who disagrees with us is either provided with different information or is irrationally constrained by their own biases.[36]

Related to the phenomenon of naive realism is confirmation bias, which triggers people to favor information that confirms their existing beliefs and preconceptions. As humans, we are highly averse to being proven wrong, often making us more likely to adopt a falsehood, even when confronted with a logical, rational argument—that is, as long as this falsehood confirms our previously held biases.[37] Thereby, confirmation bias is as much founded on heuristics as it is founded on cognitive dissonance, namely, our need to ensure that our actions and beliefs are in harmony. Information that contradicts our predispositions, beliefs, and biases causes dissonance and conflict with our need for harmony, inclining us to surround ourselves not just with like-minded people but also with confirmative information.[38] This need for cognitive coherence affects professional- and nonprofessional-information consumers alike, including journalists and academics. As gatekeepers of knowledge, particularly the latter are supposed to be open for the falsification and refutation of their arguments—something that distinguishes true science from pseudoscience. Nonetheless, academics tend to be drawn to research that supports their claims rather than research that refutes it, in the same way that journalists often seek interviewees who support their own personal or their editorial biases. Would the liberal-leaning CNN America invite a climate change denier onto the show, or would the conservative-leaning Fox News have an Islamist on air? And if so, would their argument be heard or merely presented as a straw man to be attacked?

The consequences of confirmation bias on information processing are therefore significant. We are inclined to block out evidence that runs contrary to our preconception, and we are discouraged from seeking alternative information in an effort to broaden our horizon.[39] What confirmation bias does, then, is perpetuate and deepen existing core beliefs as "data and feedback discrepant with a core belief typically either escape notice altogether or undergo reframing to be consistent with preconceptions."[40] Even when confronted with the same information, people tend to extract different conclusions from it as the "truth," which is clearly filtered through preexisting biases. That is to say, we tend to see flaws in the evidence that undermine our position while we overemphasize research and facts that support our position.[41] This explains how news events can be interpreted completely differently by journalists, experts, and analysts—particularly when the assessment is a "hot take" and under time pressure, as is often the case with breaking news coverage. Moreover, our desire to keep our existing preconceptions in harmony with new information leads us to reactively devalue information that comes from a source that we either do not trust or consider antagonistic. During the 2020 US presidential election campaign, statements made by incumbent President Trump were at times rejected outright by many

voters with liberal core beliefs in the same way as statements made by Democratic candidate Biden were often rejected by many voters with conservative
core beliefs—and all that without checking the veracity of their statements.[42]

The Social Dimension

Typically, most heuristic shortcuts tend to take the route of existing beliefs and
worldviews. Biases draw on our existing ontological predispositions, namely,
existing prisms through which we try to make sense of the world around us.
These prisms are defined by beliefs that act as templates for the individual to
process reality—templates that evolve through a process of collective experience. That is to say, our individual core beliefs about how the world works are
products of our social environment. As social beings, our individual cognitive
processes might occur on the individual level but are exposed to and shaped by
the same conditions and contexts as those of other members of our ingroup—
regardless of whether this ingroup is ideological, religious, national, or ethnic in
nature.[43] Moreover, shared cognition within our ingroup facilitates social integration. Common points of reference and shared cognitions on certain topics
and issues help us to maintain our bond with our social surroundings.[44] We
either consciously select our ingroup based on shared beliefs or develop common beliefs as a consequence of being part of a group—nowhere is this phenomenon more apparent than in the virtual socialization on social media, as
the next chapter shows. These beliefs are organized around common themes
and consist of contents such as collective memories, ideologies, and myths[45]—
contents that are often the source for group identity.[46] Hence, societal beliefs
provide shortcuts to a collective experience of "truth," which might be shared by
the great majority of group members or only part of them.

These societal beliefs "establish an order which will enable individuals to
orient themselves in their material and social world and . . . enable communication to take place among the members of a community by providing them with
a code for social exchange and a code for naming and classifying unambiguously
the various aspects of their world and their individual and group history."[47]

Societal beliefs help us to understand ourselves vis-à-vis others by placing them into "our" world.[48] This is especially the case in the context of ideology as a collective belief system that not only provides a positivist framework
explaining how the world functions but also a normative framework for how
the world is supposed to be.[49] As such, ideology is not just an abstract meaning
system used to explain social, political, economic, or political phenomena, but
is often also understood as a recurring pattern of ideas that offers a distorted
view of reality.[50] The latter pejorative approach to defining ideology as a form
of illusion or systematically distorted communication thereby underestimates

the important sociopsychological role of ideology in defining the sociopolitical landscape of the twenty-first century. A more value-neutral approach to the concept of ideology is taken here to understand how ideology as a social belief system is experiencing a resurgence after Bell famously declared the "end of ideology" in the 1960s.[51] Looking at the polarized public debates in liberal and illiberal societies today, ideologically anchored narratives appear to dominate public discourse. The storylines that are being used to make sense of the world across ideological spectrums are founded on simplistic dichotomies and patterns that try to bring order in what is for many an overly complex world of uncertainty. Being confronted with a "messy" transnational environment that is globalized, privatized, securitized, and mediatized, the individual finds refuge in ideology as it provides an illusion of sociopolitical order, either affirming an existing order or providing normative support for an alternative order.[52]

Traditionally, the political ideological landscape has been divided into "left" and "right" or "liberal" and "conservative," with the former in both dichotomies being broadly understood as embracing social change against the status quo, and the latter being opposed to social change and embracing the status quo.[53] A liberal seeks to change the current order in an effort to achieve more equality, social justice, and pluralism. Change in liberal ideology is not just perceived as the motor for progress but an integral part of a healthy evolution of sociopolitical order.[54] Conservatives, on the contrary, prioritize stability and order, system maintenance, family morals, and traditions, while accepting a degree of socioeconomic inequality as part of a merit-based reward system.[55] Though this dichotomy has evolved from a liberal political tradition that is fundamentally Western, versions of this liberal–conservative continuum exist around the world. The expression of political ideology has thereby become ever more hybrid, blending traditionally conservative and liberal predispositions. The notion of identity politics merges these hybrid forms of political ideology with grievance-based group identification, where the split between ingroup and outgroup no longer takes place along political ideological lines but rather divides itself between aggrieved individuals on both sides of the political spectrum.[56]

These ideological predispositions not only shape sociopolitical views and behavior but also determine an individual's social integration. We tend to seek confirmation within our social environment, causing us to be drawn more toward our ideological ingroup. Liberals tend to socialize more with liberals, and conservatives more with conservatives, as it provides them with identity security when their own predispositions are being confirmed—something that makes ideological ingroups vulnerable to "echo-chambering" and confirmation biases.[57] Likewise, attribution bias emerges from us dividing the world into "us" and "them," whereby our attitude of liking or disliking the purveyor of information has an impact on how we receive information.[58] That is, if information is conveyed by an authority we trust or with whom we share the ideological ingroup, we are more likely to accept this information than when the information is conveyed by an authority we do not trust—something subversion campaigns exploit.

Thereby, the perception that conservatives are more ideological than liberals in their information processing mostly stems from the observation that conservatives tend to identify as such more readily and consciously.[59] To state the obvious, however, liberals can be just as dogmatic as their ideological counterparts and are equally affected in their information processing by their ideological bias.[60] On both the "left" and "right," ideological predispositions guide selective processing of information, causing distortion and the oversimplification of complexities.[61] We therefore tend to favor narratives and stories that speak to our ideological predisposition: though a conservative might embrace the narrative that authoritarian leaders are better at upholding stability in the Middle East than democratic leaders, a liberal is more inclined to reject this narrative of "authoritarian stability"—something that explains why Russia and the United Arab Emirates tailor their narratives in a certain way, as chapters 4 and 5 show. The clash over ideologies has become most pronounced in the realm of domestic politics, where the extreme ends of the spectrum propagate irreconcilable positions, particularly on questions of immigration and multiculturalism. Conservative pledges for immigration control are often framed as xenophobia by liberals, while liberal *Willkommenskultur* (welcoming culture) is viewed as a fundamental threat to national security by the "right."[62]

Conservative ideas and beliefs seem to thrive on the basis of sentiments of fear, pain, and the prospect of loss, as the immediate aftermath of the September 11, 2001, terrorist attacks on the United States clearly shows. The social psyche of Americans having experienced the trauma of the terrorist attacks, and the subsequent feeling of helplessness, created an audience that was susceptible to conservative policies that focused on law and order, military strength, and limitations on civil liberties.[63] The perception of uncertainty and threat situationally prompts individuals to adopt more conservative standpoints regardless of their disposition—a cognitive vulnerability that can be exploited in the era of disinformation. The US reasoning in the run-up to the Iraq War of 2003 is a case in point: the framing of the Saddam Hussein regime as a threat to US national security by linking it to international terrorism and weapons of mass destruction did not only appeal to conservatives but even caused liberals to endorse more conservative policies.[64]

Hence, ideology as a belief system mediates our ability to process information objectively. Though liberals and conservatives are equally prone to use ideology-based heuristics to process information, there seems to be a correlation between general "closed-mindedness" and conservative beliefs—"closed-mindedness" here referring to the unwillingness to listen to new ideas or opinions. As Jost highlights, the willingness to accept information that challenges one's own perception, albeit constrained on both sides of the ideological divide, appears to be lower among conservatives, who show a stronger tendency of path dependency, rule following, and norm attainment.[65] The conservative preference for the maintenance of order and the status quo seems to undermine intellectual flexibility and ambiguity—making the conservative mind-set slightly more vulnerable to polarization.

The clash of the "open-minded" versus the "closed-minded," however, reveals that neither side can break away from cognitive constraints. The relative "open-mindedness" of liberals is often bounded by a liberal argument carried ad absurdum when attempting to censor anyone with what liberals perceive to be "less progressive" views. Illiberal liberalism that paradoxically prescribes a liberal belief system as a prerequisite for living in a liberal society undermines the core tenets of liberalism.[66] Taking the example of French president Macron's 2020 comments that Islam is in need of reform to subscribe to liberal values highlights how illiberal liberalism tries to impose ostensibly "progressive" ideas of secularism on a minority.[67]

Campbell and Manning look at what they call "victimhood culture" that enables liberals, under the pretext of protecting vulnerable groups, to constrain academic freedom and the freedom of speech. Both argue that this "victimhood culture" is not so much about fighting injustices such as prejudice, bigotry, and harassment but more about elevating one's own moral worth over that of alleged offenders. The threshold for what constitutes "offensive" has thereby been lowered to a level that increasingly limits independent thought and objective analysis of facts.[68] The resulting moral polarization between proponents and opponents of this "victimhood culture" has aggravated the culture wars between liberalism and conservatism as one side's overvictimization of vulnerable groups has triggered a reactionary pushback, particularly among conservatives who tend to view these liberal debates as coming from a vantage point of privilege. The antiestablishment narratives of the "right" are founded on a rejection of a "victimhood culture" that seems to thrive on political correctness imposed by what is often described by conservatives as "the elite." Political correctness has become a hollow phantom to describe liberal mainstream beliefs that no longer resonate with a growing class of socioeconomically disenfranchised and politically alienated voters.[69] Whether Donald Trump in the United States, Nigel Farage in Britain, or Marine Le Pen in France, conservative populists have used legitimate socioeconomic and sociopolitical grievances of voters to compound a widespread societal belief of victimhood—a belief that can unleash immense mobilizing power, as the following chapters show.[70] The "left," or "liberals," are being presented as the "elites" responsible for the grievances suffered by the losers of globalization—a project that is presented as liberal in itself and opposed to conservative core beliefs.

Victimhood on both sides of the ideological divide thereby functions as a cognitive barrier to "rationality" and "objectivity." Built around chosen traumas, victimhood lies at the heart of what Mishra describes as the age of anger, where the postmodern underdog with his aggravated sense of victimhood demands redemption.[71] Narratives of victimhood have thus been central to the development of conspiracy theories that present "alternative facts" to the facts presented by the omnipotent "elites" of academia, media, and government.[72] The insurgency against the "liberal" establishment led by self-victimized underdogs embracing conservative beliefs has given rise to a new "regime of truth" that favors emotions and ideological beliefs over facts.

The Emotional Dimension

Apart from societal beliefs, hot cognition—that is, cognition colored by emotions—is another important barrier for rational decision-making and information processing. We are drawn not only to information that confirms our existing ideological predispositions but also to information that speaks to our emotional state. Similar to societal beliefs, emotions constrain our rationality and make us favor information that speaks to certain, mostly negative, emotions as well as prompt our activism. To return to the earlier philosophical debate on "pure reason," to think that reason is superior to (or exists in absence of) the emotional state appears to be deceiving. As David Hume famously stated, "reason is, and ought only to be, the slave of the passions, and can never pretend to any other office than to serve and obey them."[73] Freud also saw cognition and emotions as two inseparable sides of the same coin. In his theory of the "heart" and "mind," the primary mode of information processing is primitively emotion-based, while only the secondary process is based on rational analysis.[74] Both Hume's statement and Freud's theory highlight the role of emotion in blurring our rationality,[75] particularly in the context of what has been described as the age of anger,[76] or the posttruth era,[77] where emotions and beliefs appear to be just as influential in shaping truth as facts and reason.[78]

Mishra defines the age of anger as driven by "ressentiments as the defining feature of a world where . . . the modern promise of equality collides with massive disparities of power, education, status and property ownership."[79] The self-victimized underdog, or *Wutbürger*, as Germans have coined the bourgeois conservative who revolts against the establishment,[80] is driven by anger over perceived helplessness, disempowerment, and disenfranchisement in a quest for "dignity."[81] His revolt is directed against the status quo as both the scapegoat and scarecrow of a liberal world order that, at least in the West, no longer delivers as inclusively to the public as it once did. The consequence of this per-ception of helplessness, disempowerment, and disenfranchisement are collec-tive emotions of fear and anger that not only dominate discourse on the fringes but have given way to an entirely new ontological outlook on the world: one where the "masses" are being robbed of their voice, their socioeconomic status, their political say, and ultimately their dignity.

Apart from anger, fear is a powerful emotion that is being exploited in mostly conservative populist discourse. Though anger mobilizes people to act, fear paralyzes in a first instance but creates audiences susceptible to hawk-ish policy decisions. Thereby, fear can function as an immensely powerful driver of mobilization. Securitization plays an important role in policymaking as well—namely, the process of framing risks as security threats mediated by the sociopsychological predispositions of those taking the lead in the securi-tization effort.[82] Looking at the Trump administration's approach to Iran, for example, it becomes clear how important fearmongering was in mobilizing conservative circles in Washington to embrace the narrative that Iran was an existential threat. The United States' "maximum pressure" strategy vis-à-vis Tehran between 2017 and 2020 was the result of policy mobilization that almost entirely revolved around fear as a collective emotion within an ideolog-ical and emotional echo chamber. Years of framing Iran as an existential threat to US interests ripened a fear-based consensus that Iran could be engaged only through hard power.

But what are emotions? As two sides of the same coin, cognition and emo-tion often work complementarily as emotions shape information processing, prompting us to favor one piece of information over the next.[83] As neurological phenomena, emotions have as much a social and psychological as a physiolog-ical component. They are subjective feelings that are accompanied by physi-ological, cognitive, and behavioral responses alike.[84] Thereby, "emotions serve as mediators and as data for processes of judgment, evaluation, and decision-making, which may then lead to particular behaviors."[85] And it is here, at the point of translating cognition into action or behavior, where emotions play a significant role in mediating our cognition, activating or deactivating us to take action. Thus, although psychological and physiological in nature, emotions have a strong social component as well, as emotional stimuli are a product of social-ization.[86] From an early age, we learn what triggers to look for to feel a particular emotion and how to express this emotion in accordance with social norms. The institutionalization of certain cues and triggers for specific emotions takes place through social discourse, as they are learned behaviors.[87] Thus, emotions are not mere biological reflexes but are also powerful socialized stimuli that can be triggered to be induced by extreme behavioral changes. For the information warrior, pathos (i.e., the emotional appeal of narratives) has become a crucial element of achieving a change in attitude, decision-making, and behavior in the target audience, as the next chapters show.

The predominant collective emotions in political cognition in the "posttruth era" appear to be negative, revolving around fear and anger—with hope and joy taking a back seat.[88] At the interface of cognition and behavior, emotions such as fear and anger not only determine what information we tend to engage with but, more important, determine how we react to certain input outside the information space in the physical world. As Edmund Burke famously said, "No passion so effectually robs the mind of all its powers of acting and reasoning as fear."[89] Fear arises from the perception of danger or threat posed to oneself or the ingroup, which triggers paralysis rather than activism.[90] At the core of this emotion lies a sentiment of uncertainty that has the potential to destroy hope and optimism and consolidate a pessimistic state of mind based on suspicion and mistrust. Though fear can be experienced as an individual, it has, like other emotions, a socially constructed dimension that can render it a collective emotion experienced by an entire group.[91]

Therefore, fear can be induced or exacerbated through the manipulation of cognitive frames as the case of securitization shows: framing the world through a lens of uncertainty and potential insecurity creates susceptible audiences that are willing to embrace hawkish and often violent responses to these securitized threats.[92] The post-9/11 securitization of Islamic terrorism has created a deeply ingrained fear, particularly (but not exclusively) among conservatives in the United States that continues to impair their sociopsychological ability to assess Islam and Islamism as separate from terrorism.[93] When in a state of fear, we tend to look for information that provides us with a degree of certainty amid a state of uncertainty, as the COVID-19 crisis has demonstrated. That is to say, when confronted with a complex threat environment, we seem to be looking for information that reduces complexity and provides us with clear answers, even if they might not be rationally available. So a collective state of fear breeds conspiracy theories and simplistic narratives to provide a black-and-white answer to complex problems, as the case of "global terrorism" and the coronavirus pandemic exemplifies.[94]

Anger is a more aggressive emotion that has the power to mobilize information and individuals. As a remnant of a more uncivilized past, anger is the result of a deep frustration in response to a perceived misdeed that creates a mental state of arousal that makes us both more alert and mobilizes us to take action.[95] The state of heightened arousal makes anger-infused information more viral. In other words, information that is spun emotionally travels faster because we tend to be drawn to it more than more sober, less emotionally charged stories—the Yellow Press being a case in point. Anger thus functions as an emotional contagion that creates deeper social integration between individuals sharing this anger, thereby reducing dissonance.[96] Collective anger has the power to unite individuals around information that confirms their emotional state of mind. Outrage and annoyance over a particular issue can thereby help to compound echo chambers in which individuals with similar emotional biases are drawn to the same stories and information pieces. At the same time, objective content without an emotional hook might find it harder to penetrate readership—a phenomenon that is discussed further in the next chapter in the context of social media. Research clearly shows that on social media platforms, content appears to be shared more readily when emotionally infused with anger.[97] Also, political activism appears to be most effective in the information space when inciting anger in the readership. "Objective reason" might thereby be a rather unattractive sell for journalists, politicians, and social media influencers.

CONCLUSION

The American sociologist and politician Daniel Patrick Moynihan once famously said that "everyone is entitled to his own opinion, but not to his own facts"—a statement that seems to neatly differentiate with the subjective opinion and the supposedly objective fact.[98] This chapter intended to highlight that this neat distinction is easier said than done, considering how cognitive and emotional constraints blur our ability to see reality in an unmediated manner. Though "truth" appears to be a social construct that is only ever as true as others perceive it to be, constructivist relativism should not distract from the premise that "fact" needs to be established and firmly based on a philosophical and scientific tradition that dates back centuries.

In this context, Hannah Arendt asserts that being alone and withdrawn from the social context might be the best way for us to approach "truth": "Outstanding among the existential modes of truth-telling are the solitude of the philosopher, the isolation of the scientist and the artist, the impartiality of the historian and the judge, and the independence of the fact-finder, the witness, and the reporter."[99]

However, as social animals, we do not exist withdrawn from the social context that gives meaning to our observations and beliefs. Unlike the scientific consensus that follows clearly established norms and practices in the establishment and codification of facts, "alternative facts" cannot be simply replicated in an arbitrary process of social media echo-chambering. Nonetheless, it is the insurgency against the authority of science and other gatekeepers of "truth" that in the age of anger led many people to spin facts into more palatable narratives, often throwing overboard scientific traditions developed over centuries. Though the consensus on "truth" is constantly challenged by emotionally charged opinions, it remains to be seen to what extent those who disrupt the information space by challenging the consensus can build a new consensus. As Moscovici argues, "the greater the extent to which a representation of this world is shared with other people, the more this world which is of our making, 'in here,' seems to be autonomous, existing on its own, 'out there.'"[100]

That is to say that through social discourse, we seem to shape the tools that we use to perceive and describe the "real" world around us.[101] The definition of these tools and concepts that we apply to make sense of reality is a process that relies on a social consensus—a consensus that traditionally did not seem to be hard to attain. Our gullible nature to trust others to tell the truth by default, dubbed the truth bias, appears to predispose us to falling in line with a consensus, even if this consensus is just a perceived one.[102] Research has shown that even when the majority of a group's members privately rejects a particular norm, they might go along with it when they incorrectly assume that the ingroup accepts that norm. Pluralistic ignorance draws on our need to reduce dissonance and exist in harmony with our norms and values and those of the ingroup.[103]

Hence, the process that underlies our social integration is shaped extensively by our perception of the world and shared predispositions of how the world works. Social discourse helps build communities around commonly accepted narratives that do not often rest on pure fact or reason. They are more likely drenched in myths and emotion in an effort to mobilize people.[104] The idea of the nation itself as a homogeneous community rests on narratives of what constitutes "Britishness," "Americanness," or "Frenchness." In the context of nationalism as the celebration of the nation, Aristotle's conceptualization of the pathos seems to resonate more than logos. As Aristotle asserts, we as social storytellers have difficulty conveying messages and meaning without any emotional resonance. Particularly in the complex world of the twenty-first century, we might develop an increased appetite for stories that can help us deconstruct complexity and reduce it to more accessible storylines.[105] Our "truth" is therefore not only diluted through cognitive biases and ideological and emotional predispositions but also through social deconstruction and reconstruction via coherent storylines. Narratives that frame the COVID-19 pandemic as a hoax invented by pharmaceutical companies and other "elites" have gone viral amid widespread lockdowns and the public fear of the unknown—it provided simplistic, comforting storylines that were more palatable than the uncertainties communicated by the sciences, policymakers, and the media. As it has been throughout human history, we tend to transport information most effectively via narratives—namely, storylines that wrap factuality in emotion; situate events in an ideologically curated setting; connect past, present, and future; and grant us a metaphysical place of belonging—in short, narratives provide a lens through which we can make sense of the world. Narratives, then, offer the metaheuristic for us to perceive and convey our "truth."[106]

The next chapter focuses on the aspect of dissemination that constitutes the infrastructural vulnerability in our information space that in many ways exploits and deepens our sociopsychological vulnerabilities. The new information space of the twenty-first century, which is dominated by social media, brings out the worst in us as cognitive misers, with devastating consequences for veracity and factuality in social discourse.

NOTES

1. BBC Three, "Do You Have a Gender Bias?"
2. Griffin, *First Look*, 22.
3. Nietzsche, "Truth and Lies," 77–78.
4. Postman, "Information Environment," 239.
5. Plato, *Republic*, 242.
6. Ferguson, "Plato's Simile," 25.
7. Aristotle, *On Rhetoric*, 333.
8. Griffin, *First Look*, 36.
9. Winter, "Truth or Fiction," 144.
10. Unkelbach and Rom, "Referential Theory," 111.
11. Lamore, "Descartes and Skepticism," 26.
12. Descartes, *Discourse*, 61.
13. Bacon, *Novum Organum*, 12–13.
14. Garret, *Hume*, 174.
15. Bendassolli, "Theory Building," 3.
16. Encyclopaedia Britannica, *Ideas*, 244.
17. Hegel, *Phenomenology*, 55.
18. Baldwin, "John Locke's Contributions," 179.
19. Peters and Besley, "Royal Society," 227–32.
20. Shapin, *Social History*, 42ff.
21. Foucault, "Truth and Power," 207.
22. Merton, "Note."
23. Merton, "Normative Structure," 270–78.
24. Milliken, "Study of Discourse," 229.
25. Burge, *Origins*, 15.
26. Van Inwagen, "It Is Wrong Everywhere."
27. Brand, "Hot Cognition," 5–15.
28. Keltner and Robinson, "Extremism," 101–5.
29. Fazio, "Knowledge Does Not Protect," 999.
30. Simon, "Motivational and Emotional Controls."
31. Fiske and Taylor, *Social Cognition*, 12.
32. Kahneman and Tversky, *Judgment under Uncertainty*.
33. Baumeister and Bushman, *Social Psychology*, 164.
34. Statistics show that in the United Kingdom, only 12.8 percent of all consultant surgeons were female in 2018. See www.rcseng.ac.uk/careers-in-surgery/women-in -surgery/statistics/.
35. Ward, "Psychological Barriers," 276.
36. Ward.

37. Plous, *Psychology of Judgment*, 233.
38. Festinger, *Theory of Cognitive Dissonance.*
39. Dweck and Ehrlinger, "Implicit Theories," 320.
40. Eidelson and Eidelson, "Dangerous Ideas," 182.
41. Ward, "Psychological Barriers," 268.
42. Ward, 271.
43. Gayer et al., "Overcoming Psychological Barriers," 973.
44. Eidelson and Eidelson, "Dangerous Ideas," 183.
45. Ellul, *Propaganda*, 360.
46. See Bar-Tal, "Sociopsychological Foundations."
47. Moscovici, "Notes," 212.
48. Stroud, "Goal," 155.
49. Denzau and North, "Shared Mental Models," 4.
50. Jost, "End," 652.
51. Bell, *End of Ideology.*
52. Jost, Federico, and Napier, "Political Ideology," 326.
53. Jost, Federico, and Napier, 311.
54. Erikson, Luttbeg, and Tedin, *American Public Opinion*, 75.
55. McClosky and Zaller, *American Ethos*, 189.
56. Fukuyama, *Identity*, 83.
57. Jost, Federico, and Napier, "Political Ideology," 320.
58. Tetlock and Levi, "Attribution Bias," 68–88.
59. Jost, "End," 658.
60. Eysenck, *Psychology*, chap. 1.
61. Jost, "End," 661.
62. Akrap, "Germany's Response."
63. Cohen et al., "American Roulette," 177.
64. Castells, *Communication Power*, 167–69.
65. Jost, "End," 662.
66. Orgad, *Cultural Defense*, 136.
67. Krieg, "Macron's 'Crusade.'"
68. Campbell and Manning, *Rise of Victimhood Culture*, 1–27.
69. Weigel, "Political Correctness."
70. Waldman, "How Trump and Republicans Wield the Politics of Victimhood."
71. Mishra, *Age of Anger*, 406.
72. Singer and Brooking, *Like War*, 161.
73. Ainslie and Butler, *Cambridge Companion to Hume's Treatise*, 252.
74. Moscovici, "Notes," 231.
75. See Lerner et al., "Emotion."
76. Mishra, *Age of Anger.*
77. Wharton, "Remarks," 7.
78. *Oxford Dictionary*, "Post Truth."
79. Mishra, *Age of Anger*, 31.
80. Kurbjuweit, "Der Wutbürger."
81. Fukuyama, "Against Identity Politics."
82. Buzan, Wæver, and de Wilde, *Security*, 25.
83. Castells, *Communication Power*, 146.
84. Averill, "Emotions," 385ff.

85. Bar-Tal, "Why Does Fear Override Hope?" 602.
86. Averill, "Studies," 1146.
87. Lewis and Saarni, "Culture and Emotions," 3ff.
88. Fan et al., "Anger Is More Influential."
89. Burke, *Philosophical Inquiry*, 54.
90. Libicki, "Convergence," 52.
91. Bar-Tal, "Why Does Fear Override Hope?" 603.
92. Exoo, *Pen*, 41.
93. Lewandowsky et al., "Misinformation," 490.
94. Bessi et al., "Trend of Narratives," 2.
95. Averill, "Studies," 1149–50.
96. Berger and Milkman, "What Makes Online Content Viral?" 2.
97. Paul and Matthews, "Russian 'Firehose of Falsehood,'" 6.
98. Moynihan, *Daniel Patrick Moynihan*, 2.
99. Arendt, "Truth and Politics," 311.
100. Moscovici, "Notes," 232.
101. See Bumer, *Symbolic Interactionism*.
102. McCornack and Parks, "Deception Detection."
103. Lewandowsky et al., "Misinformation," 490.
104. See Milliken, "Study of Discourse."
105. Lamb-Sinclair, "When Narrative Matters More Than Fact."
106. Singer and Brooking, *Like War*, 156.

T W O

Challenging the
Gatekeepers of Truth

The idea of the media as society's gatekeeper filtering and editing information is rooted in mid–twentieth century communications theory and defines a "process of culling and crafting countless bits of information into the limited number of messages that reach people each day.... This process determines not only which information is selected, but also what the content and nature of messages, such as news, will be."[1]

In so doing, the media is at the heart of the modern public sphere, shaping and transmitting popular opinion and discourse. By acting as the actual filter and deciding what information enters public discourse and how, the media is a key instrument in constructing the civil-societal consensus.[2] As a constituent body of civil society, the media has assumed what Edmund Burke is said to have referred to as the fourth estate, or fourth power of governance: "Burke said there were Three Estates in Parliament; but, in the Reporters' Gallery yonder, there sat a Fourth Estate more important far than they all."[3]

The media is no longer just the transmitter of messages between individuals within society; it has become the intermediary between the ruler and the ruled that allows the public to aggregate a common public position that can be used to speak truth to power.

Another important pillar of civil society is academia—namely, researchers, analysts, and experts—whose scientific judgment on what is and what is not factual have long determined the metrics for "objective truth" in public discourse. Working hand in hand with the media, academia has often functioned as an auxiliary gatekeeper, not necessarily for information but for "truth." The debate on climate change would not have been possible without pundits and experts weighing in and providing legitimacy and credibility to the various arguments made in public discourse. Of most concern are those experts who choose to distort the conversation by providing academically questionable accounts to refute the overwhelming scientific consensus that human-made climate change is real.[4]

This is the context in which this chapter examines the infrastructural domain—namely, the infrastructure of the information space—including where and how information is collected, processed, and, most importantly, disseminated. Thereby, we intend to unpack the evolution of the information ecosystem from early modernity into the twenty-first century to show the extent to which new technological innovations in the information space change the dynamics of how we process information, often exacerbating existing sociopsychological biases.

As such, the infrastructural domain is the predestined target for the operations of information warriors. Because it is here, at the heart of civil society, that weaponized narratives can not just alter public discourse but also undermine the sociopolitical consensus and potentially alter the sociopolitical status quo. In particular, disruptive narratives artificially injected and promoted in the media environment can undermine the ability of societies to reach a public consensus, leading to a polarization in the civil-societal arena that can spill into the physical domain. Although human cognition is the flag to be captured on the battlefield of information warfare, it is the vulnerabilities of the information space, particularly in liberal societies, that provide the information warrior with subtle access to the human mind. It is here where weaponized narratives catering to existing cognitive dispositions in society can be most effective in shaping societal reality.

This chapter commences by outlining the liberal idea of the public sphere and the role media takes in becoming an agent of societal consensus and "truth." It is important here to understand how mass media traditionally framed reality in order to produce "news." We continue by looking at academia as a gatekeeper for "truth," showing how instrumental the judgments and opinions of experts are in building narratives that are sustainable. Finally, the chapter shows how social media has disrupted discourses by challenging traditional gatekeepers. But instead of contributing to an increased degree of veracity in public discourse, it has increased polarization, making it harder to find a consensus on what is actually true.

THE MEDIA: BUILDING AND
SHAPING THE PUBLIC SPHERE

Any serious inquiry into the role of the media in shaping societal discourse, consciousness, and public opinion needs to commence with a look at the concept of the public sphere. The need for a public space where individuals and groups can discuss matters of collective interest appears to date back to ancient

Greece. The Greeks conceived of a distinction between *oikos*, the private space of the household, and *polis*, the public space of the community.[5] The citizen of the Greek polis had access to the agora, the market and assembly place, where matters of public concern would be discussed and debated. On a small scale, the agora presents an early form of a public sphere that not only offered a space withdrawn from the private sphere of the household but also, more importantly, a political space where citizens actively partook in policy formation. Aspects of the agora were replicated in the forum of the Roman Republic but were almost impossible to find in the rigid estate system of the Middle Ages—typified by feudalism with its serfdom, its lack of private property, and the absence of a truly private space.

For Jürgen Habermas—who famously coined the term of *Öffentlichkeit*, or public sphere—the truly modern sense of a public space emerges with the rise of bourgeois society in urban centers in the seventeenth century. Their accumulation of wealth provided for a new kind of societal power outside the feudal estates of clergy, nobility, and peasantry.[6] For the urban merchant society to thrive, it required relative freedom to maneuver, following the rules of the market, not the state. Simultaneously, the bourgeoisie started to organize in coffee houses, *salons de thé*, and societies to discuss mutual interests and form a lobby that could engage in dialogue with the ruling authority—initially, in a mere attempt to negotiate better terms for doing business. Over time, Habermas explains, these initiatives created a public space and consciousness among the educated urban middle class, providing an arena for public and, more importantly, sociopolitical discourse. Yet this public space was still constrained in terms of reach and accessibility because discourse was still mostly oral and face-to-face. Hence, in the context of the public sphere, the emergence of newspapers in the 1600s, coupled with the public need and ambition to organize collectively beyond the confines of the authority of state and estates, created something that was more powerful than the written word alone: civil society. Though the origin of the written word might have been in Mesopotamia in the third millennium BC and had been provided with new communication power through Gutenberg's printing press in the fifteenth century AD, it arguably could realize its full political power only in the context of a bourgeois public sphere—a space Habermas defines as

> a realm of our social life in which something approaching public opinion can be formed. Access is guaranteed to all citizens. A portion of the public sphere comes into being in every conversation in which private individuals assemble to form a public body. . . . Citizens behave like a public body when they confer in an unrestricted fashion—that is with the guarantee to assembly and association and the freedom to express and publish their opinions— about matters of general interest.[7]

Consequently, according to Habermas, the public sphere now being detached from the physical space of the agora rests on two premises: unrestricted access and inclusive political dialogue between its members. In the creation of this public sphere, the evolution of print media was important to push the boundaries of civil society beyond the physical realm of the coffee house or the bourgeois societies, to create a more encompassing and more inclusive public dialogue.

In the words of Rousseau, the public sphere allowed for the formation of the *volonté générale* as a community's general will. Thereby, Rousseau defines the *volonté générale* as a public consensus to which all individual wills are subservient and that as a common denominator should be representative of the plurality of all individual wills.[8] Nonetheless, although the notion of civil society being able to produce an inclusive public consensus might be overly idealistic, it is within the public sphere that societal beliefs are constructed by merging and consolidating individual beliefs into truth as a social phenomenon.[9]

It is at this stage that the rising print media provided the communication infrastructure to help civil society consolidate an aggregate public consensus that we would today classify as public opinion. This is expressed in bourgeois writing, in the then-still-infant medium of the newspaper, and was an essential ingredient of a political dialogue with the authority of the state. It allowed for the first time those in power to be held to account within the public forum of civil society.[10] It is because of civil society's check on power that the development of the public sphere is often erroneously linked with democratization. Although the natural opponent to authoritarian rule, civil-societal activism assisted by the press existed as an extraparliamentary means to exercise leverage over a largely autocratic ruling elite. For centuries, infant civil society in Europe existed in political systems that were undemocratic but were consequently exposed to a process of liberalization. Thus, civil society can exist without democracy, but democracy cannot exist without civil society. The reason is that the ability of citizens to speak truth to power enables the process of political liberalization, which might eventually set a society on the course of democratization.[11] So even in autocratic states that leave space for civil society, such as the tribal monarchies of Qatar or Kuwait, citizen activism can prompt ruling elites to at least listen to what the public has to say.[12]

In its capacity to convey "truth to power," the media is supposed to provide the communication infrastructure for individuals to convey matters of public concern to other members of society as well as to the authorities of the state. In so doing, the media becomes an instrument to interrogate those in power by setting the agenda for public interests, concerns, and grievances.[13] Whether those in power decide to respond to these concerns often depends on the nature of the sociopolitical system that is tied to the public sphere. Nonetheless, the media's role as the fourth estate, in the words of Burke, relies on its ability to assume the fourth power of governance, solely by scrutinizing the other three branches, especially the executive. Though only an informal institution, the media as an extended arm of civil society ideally operates independently from those in power, siding with the public by holding authorities to account. In Habermas's norma- tive approach to the public sphere, the media ought to be critical and investigate means to exercise "objective" scrutiny over those in power.[14]

For the media to live up to its civil-societal duty, however, it is essential that it gains the trust of the public as being truthful and objective. As Day argues, journalists "strive to keep their personal preferences and opinions outs of news stories, to achieve balance in coverage, and to rely on credible and responsible news sources [and to be] concerned with facts and impartiality in the presenta- tion of these facts."[15]

Most important, from a liberal point of view, the media should function as an arbiter of truth that independently holds the middle ground of the public's *volonté générale*.[16] Only when the media is able to capture public opinion inclu- sively and without ruling elites can it provide reliable and transparent infor- mation that the public trusts. The accuracy and the veracity of the information being disseminated by the media becomes an essential part of its arbiter role as "without truth, there is no way to speak truth to power. Truth underlies dissent. Without truth, there is no way to dissent by appealing to facts that undermine the authority of a leader. Truth underlies trust. Without trust, our institutions cannot function; their authority merely will rest on power."[17]

Where the traditional media seems to fail today in the eyes of many on the fringes of public consensus is in representing the general will inclusively. Within the increasing number of social media–curated echo chambers, public trust in the conventional media's ability to speak "truth" to power is eroding. The widespread use of the political buzzword "fake news" in reference to the media is indicative of the intellectual and ideological differences between the media mainstream and polarized peripheries of public opinion that move increasingly into the center of the bourgeois discourse. Even more, the media in the rhet- oric of conservative populists has been stigmatized as a tool of manipulation by a macro-elitist bogeyman that helps propagate a liberal worldview.[18] The pejorative *Lügenpresse*, or "lying press," dates back to nationalist, anti-Semitic pamphlets in mid-nineteenth-century Germany and was picked up by the Nazi propagandist Joseph Goebbels in the 1930s to justify his clamp-down on the free press as an expression of contempt vis-à-vis an "elitist" government-media complex.[19] This leads us to ask to what extent the public sphere has actually ever been inclusive and representative of societal reality.

Although Habermas's normative conceptual account of the public sphere prescribes inclusiveness and unrestricted access in order for the public sphere to be truly public, the reality of the public sphere in its evolution since the eighteenth century shows that from the beginning, access to this space has been rather restricted. The coffee houses, theaters, and newspapers of their time were part of a liberal, educated milieu and did not provide access to underprivileged, uneducated parts of society—an allegation many in the nonliberal spectrum of society continue to make today. Barriers to entry to the public sphere today might no longer just be education but technical and sociopsychological barriers as well.

Satellite television was first to help diversify media sources and provide individuals around the globe with more unrestricted access to discourse. Fox News and Al Jazeera are two hugely popular examples on the conservative and liberal ends of the spectrum, respectively.[20] Yet this diversification has led to fragmentation, rather than consolidation, of the public consensus.[21] Although access to satellite media is in principle less restricted, individuals are being confronted with a multitude of different public spaces and tend to get drawn to those that cater to their cognitive predispositions—a phenomenon that is discussed in the context of social media in the latter half of this chapter. As a consequence of the media's perceived liberal elite nexus, public trust in conventional media has been steadily declining since the financial crisis of 2008. The perception that the media only caters to the political and socioeconomic elites who support a so-called liberal world order—which many of the losers of globalization blame for the financial and economic crash—has led to a severe crisis of trust between parts of the public and the mainstream media establishment.[22]

The discrepancy between the idealistic role of the media and the reality of the conventional twenty-first-century media environment is owed to a range of biases that have distorted the ability of journalists to depict a reality that both resonates inclusively with the vast majority of the public while exercising checks and balances on the ruling elites.

Media Biases

The first bias that conventional media displays is ideological. Accusations made by right-wing populists that the media predominantly reaffirms liberal narratives that revolve around a progressive worldview appear to be true. Starting from the liberal premise in the 1600s that newspapers and journalists were meant to speak truth to power, journalists have tended to resist the political status quo, advocate for social reform, and endorse values of tolerance and equality. On average, a journalist is more likely to embrace a liberal view on social issues such as immigration, globalization, and climate change than the public at large. More so, many journalists are often trying to take a pedagogical approach to "educating" the public on liberal principles and values in an effort to satisfy what some consider to be their ambition as guardians of liberal political correctness.[23] As a consequence, fringe opinions outside the liberal spectrum are often underrepresented. In the United States, the argument has repeatedly been made that the liberal complex in the US media mainstream is deeply ingrained.[24] Jim Kuypers shows in his book *Press Bias and Politics* that the US media is far from being a balanced arbiter of truth and has a strong tendency to misrepresent news stories through a liberal, left-leaning prism.[25] As Bill Kristol states in his famous treatise on neoconservatism, "There is a comfortable symbiosis between our national newsmagazines, our half-dozen or so newspapers that claim national attention, and our national television networks. They are all liberal, more or less, and feel that they share the journalistic mission of 'enlightening' . . . the American public."[26]

Although the liberal bias argument is predominantly advanced by researchers and journalists on the conservative end of the political spectrum, a discourse analysis conducted on how America's main news outlets report on particular issues suggests that the main media companies in the United States, with the exception of Fox News and the *Washington Times*, are positioned to the left of the political center.[27] Jeffrey Milyo and Tim Groseclose argue that most journalists in the United States are inclined to engage experts from think tanks who are on the liberal rather than conservative end of the spectrum.

In Europe, where the conventional media landscape might not be as polarized as in the United States, the consensus among the main media companies still appears to be liberal-leaning. In Germany in particular, where state-run outlets dominate the broadcast media, Uwe Krüger argues that a liberal worldview sets the mainstream agenda.[28] The dominant narratives that are being selected by Germany's conventional mainstream media are socially, politically, and even economically liberal and cater predominantly to a liberal-intellectual complex while neglecting fringe opinions on both the far left and the conservative right. Contained within this complex, Krüger continues, is a liberal political elite with whom the media engages extensively in an effort to retain favorable access.

Krüger touches here on another important bias that is less ideological but concerns access to power. Research shows that even in liberal democracies, where the freedom and independence of the media are protected, journalists and those in power have traditionally developed a symbiotic relationship from which both sides benefit. Though policymakers are seeking favorable coverage from the media, journalists depend on access to those "in the know" to do their jobs effectively.[29] What developed, then, in the nineteenth and twentieth centuries was a media that more often than not ensured that there was a consistency with government agendas, whereby the willingness to challenge those in power was limited. Never was this symbiotic relationship more apparent than in times of war, where narratives infused with nationalism and patriotism made it practically impossible for journalists to live up to their role as the arbiters of truth. In times of crisis, the political elite often dictated the narratives from the top down, with the media becoming a de facto agent of government policy. The example of British media during World War II becoming complicit in government propaganda is a well-known case. However, embedded journalists during both the 1991 Gulf War and the 2003 Iraq War also appeared to display too much of a proximity to those in authority, making it hard for these journalists to retain an "objective distance" on what and whom they were reporting.[30] The invisible wartime whip of patriotism triggers rallying around the flag, with those journalists who fail to fall in line facing flak from the mainstream.[31] For example, in the case of the United States' controversial decision to invade Iraq in 2003, only 3 percent of all US media outlets opposed the Bush administration's decision to go to war, despite the fact that the evidence used to justify the invasion was questionable and important international allies chose not to support the invasion.[32]

As a consequence, in both wartime and peacetime, most mainstream media outlets tend to fall short of their normative role to keep the government's conscience in check. The nexus of government and media seems to undermine the ability of journalists to function as the speaking tube for the public to enter into dialogue with those in power. James Casey argues that since the late twentieth century, the public has been reduced to a mere spectator that is simply fed premade narratives by a government-media complex.[33] The rapprochement between media and governing authority consequently led to a distancing between civil society and the "fourth estate." But not all is lost. Investigative journalism in the United States continues to reveal some of the inconvenient truths that presidential administrations would rather have disappear—the media's scrutiny of the handling of the COVID-19 pandemic by the Trump White House being a case in point.

The third media bias is commercial. With the privatization of the broadcast media environment since the 1980s, giant media conglomerates started to emerge. In the West, this led to more competition in the public sphere, with public broadcasters such as Britain's BBC, Germany's ARD, and Canada's CBC losing their dominance in a competition for public attention.[34] Thus, while a diversification of media outlets created a more dynamic discourse in the public sphere, it also created the commercial pressure for private news outlets to remain profitable—sometimes at all costs. Idioms such as "If it bleeds it leads" suggest that the media's need to maximize profits often distorts the journalistic approach taken to report objectively. Drawing on our emotional biases of fear and anger, profit-oriented journalists understood how to particularly utilize fear-based editing to increase sensationalism in the hopes of increasing reach and depth of penetration.[35] Sober, rational reporting often fails to compete with reporting that directly triggers our emotional predispositions. Anger- and fear-based narratives speak directly to our emotions and are able, as discussed in the previous chapter, to mobilize our activism.[36] Dating back to the penny press of urban America in the early 1900s, sensationalism is defined by a particular focus on stories of crime, disaster, and war, along with a lurid tone of language.[37] What the "tabloids" (or so-called yellow press) do is reconstruct sometimes complex realities into emotionally charged but easily accessible narratives that more often than not intentionally omit or distort facts. As a result of an appeal to the existing biases in the public, sensationalist journalism exacerbates cognitive and emotional predispositions within the audience and presents facts and information in a more intuitive yet usually less objective manner—all to increase sales.

Additionally, confronted with the liberalization of the market for news, both broadcasters and print media face a race to the bottom in terms of the number of permanent staff they can keep on the payroll. Foreign bureaus have become understaffed or have closed altogether, and the number of foreign correspondents working in countries overseas has been reduced to a bare minimum.[38] Instead, amid the shift from a top-down to an interactive experience of news in the context of social media, the traditional media powerhouses have undergone a deprofessionalization to save costs.[39] As a consequence, the quality of international reporting has noticeably suffered (though this is not confined to the international sphere), making it harder for the conventional media to credibly fulfill the role of the gatekeeper of truth. Today, without in-house expertise, young and inexperienced freelance writers are tasked with sieving through a jungle of narratives, sometimes spinning mis- and disinformation, even if unintentionally.

The idea of the media as the arbiter of truth stems in part from the idea that it serves as an infrastructural filter sifting through the overload of information. Drawing on its own liberal, commercial, and access biases, the media functions as an effective agenda setter, privileging certain types of information over others and directing attention in the public sphere from one event to the next. As Cohen famously asserts, "The press may not be successful much of the time in telling people what to think, but it is stunningly successful in telling its readers what to think about."[40] Particularly in the relatively undiversified media environment of the mid-twentieth century, the most important agenda setters were the most dominant news agencies, a handful of newspapers and magazines, and later broadcasting stations. They preselected information and decided what was newsworthy, providing audiences with an illusion of free choice as alternative sources were unavailable.[41] Hence, the media's selection bias determined the agenda of public discourse and thereby shaped the construction of societal realities and truths. What for the public was out of sight was essentially out of mind.[42]

Debate in the agenda-setting literature revolves around the extent to which the media is actually able to set or build agendas in reciprocity with civil society and policymaking elites.[43] As the fourth estate, the media is supposedly detached from the ruling elites and scrutinizes policymaking while at the same time not simply echoing the public will without any mediation. That is to say that the media has to strike a balance as an arbiter between both civil society and the state. The process of agenda setting accounts for the media's access bias, namely, its at-times symbiotic relationship with ruling elites that allows policymakers to have considerable input in setting the agenda from the top down.[44] Agenda building, conversely, is more bottom up—the media reflects public opinion and responds to civil-societal triggers by condensing individual inputs into a wider public will.[45]

Not only does the media help set the agenda for public discourse and eventually a consensus, it also helps give meaning to events and facts by framing them within a wider ontological context: "To frame (framing) is to select some aspects of a perceived reality and make them more salient in a communicating text in such a way as to promote a particular problem definition, casual interpretation, moral evaluation, and/or treatment recommendation."[46]

Frames are essential parts of narratives, almost like scenes in a storyline defining problems, diagnosing causes, making moral judgments, and suggesting remedies.[47] In so doing, these frames speak to existing sociopsychological heuristics, societal beliefs, and potential emotional predispositions in the target audience. As Singer and Brooking point out, successful narratives require frames that resonate with audiences and that are simplistic enough to reduce the complexity of the world.[48] For example, victimization is a very effective frame that resonates among audiences feeling disenfranchised and marginalized and can be used within a narrative demonizing the elites, globalization, the European Union, or migrants as perpetrators of injustice. The media does not only create frames but, more importantly, also transports these frames to a large audience to help create a reality that is entirely transmitted through simplistic and accessible narratives about how the world works. A 2022 study that paid regular viewers of conservative Fox News to watch liberal CNN for a month found that subjects changed their political attitudes and policy preferences from conservative to more progressive—indicating how partisan media shapes the ideological framing of reality.[49]

It is here that the conventional media for centuries has played the role of the gatekeeper of truth, selecting, processing, and framing information in a way that shapes a highly subjective and literally mediated depiction of reality—a reality that is based on narratives. Adding to as well as shaping existing biases, societal beliefs, and emotional predispositions of large audiences, the conventional media evolved from the incubator cell of the public sphere to a power in its own right that no longer just spoke truth to power but has the power to actually speak "truth."

ACADEMIA AND EXPERTS
AS GATEKEEPERS OF TRUTH

The idea of truth becoming an elite product that the public consumes rather than shapes is also reflected in the role of experts and academics setting and framing the public agenda. Casey goes as far as to say that academia has become a regulator of truth: "The truth however became the exclusive domain of science. It was no longer a product of the conversation or debate of the public, or of investigations by journalists. . . . By transmitting the judgments of experts, they ratified decisions made by that class—not those made by the public or public representatives."[50]

As discussed in the previous chapter, the sciences have built their own regimes of truth that have dominated knowledge production since the 1600s. Drawing on the scientific theories of rational inquiry, induction, and deduction, academia and experts have widely endorsed an approach to knowledge generation based on facts that is trying to provide, as much as possible, an unmediated presentation of truth.

This epistemology—namely, the theory of how to generate knowledge—is inherently liberal as it is based on pluralism of thought, moderation, and open-mindedness. It is founded on means and methods that have evolved from a Roman-Hellenistic tradition and have been institutionalized in "enlightened" Europe, setting the standards for knowledge generation in the sciences. Thereby, the "regime of truth" that has dominated scientific discourse since then has in many ways been constructed around a Western, liberal experience and legacy, creating a monopoly on truth and knowledge that those who propagate "alternative facts" intend to undermine. The "regime of truth" is viewed increasingly as a paradigmatic institution of predigital modernity by those who use the tools of the digital information age in an insurgency against the "truth establishment."[51] From the scientific point of view, the rise of pseudoscience has been part of this rebellion against a liberal epistemology of truth. In absence of a clearly defined methodological regime, pseudoscience derives conclusions based on methods that are incompatible with the liberal understanding of scientific knowledge generation. Pseudoscience is not directly connected to the degree to which a theory is based on facts but to the extent to which a theory is open to falsifiability. That is, according to Popper, a scientific theory needs to be refutable so as to allow for scientific inquiry to be hermeneutic, allowing for the constant loop of thesis, prediction, testing, and questioning, which might eventually lead to a new thesis.[52] Thus, the difference between science and pseudoscience is not necessarily about one relying on facts more than the other, but a fundamental methodological difference in constructing a theory. While science tries to refute and disconfirm, pseudoscience tries to confirm relying on confirmation biases rather than rigorous attempts to challenge and evaluate existing theory. What Popper describes as a scientific attitude—namely, critical inquiry and skepticism—is what makes science scientific.[53] Yet, although method should be the metric to distinguish between science and pseudoscience, the categorization of research into science and pseudoscience has throughout history been used by different authorities to politicize inconvenient scientific truths; for example, the Church declaring Copernicus's theories as unscientific or the USSR's Communist Party considering Mendel's Laws as pseudoscientific.[54]

A good example of pseudoscientific theories are those that constitute the foundation for alternative medicine, whose physiological and psychological effectiveness is not tested scientifically but instead founded on belief. Nonetheless, pseudoscientific experts in a quest for credibility are continuously trying to provide alternative medicine with a theoretical foundation, often disregarding scientific norms of objective and critical inquiry.[55] Experimental setups are often intentionally manipulated to achieve desired outcomes and confirm a previously held belief. In the context of oncology and cancer research, alternative "cures" for cancer are not only unproven but often disproven. This comes to the detriment of patients who prefer alternative treatments to conventional ones, undermining often good chances of recovery.[56]

Hence, it is in the scientific method that science is still believed to set the standards for true knowledge generation. Scientists are often regarded as the high priests in the temple of knowledge, sitting in an ivory tower of pure reason isolated from the subjective and polarized climate of the public sphere—in reality, academia has become ever more entangled in this domain, setting the agenda in all areas where "experts" are needed. As highlighted in the previous chapter, scientific experts are subject to the same biases as other human beings, applying only more rigorous methods to arrive at a scientific conclusion.

Looking at the process of knowledge generation through constant inquiry, testing, and application to the real world, a key component of the sciences' generation of knowledge is peer review, where a scientist's thesis and evidence are scrutinized in depth and anonymously by others in the field. A publication in an academic, peer-reviewed journal or book becomes the only way to make an academic argument both credibly and legitimately. However, the process becomes quite subjective and often creates academic rivalries over interpretation, particularly in the social sciences and humanities. Though peer reviewers whose main arguments might be undermined by the argument under review might be inclined to reject the research, those whose main arguments are supported by the argument might be more inclined to endorse it. Apart from that, editors of academic journals play an important role as arbiters potentially overruling comments made by peer reviewers. Personal relationships between editors and researchers can thereby blur the former's judgment, increasing the potential for research to be published that might not stand up to scientific scrutiny. Thus, personal biases of both reviewers and editors effectively mediate scientific knowledge generation.

Further, as with the liberalization of the market for news, academia has witnessed an explosive growth in the number of new, supposedly scientific outlets online. Amid growing pressure for academics to "publish or perish," new journals have emerged that pretend to undergo a rigorous peer review process.[57] Put out by companies based in Africa, Asia, or the Middle East, and offering opportunities to publish in English, these journals provide mostly junior academics with easy avenues to academic publication, often in exchange for money. Skipping the peer review process and guaranteeing publication, these journals deliver a noncompetitive alternative to the established and renowned academic journals. According to an investigation conducted by the German public broadcaster ARD together with the newspaper *Süddeutsche Zeitung*, more than four hundred thousand academics have published in such journals worldwide.[58] These journals actively undermine the authority of science by granting pseudoscientists with opportunities to give nonscientific theories of homeopathy and alternative medicine the appearance of science. They can help market placebos or at times even harmful treatments more legitimately.

The most problematic pseudoscientific studies published under an allegedly scientific banner are those of the antivaccine movement trying to make a scientifically fraudulent case that vaccination can lead to abnormal development in children—a study linking vaccination to autism might be the most infamous one.[59] During the COVID-19 pandemic, much of the disinformation around the coronavirus emerged from these communities using mis- and disinformation, at times deliberately, to mobilize dissent against government public health measures. More than that, climate change deniers have found means in pseudoscientific journals to contest the scholarly consensus of 97 percent that human-made climate change is real. Hoax theories about climate change are thereby being fueled by "experts" who generate pseudoscientific conclusions that cater to the interests of carbon-intense industries for which facts about carbon emissions are commercially disadvantageous.[60] Instead of providing substantiated refutations of the established scholarly consensus on climate change, pseudoscientific journals often present non-evidence-based opinions that are successful in calling the scholarly consensus into question. As long as the scholarly consensus, albeit overwhelming, appears contested, it offers skeptics enough fuel to satisfy their confirmation bias. Most important, it offers laypeople enough substance to label the climate change debate "contested."[61] It fuels conspiracy theories that, wrapped in accessible narratives, are adopted by the media and transported into the public sphere. There, they can become a contagion that cannot be contained by mere objective or rational argument.[62] A reverse Dunning-Kruger effect might be at work here: the pseudoscientist's skepticism is diminished as the less he or she knows, the less he or she is able to recognize how little he or she knows, and thus, the less likely he or she is to accept sociopsychological biases and deficiencies.[63] For the scientist as a professional skeptic, the reverse might be true: the more he or she knows, the more he or she knows that he or she does not know. As a consequence, the scientist presents his or her findings in a tentative manner, leaving room for skepticism. The pseudoscientist, conversely, presents his "findings" confidently in a deterministic manner. For the public, the latter might appear to speak with more authority on what are essentially nonscientific findings.

Aside from "fake science" based on pseudoscientific methodology, the sciences have also repeatedly been haunted by scientific fraud, whereby established academics conduct studies based not only on sloppy scholarship but even on deliberate disinformation. One of the most prominent recent examples shook the academic world in the Netherlands to its core: the Dutch sociopsychologist Diederik Stapel had fabricated experimental results in an effort to generate conclusions that would tell the world what it wanted to hear about human nature.[64] Scientific misconduct appears to be widespread, as Julian Kirchherr writes in the *Guardian*: "Fourteen per cent of scientists claim to know a scientist who has fabricated entire datasets, and 72% say they know one who has indulged in other questionable research practices such as dropping selected data points to sharpen their results."[65]

Although numbers can be manipulated in quantitative research, qualitative research based on interviews, surveys, or discourse analysis is equally vulnerable to scientific misconduct particularly affecting the social sciences and humanities. Historians have similarly tried to write "fake history" to deny or relativize the Holocaust or give credibility to white supremacist theories.[66]

Equally powerful are foreign policy analysts and pundits who are paid for by external powers and could be inclined to distort academic discourse to favor particular narratives. With foreign and security policy analysis being increasingly outsourced to academia and the think tank world, most extensively in Washington, there have been increasing attempts at subversion by external parties to influence foreign and security policy reports that do not only feed into policy discourse but also feed into discourse in the public sphere.[67] As Darren Tromblay argues, "Think tanks' need for financial sustenance makes them vulnerable to foreign governments that are more than willing to engage in 'pay to play' activities by providing funding in exchange for a think tank's advocacy vis-à-vis US policymakers."[68]

The same is true for many universities and academic centers of excellence that are often underfunded and have to raise funds externally. In particular, the Arab Gulf monarchies have been actively funding academic programs and think tanks in the international relations discipline, trying to shape public discourse to a varying degree, as subsequent chapters will show. Masked as altruistic charity for the sake of scientific research, foreign policy think tanks in the West in particular have been courted by foreign governments to provide legitimacy to their strategic narratives.[69] In a highly polarized domain of academic discourse on matters of foreign and security policy, opinion pieces written by academics can be just as influential in the media and policy spheres as scientific papers or books.

Academia and "experts" are therefore important gatekeepers of truth in the public sphere whose judgments and opinions as well as their research weighs heavily on policymaking and the shaping of public opinion.[70] Their agenda-setting power unfolds when linked with the reach of the media. Whereas research in the ivory tower of academia might shape scientific discourse off the radar of public opinion, it is the impact factor of academic research and opinion in the public sphere, augmented by the media in constant need for "credible sources," that make it a potent component of information warfare.

Social media as the insurgency medium in the information space challenges both media and academia as the gatekeepers of truth, presenting alternatives to the liberal epistemology of an elitist class of scientists. The collective intelligence of the online sphere (probably more accurately described as collective credulity) has in many ways started to not just undermine conventional agenda setters but also to set a new metric for "truth."[71] It is for this reason that Marc Owen-Jones describes social media as an integral part of a new "deception order," because it is here that information travels freely decoupled from traditional values of veracity or factuality.[72]

THE RISE OF INSURGENCY MEDIA

The rise of social media in the 2000s has turned media consumption on its head, creating a new globalized agora for civil-societal activism that is no longer hierarchical but heterarchical.[73] While conventional media long played the role of an intermediary between civil society and the ruling elites, social media has built networks between individuals and groups that blur the existing boundaries of media producer and consumer. The ability to consume information as a globalized social experience without the restriction and regulation of a gatekeeper and mediator has truly opened up the public sphere to the masses, eroding social distances as new virtual communities coalesce around shared beliefs, emotions, and narratives.[74]

The public sphere created by social media is inclusive, diverse, and accessible to everyone. And unlike the analogue public sphere, it is participative, performative, and discursive. Those who had previously been passive consumers of information are now actively participating in shaping and disseminating information, thereby engaging interactively in a discourse that is not mediated by conventional gatekeepers. Thereby, as Rid writes, "the Internet first disempowered journalism and then empowered activism."[75] The disintermediation from producer to consumer is revolutionary in human communication behavior and might be one of the most significant communication developments in human history, on par with the advent of the written word, the printing press, and the telegraph.[76] However, while the printing press and the telegraph had just created a more efficient way to disseminate information, social media has revolutionized communication altogether, reaching the farthest corner of the Earth and connecting some of the most remote communities through an inescapable global network. Communication has moved from face-to-face over point-to-point to multidirectional, interactive, and collaborative network communication, in which the traditional gatekeepers and intermediary authorities are just one communication node of many.

Thus, social media has become the quintessential insurgency tool used to bypass the arbiter function of conventional media, allowing the individual to speak to those in power directly. Under the Twitter handle @realDonaldTrump, the forty-fifth president of the United States spoke directly and without filter to his more than 89 million followers before his account was suspended in early 2021. It provided a means for anyone to comment and reply to whatever the "insurgent president" tweeted, providing followers with the illusion of proximity. More importantly, Donald Trump started on social media to build his political profile, lashing out not just at other celebrities but also increasingly commenting on political issues. Unlike political elites whose Twitter feeds were polished by public relations firms and strategic communication experts, Trump was able to build a solid base of followers by appearing genuine without a filter of political correctness. At a time when mainstream media would not take the political statements of a New York real estate tycoon seriously, Trump was still able to speak to audiences that would later make up his key constituency: those feeling alienated and disenfranchised by "the establishment." When he formally announced his candidacy for US president in 2015, he had already built a followership on Twitter through messaging that was simple, impulsive, and running to political correctness.[77] Trump used this base to commence his insurgency campaign against the "mainstream" and the "Washington swamp."

Social media has undermined the monopoly of the conventional media in sociopolitical discourse, bypassing its role as the agenda setter and gatekeeper of "truth." Like other emerging communication technologies throughout history, social media challenges existing authorities, both political and civil-societal.[78] It has provided any individual with political views with a platform to market them and the potential to attract followers without being constrained by the authority of the state, the media, academia, or other established civil-societal forces. Fringe opinions and mis- and disinformation that might have been previously filtered out by the established gatekeepers in media and academia can now be marketed on a large scale from anywhere in the world with little or no budget at all. As the existing gatekeepers have lost trust, individuals with rebellious antiestablishment and antimainstream viewpoints are increasingly drawn to social media as alternative information sources.[79] The self-victimized underdog, feeling disenfranchised by "the system," found a new home in the social media sphere where conspiracy theories and simplistic narratives speak louder than in the conventional media sphere, which is constrained by everything that makes it journalistic: tone, fairness, facts-based arguments, and context over conclusions.[80] Social media is thereby not developing into a medium of moderation but into one that disproportionately empowers the extremes. Research shows that the more politicians deviate from the political center and mainstream, the more they can attract followers on Twitter or Facebook.[81] The reason for this is that these politicians have found ways to polarize the political debate on social media, often abandoning norms of political correctness and decency. And the rules for virality on social media seem to reward those who swap facts-based moderation and balance for impulsive, emotion-driven narrative.

Online virality does not depend on veracity or factual correctness but on its attractiveness to keep the audience's attention amid an ever-growing volume of information and an ever-smaller attention span. Thereby, social media giants have found ways to commercially exploit our sociopsychological vulnerabilities, transforming us into dopamine junkies seeking approval and confirmation on their platforms. Attention has become a currency on social media that can be sold—as "likes," "shares," and "comments"—and become the new metric for relevance and ultimately "truth."[82] The liking and sharing of content is part of our interaction with like-minded peers online. The sharing of information has a social exchange value that facilitates social integration, in particular when information is emotionally charged. As activity is a social experience rather than a professional journalistic exercise, information tends to be fused with emotions. As discussed in the previous chapter, anger and anxiety are the most important emotions stimulating arousal that becomes an essential trigger for content going viral on social media. That is to say, the content that evokes high-arousal emotions such as anger and anxiety is more likely to go viral, regardless of its valence.[83] Thus, similar to sensationalist journalism, social media facilitated through its contagion effect of perpetuating "shares" and "likes" creates virality through emotional stimulation. As Boyd highlights in a 2009 talk, "Our bodies are programmed to consume fats and sugars because they're rare in nature. . . . In the same way, we're biologically programmed to be attentive to things that stimulate: content that is gross, violent, or sexual and that gossip which is humiliating, embarrassing, or offensive. If we're not careful, we're going to develop the psychological equivalent of obesity. We'll find ourselves consuming content that is least beneficial for ourselves or society as a whole."[84]

In a public sphere of unmediated content, information competes with mis- and disinformation, whereby information that appears more scandalous, emotionally arousing, and novel is more likely to receive public attention than information that, albeit more factual, seems ordinary. Surprisingly, novel information not only breaks our expectation but is also more valuable for our brain from an evolutionary point of view. As it updates our knowledge of the world, novel information increases our chance to survive, causing our brain to process novel and more curious information quicker than ordinary information.[85] In this regard, in a social media sphere where everything goes, virality is not a product of veracity but of novelty, simplicity, and emotionality.

Creating Global Echo Chambers

The social media sphere is a human-made and algorithm-empowered environment, which displays different characteristics from the analogue public sphere where interaction has either been physical or mediated by a limited number of gatekeepers. Without filters imposed by traditional gatekeepers, the glut of information in the social media sphere is being managed by algorithms that direct consumers' attention to what the social media provider thinks would interest them based only on past behavior. Thus, while information on social media might be unmediated by journalists, editors, academics, or state authority, consumers are being spoon-fed by information feeds that are curated by algorithms and tailored to our previous information-processing behavior.[86]

Social media therefore follows a trend that has reshaped conventional media since the 1980s: the move from largely consensual media to specialized media that speaks to particular audiences. Responding to demands of audiences and catering to their emotional, psychological, and ideological predispositions, the liberalization of the media environment over the past four decades had already set the foundation for social zoning. The public sphere had already been effectively depublicized by creating echo chambers where information is consumed not for critical reflection or contextualization purposes but purely based on confirming existing biases.[87]

Algorithms have helped predict consumer preferences and selectively expose consumers to the information they most likely want to hear. It is here where digital marketing and strategic communications can micro-target social media users. Social media provides communication professionals not just with a means to tap into an unprecedented wealth of data on consumer preferences, as well as their ideological and emotional predispositions, but at the same time with a means to exploit these data to tailor messages to consumers. In the context of weaponized narratives, social media allows for consumers to be selectively exposed to information based on their communication profile.[88] For example, Facebook allows political campaigners to micro-target potential voters in a socioeconomically deprived community with ads that spin narratives drawing on local fears of further job loss. During the 2016 and 2020 US presidential campaigns, communication professionals used social media to directly speak to voters in America's rural and often economically deprived Midwest to endorse Trump's antimigration stance by relying on narratives that would correlate immigration with further job loss.[89]

Thereby, on social media, information is being curated to make information processing more "efficient," leaving no room for critical reflection or interrogation but providing us with the information that responds to our immediate needs. Providers such as YouTube, Facebook, and Twitter show us information that is not only more relevant to our search history but also conforms more to our previously held biases. Personalized information feeds thrive on homogeneity of content and conformity with previously consumed information, while veracity and factuality take a back seat.

The social element of this new experience of processing information adds to the phenomenon of exposure selectivity as we are drawn to content that mostly resonates not just with our own predispositions but also with those of our online friends, followers, and subscribers. Like a magnet, we as social media users are attracted to content clusters online that confirm our previous engagements with content.[90] The more polarized online debates are, the more we are drawn to the poles, often leaving no room for a moderate middle ground. Our cognitive need for harmony between sensual experience and previously held beliefs and opinions prompt us to cluster together in online "tribes" that comfort us with reaffirmation while protecting us from cognitive dissonance.[91] The new decentralized and dynamic complexity of the social media environment provides the perfect context for an emergent network effect, whereby online "tribes" connect across a global geographic space and are more connected to each other than those outside the "tribe." Cialdini and Goldstein intimate that opinions and narratives in clusters go viral more easily as subscribers to the cluster are peer-pressured into conforming with trending narratives and opinions.[92] The echo chamber is becoming so airtight that "outsider" perspectives have no chance of penetrating the digital bubble. The consequence of these online echo chambers was already illustratively outlined by Sunstein in 2001: "If people want to restrict themselves to certain points of view, by limiting themselves to conservatives, moderates, liberals, vegetarians, or Nazis, that would be entirely feasible with a simple point-and-click. If people want to isolate themselves, and speak only with like-minded others, that is feasible, too. . . . The implication is that groups of people, especially if they are like-minded, will end up thinking the same thing that they thought before—but in more extreme form."[93]

Hence, as social media becomes an increasingly important component of our information and news diet, journalists, analysts, academics, and policymakers alike willingly (or unwillingly) become members of online "tribes," exposed to varying degrees of "echo-chambering" where truth becomes a repetition-induced illusion. In the echo chamber, information consumption becomes increasingly homogenous, creating a false sense of consensus, which may foster an Orwellian illusion of truth. As Orwell famously states in his novel *1984*, "If all records told the same tale—then the lie passed into history and became truth."[94]

In the digital echo chambers, information bounces off other users, creating a sense of repetition as they share or positively engage with content. These environments thus generate a repetition-induced truth effect, whereby information is deemed more truthful through repetition. As Gustave Le Bon explains, "It was Napoleon, I believe, who said that there is only one figure in rhetoric of serious importance, namely, repetition. The thing affirmed comes by repetition to fix itself in the mind in such a way that it is accepted in the end as a demonstrated truth."[95]

Research has shown that repeated exposure to information increases the ease with which information is being processed regardless of its veracity.[96] Repetition works thereby as a heuristic shortcut allowing us to infer accuracy or veracity from repeated exposure to the same information. The cognitive ease of processing repeated information, as opposed to new information, makes us gravitate to repeated information, prompting us to internalize such information more easily as truthful—something that can be tested neurologically.[97] This illusionary truth effect is particularly strong when information is presented in a contested or ambiguous manner.[98] Looking at public and foreign policy debates on social media, which tend to be contentious and polarized, a single previous exposure to a statement is sufficient to increase perceived accuracy and the veracity of any successive statement confirming the previous one, regardless of whether the statement is factually accurate or not.[99] More than that, research has shown that repetition is more powerful than actual knowledge. In a study where participants were repeatedly exposed to false statements that contradicted their previous knowledge, the participants eventually accepted these statements as true, even though stored knowledge could have been used to detect a contradiction.[100]

Overwhelmed with a flood of (dis/mis)information, repetition provides us with a heuristic shortcut to a subjectively constructed truth. The repetition-induced truth effect becomes most potent when a statement or narrative correlates wholly or partially with prior knowledge or beliefs. For example, for social media users who believe that most immigrants are criminals, even a false statement that suggests that migrants are involved in a murder case will be considered true. Here, Pennycook, Cannon, and Rand show that the repetition-related truth effect is more powerful than confirmation bias or partisanship: if exposed often enough to the same information, we might eventually accept information as true that contradicts our own biases.[101]

It is therefore in this context of social media echo chambers that urban myths and conspiracy theories flourish, as veracity is not a product of comprehensive and critical interrogation but more often a product of consensus within an artificially constructed echo chamber. The idea of the public sphere is thereby turned inside out: although people are able to express their opinions in an increasingly unmediated way independent from conventional gatekeepers, the characteristic of the decentralized, network-centric social media sphere leads to a "tribalization" of the public sphere into smaller content clusters. In these clusters, information, whether factually true or false, travels within the constraints of algorithms that tend to expose the social media user to repetitive content that provides the user with the illusion that something is truthful merely based on the metric of social shares. Twitter, which might be less mediated by algorithms than other social media competitors, has become a major source for open intelligence for professionals and laypeople alike, sometimes providing a false sense of accuracy and veracity based on tweet endorsements. The opinions of Twitter influencers with elaborate followings receive the most "likes" and "retweets," catapulting their tweets into Twitter trends, thereby increasing virality. As others engage with these tweets, the content gets repeated, suggesting to others that it must be true.

What is considered truthful on social media is relative, given that it is the product of our homophily, meaning our tendency to associate with like-minded individuals, following the maxim of "birds of a feather flock together." Here, both cognitive and emotional predispositions function as social integrators online where users flock together based on shared beliefs and emotions. Anger in particular becomes a digitally experienced, social phenomenon, enabling social media users to find each other based on shared outrage over certain issues.[102] Thereby, anger over inaction against climate change on the political left is just as effective in bringing emotionally charged individuals together as anger over mass immigration on the political right. Outrage over the other side's outrage then becomes a self-perpetuating trend that drives virality of a particular issue while fostering negative integration around emotional and cognitive like-mindedness. For example, in a debate over gun control in the United States, where liberals tend to endorse a more rigid policy of gun control and conservatives tend to advocate for a laxer policy of gun control, the outrage over opinions advanced on the other side of the ideological divide binds liberals and conservatives closer together. The same dynamics can be observed in social media debates on Brexit in the United Kingdom, where emotions drive user aggregation in both the pro- and anti-Brexit echo chambers. This process is helped by the fact that social media giants such as Facebook have manipulated their algorithms to ensure that controversial posts triggering negative emotions, such as anger or hatred, attracted more views than those triggering positive emotions.[103]

Not only does social media provide us with the ability to more easily connect to people who share our cognitive and emotional predispositions; it also allows us to become producer and consumer of information at the same time. In a consensual universe of social media echo chambers, our endorsement of each other's content creates a fiduciary truth based on trust not just in information shared but also in who shares it—something called attribution bias, which is where the attitude of liking or disliking the purveyor of information is key to successful persuasion.[104] Our need for social approval and recognition within the social media sphere make us dopamine-driven users who become addicted to "likes," "retweets," and "shares," which become metrics not just of veracity but also of social status and validation.[105] The urge to "go viral" becomes increasingly powerful, triggering us as social media "producers" to become ever more sensationalist and provocative in what we share—and, as discussed above, sober factuality is rarely a recipe for virality.

Trolls, Bots, and the Distortion of Public Debate

The purportedly unmediated social media environment might have challenged existing gatekeepers, but it has been subject to new digital ones that distort content trends and thereby manipulate public debate. Apart from algorithms as content curators, trolls and bots have become very potent discourse saboteurs in this new human-made cyber agora. In a context where emotionality and sensationalism drive virality, trolls and cyber bullies have the power to attack public discourse en masse in a way that was impossible at a time of conventional top-down media production. In the network-centric digital bubbles of the social media sphere, however, trolls can often evade scrutiny and criminal liability when engaging in online harassment, denigration, impersonation, and ostracization of others.[106] Trolling refers to the "deliberate provocation of others using deception and harmful behaviour on the Internet which often results in conflict, highly emotional reactions, and disruption of communication in order to advance the troll's own amusement."[107]

Although trolls are often individuals driven by their need to satisfy their narcissistic and sadistic personality traits, they consciously operate in the public sphere to distort what is said by whom. With a principal objective of creating anger and injecting emotions in civil-societal discourse, trolls not only have the ability to intimidate and silence other users but also have a competitive advantage when attacking authorities online in that they (unlike policymakers, journalists, or academics) do not have to respect political correctness. Knowing that individuals in roles of authority must use their words wisely and responsibly, trolls provoke, making attempts to bait the attacked to respond on the same level, thereby undermining his or her credibility.[108]

In so doing, trolls can be an effective tool to usurp public discourse, because armies of trolls can bombard analysts, journalists, or policymakers with counterfactual content. They not only do this to play devil's advocate but, more importantly, to lure the attacked into an emotional and seemingly unobjective discourse. Further, trolls can drive trends by putting out mis- or disinformation to divert attention away from factual information. The more sophisticated and organized troll armies are even able to drive their own trends based on disseminated narratives that can outperform other narratives.

Authoritarian regimes such as Russia and Saudi Arabia have become major troll powers in the social media sphere, maintaining so-called troll farms that provide jobs for locals whose roles revolve around manipulating discourse in an effort to hack free speech. The most famous troll farm is Russia's Internet Research Agency, which has been at the forefront of the battle to conquer hearts and minds in the West through narratives that would speak to predispositions of specific social media echo chambers. Hundreds of youngsters are employed by the Internet Research Agency to maintain a range of social media accounts and feed them with narratives.[109] In Saudi Arabia, a similar troll farm has been set up to harass and intimidate critics online while disseminating narratives that do not just support the official line of the deep state of Crown Prince Mohammed bin Salman but also undermine narratives of those deemed enemies of the regime.[110]

Equally powerful on social media are bot armies that operate as automated surrogates, providing trolls with virtual endorsements and amplifying their messages. With fake followers and bots for sale, botnets consisting of hundreds of thousands of bot accounts can shift the entire course of a debate online. It is estimated that between 5 and 10 percent of all Twitter accounts are bots.[111] As social media companies are interested in traffic and new users, they are often reluctant to delete fake accounts.[112] Bots can post up to one thousand times a day and therefore have the ability to increase virality of selected messages and narratives, completely distorting social media trends.[113] Wooley distinguishes between three types of bots that all serve different purposes in the war over narratives on social media:

- First, *follower bots* merely boost follower counts and conduct retweets in an effort to create a false online consensus.

- Second, *roadblock bots* send barrages of posts and tweets so as to prevent particular target groups from constituting a social media trend.
- Third, *propaganda bots* actively seek to disseminate the political message of foreign governments, such as those working for Russia and Saudi Arabia.[114]

A 2017 study released by Oxford University's Computational Propaganda Research Project shows that bots have been deployed by the governments of more than eleven countries in an effort to manipulate public debate.[115] Hence, the "insurgency media" has gone "from being the natural infrastructure for sharing collective grievances and coordinating civic engagement to being a computational tool for social control, manipulated by canny political consultants and available to politicians in democracies and dictatorships alike."[116]

CONCLUSION

The infrastructural domain of the information space has become increasingly technologized, providing new opportunities for the members of the public to communicate with one another and those in power of governance. Civil-societal dialogue in the public sphere of the social media age at first sight appears to be more inclusive and unrestricted. Anyone with a smartphone can actively participate in public debate as both consumer and producer of content. The ability to speak truth to power no longer rests with the editors of large conventional media outlets or experts in academic ivory towers. The conventional gatekeepers of truth that would normally set the agenda of public and political debate are often bypassed or at least have been severely challenged in their monopoly of filtering and framing information.

Even more, the conventional gatekeepers in the media and academia are increasingly subject to social media's role as the new agenda setter. There is a burgeoning symbiotic relationship developing between microblogging, and news as trends on Twitter have become just as important as the ticker of news agencies that themselves often follow social media trends to set priorities.[117] The "collective evidence" provided by social media clusters thereby does not only tell us what to think about but increasingly also what to think. Yet, while social media has made it easier to get access to primary sources and their information on the ground, it has also become increasingly easy to mimic primary source intelligence. Activists in Gaza have used graphic images from other conflicts in the region to show how residents in the enclave have been affected by Israeli bombing in 2014.[118] In other cases, seemingly independent journalists report "on the ground" in Syria, spreading conspiracy theories about the opposition, thereby supporting the narratives of the Assad regime.[119] Particularly in an insurgency environment, the distinction between citizen, journalist, and activist becomes more and more blurred.[120] Nonetheless, information that seemingly emanates from the ground of complex conflict environments cannot be ignored by journalists, who at the least tend to triangulate their reporting with social media feeds, meaning that the thoughts of highly polarized masses can fill the gaps—often without an adequate filter.

Hence, what happens on social media matters. It drives conventional media reporting, and it can incite civil-societal activism and ultimately set the agenda for policymakers. With journalists, academics, and policymakers feeding off the social media sphere, trending messages and narratives find their ways into newspaper articles, the commentary of TV pundits, think tank reports, and policymaking debates. #MeToo, #BlackLivesMatter, #BringBackOurGirls, and #Ferguson have become extremely powerful hashtags on Twitter that have driven global public opinion and awareness.

In so doing, social media has evolved from a mere distraction machine into a tool of sociopolitical power, galvanizing public awareness and civil-societal activism. The disintermediation of the public sphere has provided a voice for the voiceless but has not made it necessarily easier to build a public consensus. Without a regulator or traditional gatekeeper, information in the hybrid space of social and conventional media is mediated by algorithmic filters, the mood of certain influencers, and the oligarchic decision-making of a few social media tycoons who are commercially exploiting our sociopsychological vulnerabilities. With more people being able to speak but not everyone being heard, gatekeeping has been diverted from editorial chairs to swarms of social media users whose biases and sociopsychological vulnerabilities are being exploited within an algorithm-empowered as well as troll- and bot-infested information space.[121]

What insurgency media has done is taken the scepter of gatekeeping away from the conventional media and policymakers and handed it to the masses, who, unconstrained by professional journalistic norms and values, have taken the opportunity to test the boundaries of political correctness and the ideological mainstream. Echo chambers catering to the extreme fringes favor radicals, while moderates fall victim to virality and sensationalism. The social experience of news has created a reality where facts are matters of consensus within ever more homogeneous echo chambers and where emotions trump sober rationality. Outside the echo chambers consensus quickly collapses along ideological lines making "facts" mere matters of opinion.

Truth becomes ever more relative as within a bottomless ocean of information, homophily drives our heuristic shortcuts and our new social media tribes help us construct our truth, making it ever more difficult for us to understand others outside the tribe. It is this infrastructural vulnerability of the information space that can be exploited in an effort to shape the process of constructing our reality. For the twenty-first century's information warriors, this strategic vulnerability provides an access point to implant weaponized narratives.

NOTES

1. Shoemaker and Voss, *Gatekeeping Theory*, 8.
2. Shoemaker et al., "Individual and Routine Forces," 233.
3. Carlyle, *On Heroes*, 257.
4. Brüggemann, "Die Medien," 137.
5. Roy, "'Polis' and 'Oikos.'"
6. Habermas, *Structural Transformation*, 24.
7. Habermas, "Public Sphere," 49–50.
8. Rousseau, *Social Contract*, 12.
9. Griffin, *First Look*, 102.
10. Marschall, "Lügen," 20.
11. White, "Civil Society," 77–78.
12. See Krieg, "Gulf Security Policy."
13. Exoo, *Pen*, 5.
14. Habermas, "Wahrheitstheorien," 211ff.
15. Day, *Ethics*, 37.
16. Hermida, "Nothing but the Truth," 47.
17. Stanley, *In Defence of Truth*, 74.
18. Reinemann, "Die Vertrauenskrise," 88.
19. Schneider, "Zwei mal drei macht vier," 120.
20. Bennett and Livingston, "Disinformation Order," 125; Seib, *Al Jazeera Effect*, x.
21. Chalif, "Political Media Fragmentation," 46.
22. Nervala, "Lügenpresse," 20.
23. Pöttker, "Die Aufgabe Öffentlichkeit," 223.
24. Lichter, Rothman, and Lichter, *Media Elite*.
25. Kuypers, *Press Bias*.
26. Kristol, *Neoconservatism*, 383.
27. Milyo and Groseclose, "Measure."
28. Krüger, "Medien Mainstream," 254.
29. Taylor, *Global Communications*, 62.
30. Boyd-Barrett, "Understanding," 30.
31. Robinson, "Researching US Media State Relations," 98.
32. Exoo, *Pen*, 99.
33. Casey, "Mass Media," 14.
34. Calabrese, "Privatization," 2.
35. Stephens, *History*, 100.
36. Serani, "If It Bleeds."
37. Sachsman and Bulla, *Sensationalism*, xx.
38. Kaphle, "Foreign Desk."
39. Haller, "Transparenz schafft Vertrauen," 235.
40. Cohen, *Press*, 13.
41. Griffin, *First Look*, 391.
42. Sonwalkar, "Out of Sight," 207.

43. Dearing and Rogers, "Agenda-Setting Research."
44. Berkowitz, "Who Sets the Media Agenda?"
45. Dearing and Rogers, "Agenda-Setting Research."
46. Entman, "Framing," 52.
47. Entman.
48. Singer and Brooking, *Like War*, 158–60.
49. Broockman and Kalla, "Manifold Effects."
50. Casey, "Mass Media," 14.
51. Crano, "Neoliberal Epistemology," 20.
52. Lakatos, "Science."
53. Popper, *Conjectures*, 66.
54. Lakatos, "Science."
55. Sampson, "Antiscience."
56. Vickers, "Alternative Cancer Cures."
57. Colquhoun, "Publish-or-Perish."
58. ARD, "Fake Science."
59. Davidson, "Vaccination."
60. Brüggemann, "Die Medien," 143.
61. Van der Linden, "Conspiracy-Effect," 173.
62. Bessi et al., "Trend of Narratives."
63. Pryor, "How to Counter the Circus."
64. Bhattacharjee, "Mind of a Con Man."
65. Kirchherr, "Why We Can't Trust Academic Journals."
66. Kakutani, "Death of Truth."
67. See Nicander, "Role of Think Tanks."
68. Tromblay, "Intelligence," 2.
69. Tromblay, 6.
70. Castells, *Communication Power*, 207.
71. Mocanu et al., "Collective Attention," 1199.
72. Owen-Jones, *Digital Authoritarianism*, 58.
73. Castells, *Communication Power*, 21.
74. Eickelman and Anderson, "Preface," xii.
75. Rid, *Active Measures*, 13.
76. Eickelman and Anderson, "Redefining Muslim Publics," 8.
77. Ott, "Age of Twitter," 60–62.
78. Castells, *Communication Power*, xxi.
79. Mocanu et al., "Collective Attention," 1202.
80. Herrman, "In the Trenches."
81. Hughes, "Highly Ideological Members of Congress."
82. Hendricks and Vestergaard, "Verlorene Wirklichkeit?" 6.
83. Berger and Milkman, "What Makes Online Content Viral?" 9.
84. Boyd, *Streams of Content*.
85. Vosoughi, Roy, and Aral, "Spread," 1150.
86. Kissinger, "How the Enlightenment Ends."
87. Nervala, "*Lügenpresse*," 25.
88. Libicki, "Convergence," 52.
89. Singer and Brooking, *Like War*, 178.
90. Del Vicarioa, "Spreading," 554.

91. Törnberg, "Echo Chambers," 2.
92. Cialdini and Goldstein, "Social Influence," 55.
93. Sunstein, "Daily We."
94. Orwell, *1984*, 33.
95. Le Bon, "Leaders," 121.
96. Fazio, "Knowledge Does Not Protect."
97. Wang et al., "On Known Unknowns," 739.
98. Dechene et al., "Truth about the Truth," 239.
99. Pennycook, Cannon, and Rand, "Prior Exposure," 4.
100. Fazio, "Knowledge Does Not Protect."
101. Pennycook, Cannon, and Rand, "Prior Exposure," 33.
102. Fan et al., "Anger Is More Influential," 1.
103. Merill and Oremus, "Five Points."
104. Moscovici, "Notes," 233.
105. Singer and Brooking, *Like War*, 4.
106. Awan, "Cyber-Extremism," 141.
107. Sest and March, "Constructing the Cyber-Troll," 69.
108. Singer and Brooking, *Like War*, 164.
109. Seddon, "Documents."
110. Benner et al., "Saudis' Image Makers."
111. Owen-Jones, *Digital Authoritarianism*, 41.
112. Singer and Brooking, *Like War*, 140.
113. Timberg, "Spreading Fake News."
114. Woolley, "Computational Propaganda," 16.
115. Bradshaw and Howard, "Troops, Trolls and Troublemakers," 11.
116. Timberg, "New Report."
117. Jamieson, *Cyberwar*, 43.
118. BBC Trending, "#BBCtrending."
119. BBC Trending, "Syria War."
120. Singer and Brooking, *Like War*, 70.
121. Törnberg, "Echo Chambers," 2.

THREE
....

Subversion and the
Contest of Wills

In the summer of 1977, news broke that the United States had successfully tested the neutron bomb, a low-yield thermonuclear weapon to be used tactically against Soviet armor. Western civil society was up in arms, particularly in Europe, where these weapons might potentially be used. Newspaper articles warned of the "death ray" and the dangers of radiation contamination from a weapon that might be more readily used than conventional, strategic nuclear weapons.[1] Activists were organizing protests across Europe, turning the question of deployment into a matter of public concern. Politicians responded by fielding motions in national legislatures in an attempt to pressure governments to prohibit the deployment of such weapons on the European continent.[2]

What was founded on genuine civil-societal activism was then amplified by a KGB operation. The aim of this KGB information operation was to prevent the deployment of such weapons on the European continent as well as polarize the debate within NATO, pitting the European nations against Washington.[3] Soviet Bloc media had pushed out thousands of news stories securitizing the "N-bomb," while communist parties in Europe as well as KGB front groups such as the World Peace Council helped channel civil-societal grievances toward mass protests.[4] Tapping into genuine grievances, the Soviet campaign eventually managed to undercut America's plans to deploy neutron bombs in Europe—a huge success that demonstrated the strategic depth of the KGB's "active measures."

This case study goes to show that information warfare is an old phenomenon. The exploitation of sociopsychological and infrastructural vulnerabilities in the information space to achieve political objectives in the physical world had been a constant component of what the Soviets defined as "active measures" throughout the Cold War. Yet only a few of these operations ever spilled over from the virtual information environment into the physical domain and actually changed the attitudes, decisions, and ultimately behaviors of key decision-makers and members of the public.

As this chapter demonstrates, the liberalization of the information environment, with its increased infrastructural vulnerability, allows information warriors today to more readily exploit and subvert what the Russians might define as the information-psychological stability of the opponent.[5] That is to say that weaponized narratives tailored to the cognitive and emotional predisposition of audiences can not only change attitudes and decision-making but also eventually even behaviors of individuals, communities, and policy elites. In the most extreme case, weaponized narratives can mobilize groups both online and offline to act reflexively based on the intent of the subverting power—a reality that can undermine the sociopolitical consensus and at times even the sociopolitical status quo. Essentially, narratives can be more effectively weaponized in the twenty-first-century information environment to alter people's will than they could during the Cold War—both on the individual and collective levels. This is done without the need for the use of force or other means of coercion, predominantly through the power of influence.

This chapter begins with a historical overview of information operations ranging from political warfare to information operations and psychological warfare over public diplomacy. At the heart of this chapter lies the definition of subversion as an antagonist's strategic exploitation of sociopsychological, infrastructural, and physical vulnerabilities in the information environment to erode a sociopolitical consensus or status quo. The second section of the chapter unpacks the ends, ways, and means of information warriors to use subversion as a means of strategic power as an alternative to conventional coercion. It concludes by outlining a six-step process that information warriors follow to design narratives that can succeed in altering the wills and behaviors of communities and individual policymakers alike.

A SHORT HISTORY OF
INFORMATION OPERATIONS

The idea of achieving victory without fighting appears to be as old as military thinking. In his *Art of War*, the Chinese military strategist Sun Tzu is quoted as defining the greatest victory as the one that does not require fighting: "Hence to fight and conquer in all your battles is not supreme excellence; supreme excellence consists in breaking the enemy's resistance without fighting."[6] In much of Sun Tzu's writing, overwhelming force and violence take a backseat to the smart and economical application of a broad spectrum of power. Information and intelligence are often as important as kinetic military force—the art of war is to persuade the opponent to change his or her behavior without going to battle.

Although more preoccupied with the delivery of violence, the Prussian military theorist Carl Von Clausewitz also condenses warfare to a "contest of wills," whereby force is employed to "compel our enemy to do our will."[7] Even after removing this statement from the context of the Napoleonic Wars, subversion operations might still fall within Von Clausewitz's parameters of war. Moving away from his preoccupation with the delivery of force as a means to compel and coerce, subversion aiming to change our adversary's will without resorting to violence might not necessarily negate Von Clausewitz's fundamental observations about war, as argued in the second half of the chapter. Thus, as the thinking of these two strategic heavyweights goes to show, the ambition to use information to shape the information-psychological center of gravity of the opponent is not exclusively a modern one.

However, though both Sun Tzu and Von Clausewitz appreciate the role of information and intelligence in a contest of wills, information operations for them are mere force multipliers for other modes of power. In the case of Von Clausewitz, information and intelligence support more conventional military operations. For Sun Tzu, it takes a support function in a much broader understanding of what we might consider political warfare today. Thus, the idea that subversion might be a stand-alone means to achieve strategic political objectives, as advanced in this book, fundamentally breaks with the historic precedents of information operations. But what is the conceptual context within which this book examines the subversive weaponization of narratives?

Fundamentally, the idea of using information to influence, disrupt, corrupt, and manipulate an adversary's decision-making falls within the realm of information operations, which has developed into a very broad umbrella concept including any action that undermines information systems.[8] In Western doctrinal thinking, information operations often refer to electronic warfare and computer network operations in the cyber domain, meaning operations that target the logistical tools of information processing.[9] The term "information operation" is often used interchangeably with "information warfare," which has a more offensive connotation and is often viewed as an adjunct of military operations.[10] Russian and Chinese strategic thinking on information operations and warfare have retained a more holistic and integrated view.[11] In Chinese strategic thinking, information warfare, or *xinxi zhanzheng*, "is the struggle to dominate the generation and flow of information in order to enhance and support one's own strategic goals while degrading and constraining those of an opponent."[12] Targeting communications through a variety of electronic cyber warfare, psychological operations (psyops), and military deception lies at the heart of both information operations and warfare.

Subversion in this book falls into the wider category of psychological operations that NATO defines as "planned activities using methods of communication and other means directed at approved audiences in order to influence perceptions, attitudes and behavior, affecting the achievement of political and military objectives."[13]

Aimed primarily at the sociopsychological dimension of the information environment, the first use of the concept of psychological warfare to attack the "intellectual battlespace" with "weapons of mind" might be found in the writings of the British historian J. F. C. Fuller. In 1920, after the end of World War I, he imagined a future battlefield where psychological warfare would be integral to a clash of wills.[14] During the Cold War, the idea of a psychological war gained prominence amid the ideological clash between East and West, with both sides trying to score a victory in a battle over strategic narratives. However, here psychological warfare was not understood as a substitute but an auxiliary in war, helping to achieve and maintain a moral high ground while at war. Especially in Western terminology, the utility of psychological operations is about creating friction, uncertainty, and even paralysis in a military opponent with the ultimate objective to reduce their will and capacity to fight.[15] Martin Libicki posits four categories of psychological operations: (1) operations against the national will, (2) operations against opposing commanders, (3) operations against troops, and (4) cultural conflict. Again, these categories predominantly focus on the force-multiplying role of information targeting the willpower of commanders, troops, and the home front.[16] The aim is to create confusion and disorientation among the opponent's military personnel and thereby undermine or subvert their willingness to fight.

Going beyond the Western conceptualization of psychological warfare as a nonlethal force multiplier, China's dictionary defines psyops more widely as permanent operations below the threshold of war that continue in peacetime and wartime.[17] They are distinct from any conventional military operation and target civilian as well as military audiences. Apart from operations against military personnel, China's understanding of psychological warfare incorporates an element of alienation—an attempt to generate friction and fracturing between the enemy's population and its political leadership. Mobilizing dissent, it looks to weaken the enemy from inside—something that does not necessarily have to be exploited by any kinetic military operation.[18]

For China, psychological operations include a component of public diplomacy in the form of strategic communication, which has a mostly defensive intent by presenting China's actions as just, legitimate, and moral to audiences at home and abroad. Always in direct relation to China's actions, strategic communication and public diplomacy are about positively influencing target audiences about the "why" of its behavior.[19] They are thus typically defined as "a government's process of communicating with foreign publics in an attempt to bring about an understanding for its nation's ideas and ideals, institutions and culture, as well as its national goals and current policies."[20]

Public diplomacy, at least in the Western vernacular, has a more positive and less disruptive aim than psychological operations. Not aiming at subverting the information-psychological stability of a target audience, public diplomacy employs narratives in a defensive capacity in an effort to manage a country's reputation and brand overseas.[21] In a first instance, public diplomacy as strategic communication can set the scene in the information environment to make audiences more receptive to a particular message and narrative. Diplomats maintaining positive relations and networks with foreign audiences might therefore be taking a first step in positive engagement that can create openings for further, more offensive, and potentially hostile psychological operations.

The concept of subversion, here, touches on all elements of information operations, ranging from defensive public diplomacy as strategic communication to more subversive psychological operations. At the higher end, these operations probably more adequately correlate with the Chinese definition of psychological warfare and Soviet-style covert psyops, more commonly known as "active measures," or *aktivnyye meropriyatiya*.[22] Amid the clutter of concepts, the widely used and somewhat self-evident term "political warfare" appears to come closest to the concept of subversion as understood in this book. It takes a more holistic approach to psychological operations in wartime and peacetime, as stand-alone and force-multiplying options, both overt and covert, with the aim of influencing the information-psychological center of gravity of a target community. It entails China's idea of "unrestricted warfare," the Soviet concept of "active measures," and Russia's "next generation warfare," all of which exceed the boundaries of a traditional Western understanding of information operations.[23] In American and British conceptualizations, information operations either focus too heavily on the cyber element when discussing sabotage and espionage or on the cognitive domain when focusing on psyops.[24] None of these Western concepts coherently merge the exploitation of sociopsychological and infrastructural vulnerabilities with the mobilizing potential of political warfare in the physical domain. It is here, at the spillover of activism from the virtual domain onto the "street," where subversion can generate a potentially violent effect.[25] Most important, Western concepts fall short of understanding subversion as a full-spectrum conflict that is conducted via networks that are not state-centric.

Although the Clausewitzian view is that all warfare is inherently political, the term "political warfare" was chosen by the American diplomat George Kennan in 1946 to distinguish "political" operations under the direction of the US State Department from conventional military operations.[26] Kennan's idea was meant to be a stand-alone policy instrument to be used below the threshold of war to cultivate and mobilize front groups behind the Iron Curtain in an effort to destabilize target communities. In so doing, Kennan's approach was inherently subversive, with the objective to overthrow established authority in a country through a variety of different overt and covert actions—psychological operations being one of them.[27] Throughout the Cold War, the subversive element of political warfare in the West became ever more closely associated with covert intelligence operations by the Central Intelligence Agency (CIA). In a 1989 book, the American historian Paul A. Smith provides a definition of political warfare that most closely correlates with the concept of subversion in this book: "Political war is the use of political means to compel an opponent to do one's will, political being understood to describe purposeful intercourse between peoples and governments affecting national survival; . . . its chief aspect is the use of words, images, and ideas, commonly known, according to context, as propaganda and psychological warfare."[28] Smith makes a reference to the nonlethal contest of wills—predominantly relying on information to change an adversary's will and behavior.

Dating back to ancient times, the history of war is filled with examples of psychological operations intended to undermine the morale of enemy forces. The writing of war propaganda by the ancient Greek historian Herodotus called on the Ionians to abandon their Persian allies and to fight with the Athenians in the fifth century BC.[29] Rome's general Scipio Aemilianus's decision to completely flatten Carthage in the Third Punic War in the second century BC equally targeted local hearts and minds.[30] And the Mongols under Genghis Khan were certainly experts in terrorizing the enemy by acts of slaughter and great cruelty.[31]

Yet, as much as these operations might have been psychological in nature, they were a mere adjunct to military operations, employed either before, during, or after conventional war. In this way, these psychological operations might have followed Sun Tzu's idea of winning without battle while internalizing Von Clausewitz's maxim of changing the enemy's will. However, they have little in common with the type of subversion this book examines. The roots of the so-called political war can be found in the final years of World War II and the extensive covert effort by both Allied and Axis forces to target the morale of the other side, both civilian and military. Though covert operations and "black propaganda" supported the overall war effort, they also created the infrastructure in both the United States and the Soviet Union that would later be used during the Cold War to further wage political warfare.

In the wake of the collapse of Nazi Germany in 1945, the ideological differences between the United States and the Soviet Union became ever more pronounced, causing the wartime allegiance between Washington and Moscow to rapidly deteriorate. It became apparent that the confrontation that unraveled was at its heart a war over narratives between East and West, in which the psychological component would be central—especially once it became clear that in the face of a nuclear standoff, new subthreshold means of warfare had to be developed. In the race for postwar hearts and minds, public diplomacy would be as important as psychological operations in spreading ideological narratives. Narratives would be tailored to respective audiences and transported by networks of both overt and covert information surrogates in an effort to break into civil-societal space, where they could change not just attitudes but also behavior.

The Soviets' instrumentalization of the World Peace Council in 1949 was one of the first attempts to create a surrogate front organization that could operate in the physical domain of the information environment. Under the ostensibly harmless banner of promoting peaceful coexistence, this front would not only attract engagement from Eastern Bloc intelligentsia and civil society but also serve as a platform for the spread and legitimization of pro-Soviet narratives in the West. As Philip Taylor outlines, "'Front' organizations were required so as to disguise the fact that Moscow was conducting the orchestra: far better to have foreigners playing the tune in their own countries than musicians with a Russian accent."[32]

Behind the facade of a pacifist international organization, the Soviet KGB began implanting disinformation narratives. In 1952, the World Peace Council was not only promoting North Korea's invasion of the south but also became instrumental in spreading disinformation in the Far East in an effort to discredit the United States. The disinformation narrative was spread by two members of the World Peace Council, the Australian journalist Wilfred Burchett and the East German scientist Heinrich Brandweiner. They alleged that the United States was using germ warfare to weaken the North Korean army, which was not true. Burchett, who was directly paid a stipend by the KGB, reported the story first, while Brandweiner used his academic affiliation to verify the false reports while leading an international delegation to China.[33]

Instead of merely relying on the power of appeal, the KGB understood the value of targeted disinformation as early as 1923. According to Ion Pacepa, a high-ranking defector from Romania's secret police, the concept of disinformation was originally an invention by Stalin himself who, during World War II, was looking for a subversive instrument to take revenge against Nazi Germany.[34] *Dezinformatsiya*, or information that is intentionally manipulated, is defined in the KGB dictionary as "especially prepared data, used for the creation, in the mind of the enemy, of incorrect or imaginary pictures of reality, on the basis of which the enemy would make decisions beneficial to the Soviet Union."[35] It would become the core of Soviet "active measures," or political warfare. It is here that the Soviets went beyond what the West would call "white subversion" or "gray subversion"—that is, the use of public diplomacy to promote one's

narratives and the creation of front groups, respectively. The KGB's disinformation campaigns were considered "black subversion," involving spreading false
rumors and disinformation-based narratives; duping politicians, journalists,
and academics; and disseminating forgeries and fake documents.[36] The aim in
the Cold War was mostly limited to mere influencing and persuasion campaigns
to discredit the opposing ideology, but the ultimate aim of disinformation is to
disrupt and subvert the information-psychological stability of target communities, bringing about information paralysis and undermining decision-making
capability.

Washington's aims during the unfolding "political wars" with Moscow were
less ambitious but equally driven by a desire to influence the information-
psychological center of gravity of key audiences. At a time when the Soviet
Union had already embarked on its program of "active measures," US president
Harry Truman set up the Psychological Strategy Board to advise the National
Security Council. Truman saw the Cold War as a war over strategic narratives:

> We are now waging a cold war. The cold war must have some objective oth-
> erwise it would be senseless. It is conducted in the belief that if there is not
> war, if two systems of government are allowed to live side by side, that ours,
> because of its greater appeal to men everywhere, to mankind, in the long run
> will win out. That it will defeat dictatorial government because of its greater
> appeal to the human soul, the human heart, the human mind.[37]

Truman defined the battle for the human soul, heart, and mind as a "Campaign of Truth," whereby a network of information platforms in the Western
Hemisphere and Europe would be used to undermine the Soviet narrative.[38]
Under the umbrella of the new US Information Agency (USIA), Washington set
up an infrastructure in 1953 that was exclusively committed to weaponizing
narratives. A statement by Edward Murrow, president of the agency in 1963,
indicates how important the role of the USIA had become in the toolbox of
influence and persuasion: "Our arsenal of persuasion must be as ready as our
nuclear arsenal and used as never before."[39] At the height of the Cold War, the
USIA employed more than 10,000 people and had a budget of roughly $1 bil-
lion.[40] Other Western US partners such as Britain invested in similar outfits. The
innocently titled Information Research Department had been created already
in 1948 by the United Kingdom to disseminate anticommunist counterpropaganda to opinion leaders domestically and abroad.[41]

Although predominantly dedicated to public diplomacy, the USIA's network
also directly tried to undermine the appeal and influence of their Soviet counterparts. The Voice of America, Radio Free Europe, and Radio Liberty were at
the forefront of US political warfare during the Cold War, spreading positive

messages about liberalism, democracy, and capitalist prosperity to audiences on the other side of the Iron Curtain. This network of overt and covert radio stations sponsored by the United States became an important source of information power, particularly toward the end of the Cold War, when Radio Liberty had become a means of spreading dissident voices and narratives of liberalization amid an increasing socioeconomic and sociopolitical decay of the USSR in the 1980s.[42]

Although the United States and the USIA always highlighted the "white" and "gray" operations of its political warfare network, the CIA also used "black" operations via its own radio stations to spread subversive disinformation. During the 1950s and 1960s, the CIA operated a black radio station called Radio Swan on Swan Island in the Caribbean with the sole purpose of spreading false narratives about Fidel Castro, who had then recently come to power in Cuba. The ambition was to create dissent in Cuba that would entice the public to rise up against the popular revolutionary who had chosen to align with the Soviet Union in America's backyard.[43] After the CIA's failed surrogate invasion of Cuba in the Bays of Pigs in 1961, during which Radio Swan had broadcasted for twenty-four hours straight, the radio station was ordered to change from information warfare to public diplomacy in the Americas.[44]

A decade earlier, the CIA had used the press extensively in Iran to spread narratives against Mohammad Mossadegh. Mossadegh had been elected Iranian prime minister in 1951, promising to nationalize Iran's oil industry, which would have undermined British hydrocarbon interests in the country. For the United States, Mosaddegh was considered more of an ideological threat, as he was seen to empower the communist Tudeh Party inside Iran. The joint CIA/MI6 operation, code-named "AJAX," relied on "black" operations in an effort to target the sociopsychological support for Mossadegh with key target audiences.[45] Posing as communists, CIA operatives would stage false flag incidents to create fear among the religious establishment that a communist takeover under the watch of Mossadegh was imminent. Cartoons and articles were put in Iranian newspapers that spread narratives of "communist savagery," referring to the CIA-staged incidents.[46] This strategic narrative was directed precisely at the religious elites and the security sector to mobilize internal pressure on the shah to dismiss Mossadegh, which eventually happened in August 1953. Washington and London even managed to mobilize demonstrations in Tehran against the ousted prime minister, which turned violent.

Throughout the Cold War, "political warriors" in Washington and Moscow had invested heavily in a range of subversive operations to undermine the credibility and legitimacy of the other side's narrative. Equally, both sides responded with counternarratives to defend against incoming messages. Estimates indicate that the USSR had built between 2,500 and 3,000 jamming stations by 1962 to disrupt incoming Russian-language radio programs produced and disseminated by the United States—paradoxically spending more on jamming than the United States did on broadcasting.[47] Hence, only a few disinformation campaigns were actually able to change the attitudes, decisions, and behaviors of target audiences. Apart from information operations against the neutron bomb in 1977 and 1978, there were only a few instances in which KGB active measures were able to mobilize limited civil-societal actions as a physical effect. In 1959, KGB operatives daubed Cologne's Jewish synagogue with red swastikas—an act that was exploited by a Soviet-led global disinformation campaign designed to harm the reputation of West Germany. This operation managed to mobilize global condemnation of West Germany's failed de-Nazification strategy, culminating in protests involving fifty thousand Londoners marching on the West German embassy.[48] In 1983 the KGB executed Operation DENVER, aimed at undermining the United States' global reputation through the release of false reports in USSR-aligned outlets that the then-novel AIDS epidemic had originated in an American biowarfare lab—a piece of disinformation that continued to circulate widely throughout the 1980s.[49] Though able to influence global public opinion, these KGB operations caused only limited mobilization and never really affected policymaking. The CIA's covert efforts to tarnish the reputation of Mossadegh might have come closest to spilling into the physical domain and changing policy. However, if it had not been for the coercive nature of joint US and British sanctions against Iran, accompanied by diplomatic pressure, it remains debatable to what extent the subversive operations would have been a success.

The advent of new communication infrastructures in the twenty-first century, which allows for more rapid, instant, and micro-targeted dissemination of information, provides opportunities to build on these lessons from the Cold War.

WEAPONIZED NARRATIVES AND THE SUBVERSION OF POLITICAL WILL

The concept of subversion as defined in this book builds on the experience of "active measures" during the Cold War. It is meant to be a stand-alone lever of power that intends to achieve political ends without the use of kinetic force. It mostly exists outside military operations and therefore beyond the bounds of conventional war. Subversion is here defined as the strategic exploitation of sociopsychological, infrastructural, and physical vulnerabilities in the information environment by an external adversary to alter or erode a sociopolitical consensus or status quo. The strategic end is shaping the attitudes, decisions, and ultimately behaviors of communities as well as key communal influencers and policymakers. In line with a Russian understanding of information-psychological operations, subversion aims at shaping individual and mass consciousness and, in its most extreme form, mobilizing regime change.[50]

The vehicle of choice used to transport information to the target audience are narratives, which are carefully constructed predispositions of both how the world works and how it is supposed to work, conforming to interests and values that are clearly set out. They structure our reality, build identity, and provide meaning to individuals and communities alike. Narratives are the storylines that exploit our sociopsychological weaknesses to create "truth" as a socially constructed phenomenon. Narratives wrap factuality in emotion; situate events in an ontologically curated setting; connect past, present, and future; and grant us a metaphysical place of belonging. Thereby, narratives are metaheuristic shortcuts that help us make sense of the complex world around us, dividing the world into good and evil, moral and immoral, and legitimate and illegitimate. The weaponization of narratives implies a deliberate manipulation of existing narratives with the aim of subverting existing civil-societal and political discourse within a community that can lead to a change of attitudes, decisions, and behaviors. Weaponized narratives become means to offensively target the information-psychological center of gravity of communities, undermining the trust in the integrity of the communication networks between individuals, communities, and institutions that ultimately feed policymaking. As Bradley Allenby and Joel Garreau argue, "Weaponized narrative seeks to undermine an opponent's civilization, identity, and will by generating complexity, confusion, and political and social schisms. It can be used tactically, as part of explicit military or geopolitical conflict; or strategically, as a way to reduce, neutralize, and defeat a civilization, state, or organization."[51]

Hence, subversion based on weaponized narratives alters patterns of communications between governed and governing as well as between the various stakeholders in the policymaking process such as the media, academia, subject matter experts, civil servants, and politicians—namely, those who make up the physical domain of the information environment. To undermine the sociopolitical consensus or status quo, weaponized narratives need to achieve a high mobilization effect and a high level of orchestration across a variety of domains (see figure I.1 in the book's introduction). Thus, not every weaponized narrative is necessarily subversive if not integrated into a wider, orchestrated campaign or when failing to achieve high levels of mobilization, where either civil-societal activism spills violently into the streets or policymakers feel obliged to react.

The notion of "reflexive control" most closely correlates with influence, whereby the term "influence" is not only a highly overused buzzword in the era of strategic communication but has also become increasingly hollow in substance. Influence is about the capacity to generate a strategic effect by gradually changing the attitudes, decisions, and behaviors of individuals, communities, and ultimately policymaking elites. Influence is thereby not just the product of a narrow Western understanding of information operations but also a more holistic approach adopted to target the adversary's information-psychological center of gravity. Influence is about prevailing in a contest of wills with the adversary or competitor changing his or her behavior, in the context of subversion, doing so entirely without coercion. Thus, influence on the subversive end of the continuum in figure I.1 leads to a reflexive control of will. As Kramer and others define it, the "deliberate influence on an adversary with the goal of inclining him to make a decision predetermined by the controlling party."[52] Thomas incorporates the explicit tailoring of information in his definition that looks at reflexive control as "a means of conveying to a partner or an opponent specially prepared information to incline him to voluntarily make the predetermined decision."[53] This type of influence is defined in this way by the Russian General Staff Military Academy's glossary as "agitation": "One of the forms of information-psychological influence on the emotional plane of the target or group of targets with the aim of achieving a specific psychological state which will lead to active and specific actions being taken."[54]

Hence, influence aims at inserting specific narratives into the adversary's policymaking discourse through an orchestrated information network comprising a variety of different domains. Particularly in complex policy fields, such as foreign and security policy, agents of influence can operate in the civil-societal space as well as within academia and policymaking circles. All three components are integral parts of the physical domain of the information environment, where narratives are translated into behavioral change either by mobilizing or demobilizing civil-societal activism or by policymakers responding to civil-societal demands by adapting their policy decisions. For the subverting party, the aim is to disrupt and alter consensus among key constituencies and audiences in the policymaking nexus to have the target organization change strategic policy decisions.

Changing the sociopolitical status quo on the higher end of the continuum in figure I.1 aims at strategically disrupting and paralyzing the public sphere with the ultimate aim of undermining sociopolitical relations between the governed and the governing. The sociopolitical status quo is changed when governments are either overturned or feeling under the weight of created sociopolitical pressure to U-turn on fundamental policy decisions. First, this type of destabilization is founded on the aforementioned infocalypse, namely, the pollution of the information environment with conflicting information, misinformation, and disinformation. The result is policy paralysis, in which the subjected public and policymakers find it increasingly impossible to sieve through an impenetrable clutter of information and come to reasonable policy decisions.[55] Ovadya describes the resulting phenomenon as reality apathy when people start losing trust in information altogether.[56] The consequence would be an increased lack of informedness among voters, which would severely challenge the functioning of liberal democracies. The liar's dividend will pay off eventually: "When nothing is true then the dishonest person will thrive by saying what's true is fake."[57] Not only does this imposed information overload help information warriors cover their tracks in times of crisis, but it can also generate a wider sense of uncertainty and indecisiveness at all levels, effectively degrading the opponent's decision-making processes.[58]

Second, amid the unfolding inability to make effective policy decisions, the trust in and legitimacy of governing bodies gradually erodes. Sowing confusion and stoking negative emotions of anger and fear effectively disrupts the social fabric and polarizes public discourse. Having to respond to polarized public discourse, policymakers, especially in liberal democracies, face sociopolitical friction that can lead to policy paralysis, where the gap between government performance and public expectations widens. The resulting grievances of perceived government inadequacies among the public cause dissent that can eventually evolve into political violence and insurgency.[59] Such operations targeting the information-psychological stability follow the concept of *myatezhevoyna*, or "subversion war"—a term coined by the exiled Soviet military thinker Evgeny Messner, who wrote in the 1960s and 1970s about the idea of using information to target sociopolitical vulnerabilities in communities in an effort to incite dissidence and potentially insurgency.[60] For Messner, subversion war was about encouraging or fueling internal conflicts through the means of weaponized information to "estrange the masses from their government."[61] Messner's idea corresponds with cybernetic objectives of understanding the control and behavior of social systems as sociopsychological organisms.

Aleksandr Dugin, who conceived the idea of Russia as a Eurasian power, draws on Messner's ideas that have become ubiquitous in the writing on information warfare in resurgent Russia. Dugin's concept of net-centric war exceeds the Western concept of network-centric warfare, which narrowly revolves around electronic networks, to also include social networks that can be exploited to advance mutual interests. Among disenfranchised and alienated minority groups in particular, Dugin sees the potential for front groups that can be mobilized by external political actors to move against domestic authority structures.[62] Grooming influencers and provocateurs within these networks provides external political actors with access to a public space that is highly unregulated, especially in liberal democracies. It is from here that civil-societal activism can be steered not just to alter the policymaking process but also to move against any sociopolitical system from within. Ultimately, challenging the sociopolitical status quo attempts through weaponized narratives to erode trust within communities and causes sociopolitical friction that leads to political violence. Breaking sociopolitical consensus is therefore the gradual, cumulative effect of subversion consisting of a range of activities by externally controlled networks of actors, who in the most extreme case can bring about death by a thousand cuts leading to regime change.

Thus, though the previous two chapters unpacked the sociopsychological and infrastructural vulnerabilities of the information environment, the focus of this chapter is the third vulnerability in the physical domain. It is here at the intersection of the virtual domain of the information space and policymaking that carefully drafted narratives affect civil-societal discourse before gradually spilling into activism in the physical domain. Influence also becomes strategically relevant because it no longer just mobilizes social media followers and academic peers but also activism on the streets, influences voting behavior at the ballot box, and potentially shapes policymaking. When narratives get picked up by grassroots groups and inspire civil-societal campaigns, policymakers in liberal democracies will be unable to ignore what appears to be an expression of the voters' will. Once narratives translate into policy-relevant discourse in high-impact media outlets, academic publications, and think tank debates, narratives also shape an elite nexus that transcends into the civil service, parliament, and government. The revolving door between academia and policymaking means that seemingly independent and objective "experts" and "analysts" are able to transport information into the policymaking nexus. The example of two prominent Middle East experts in Germany illustrates this point: Günter Meyer and Michael Lüders have seemingly used their reach in the German media to spread disinformation-based narratives on Syria that originated from websites fed by the Assad regime. Both Meyer and Lüders contested the official report of UN chemical weapons experts that the infamous chemical weapons attack on East Ghouta in 2013 was perpetrated by the regime in Damascus.[63] Despite widespread criticism from peers, both of them enjoy a proximity to policymakers in Berlin and could use their scholarship to legitimize disinformation-based narratives disseminated by both Moscow and Damascus.[64] With the subversion of the old gatekeepers of truth, information warriors have found ways to access the policy arena where they can either directly engage with policy-relevant elites or indirectly mobilize civil-societal activism that can set the policy agenda, at least in liberal democracies.

Can Subversion Be War?

The question of whether subversion can be war is part of the same debate about whether psychological war, information war, or political war are actually war. The term "war" has been used so widely and broadly that its meaning today might be entirely insignificant. Yet here I am not trying to enter into the twenty-first-century debates on the definition of war but instead to examine to what extent subversion complies with some of the conventional parameters and metrics of war—acknowledging the fact that the concept of war is a highly contested one.

To return to the previous section on the history of information operations, the most fundamental aspect of war, according to Von Clausewitz, is the use of violence in what he describes as a clash of wills.[65] In a struggle to make our opponent do our will, coercion and compellence administered through the use of force are a recurring feature of war. As Freedman notes, "without the element of violence the study of war loses all focus."[66] But violence takes different shapes and forms. In the case of war, it should be organized, collective, state-sanctioned, and regulated. Deutsch and Senghaas explain that "by 'war,' we mean actual large-scale organized violence, prepared and maintained by the compulsion and legitimacy claims of a State and its government, and directed against another State or quasi-State, i.e., a relatively comparable political organization."[67]

As Strachan and Scheipers highlight, war requires reciprocity, namely, one party administering violence and another party responding to it; otherwise, violence leads to murder, massacre, and occupation.[68] The defining feature of war is thus the use of violence by two or more parties, which are political organizations that administer organized violence through their armed forces.[69] In war—to distinguish it from mere crime—violence is a group activity that does not merely serve private but also collective, public interests.[70] In Von Clausewitz's words, war is a human activity that needs to serve political ends so that fighting and violence are not just ends in themselves.

That being said, the characterization of subversion as a stand-alone lever of power to be orchestrated by heterarchical information networks in coordination as well as in the absence of conventional military operations seems to display little resemblance with the more conventional definitions of "war." Subversion purposefully avoids crossing the threshold of war while still allowing the subverting party to achieve a change in opponents' behavior, albeit not through the means of coercion and compellence. Subversion is designed not just to blur the boundaries between war and peace but also to make it a constant and enduring activity that allows subverting powers to remain committed longer to protracted conflicts. Though there is no real consensus on how long a contestation between two parties has to last for it to qualify as war, subversion does not conform to any clear beginning or end—a feature that is typical of many measures and levers used in the gray zone of subthreshold war.[71]

The conflicts of the twenty-first century take place in an international system where the redlines of interstate conflict are rigidly defined and upheld by all major powers that subscribe to the nonintervention principle. In order to be able to engage in such conflicts and potentially determine their outcome, states need to draw on the full spectrum of state power, requiring a whole-of-government approach, of which the kinetic military component might be just one of many. With resurgent powers such as Russia, China, and Iran stretching and exploiting the threshold of war, nonviolent means are becoming increasingly potent to achieve strategic objectives.[72] And subversion seems to fall into the category of "measures short of war," as Kennan defined them in his lectures in the late 1940s.[73] According to Kennan, these range from negotiation, embargo, and diplomatic intimidation to what he defines as "covert subversion." And in the list of different measures short of war that allow a protagonist to achieve political ends without crossing into the realm of war, subversion appears to be the odd one out, because all other elements contain a degree of coercion.

Like other measures short of war, subversion provides the protagonist with a means to engage in protracted conflict without bearing the consequences of major military escalation—or as Connable, Campbell, and Madden call it, high-order war. In their RAND study, they define high-order war as "a large-scale protracted or strategically decisive conventional combat."[74] In this way, subversion is a noncoercive means to potentially get a target audience to abide by a protagonist's will—and although eventually fueling political violence, remain themselves below the threshold of combat operations. In many ways, then, subversion stretches the norms of war, including principled beliefs about moral action, providing protagonists with means to achieve objectives similar to war without necessarily crossing its threshold. But does this mean subversion abstains from violence?

As Fridman puts it, hybrid, political warfare promotes the widening of the concept of violence beyond the use of kinetic, physical violence into nontraditional domains of violence that are not necessarily purely military in nature.[75] Nonetheless, these nontraditional domains of violence—such as economic violence administered through sanctions affecting the livelihoods of people; structural violence that, according to Galtung, is present when individuals are deprived because of structural vulnerabilities to achieve their full potential;[76] or political violence, such as riots or protests—are events when violence is a by-product of mass social upheavals.[77] Particularly on the higher end of the scale, the attempt by subversive actors to undermine the sociopolitical consensus, violence almost inevitably occurs as a follow-on effect of mobilizing parts of the public sphere against an existing political authority structure. For military thinkers in today's Russia, information-psychological warfare is so effective that it should be considered violent, albeit not overtly or directly violent, as is discussed further in chapter 5.[78]

The question, then, is what level of violence is violent enough to breach the threshold of war. Deutsch and Senghaas make the case that war requires scale and impact, arguing that the baseline is one thousand battle-related deaths, but this does not count indirect victims of war from famine, deteriorated public health, or lack of shelter.[79] For subversion to remain under the threshold of war, it is limited in terms of direct impact and direct violence. However, subversion might generate secondary effects in the physical domain of the information space that in scale can be as violent as conventional military operations. Subversion can steer protests and potentially drive tens of thousands to the street, which would be met by a reciprocal response by state authorities. Looking for illustrative purposes at the first few months of the Arab Spring, which were all but the effect of a subversion campaign, the death toll in individual countries had spiraled from a few hundred in Tunisia, Bahrain, Egypt, and Yemen to thousands in Libya and Syria, where regimes were more heavy-handed in their response to mass protests.[80]

That is to say, although nonviolent in its primary effect, the weaponization of narratives can cause follow-on effects that could be physically violent. According to Rid, subversion would fail the "violence test" because an information operation is "less physical, because it is always indirect. It is less emotional, because it is less personal and intimate. The symbolic uses of force through cyberspace are limited. And, as a result, code triggered violence is less instrumental than more conventional uses of force."[81]

Despite his caveat that the information-psychological effects of such operations are highly disruptive, Rid argues that because violence in the information environment is a more complex, mediated sequence of causes and consequences, information operations do not qualify as war. The reason is that information is never the direct cause of violence but requires an intermediary to actually create violent symptoms; in the case of subversion, this intermediary is human cognition exposed to the infrastructural vulnerabilities of the information environment. Violence can, if at all, only occur as a cumulative effect of a sequence of actions and reactions.

Kello is skeptical about Rid's argument that therefore subversion cannot count as a means of warfare. He argues that, instead, within a "state of unpeace," under the threshold of high-order war, actions are not overtly violent but more harmful than merely disruptive.[82] Particularly when looking at the potentially violent ripple effects of the subversion of information-psychological stability, the usurpation of an opponent's will can mobilize activism in the physical domain of the information environment that serves strategic, political ends and has a violent potential, albeit indirectly.

The question of whether subversion can be classified as a means of warfare, therefore, brings me back to Von Clausewitz and the three parameters he set for war. First, it must be violent; second, it must be political; and third, it must affect the will of people. These three parameters are hard to translate in the information space, where, as Rid rightly contends, effects are never directly violent and at times are not even violent at all. Thus, I propose to look at violence more widely to include more than physical violence, which, in the case of information-psychological stability, most likely occurs as a secondary or tertiary effect. It might be more adequate here to look at concepts such as political violence triggered by civil-societal activism. The meaning and threshold of violence in the context of political violence remain highly contested, as Della Porta highlights, arguing that "political violence is generally understood to mean behavior that violates the prevailing definition of legitimate political action."[83] Though this might be a fairly subjective metric, it highlights that violence in the nonmilitary and nonkinetic realm could also be understood as severely undermining existing norms of political behavior by state and nonstate actors. In the case of subversion, what is and what is not acceptable behavior of a foreign power trying to influence or destabilize the information-psychological center of gravity is hard to determine, as subversion "may remain entirely within the boundaries of the law, especially in free and open democracies."[84] The British insurgency expert Frank Kitson, however, argues that subversion, although a measure short of war, is an illegal activity that may or may not act as a force multiplier to existing sociopolitical rifts within a community.[85] Kitson says little about the fact that, although subversion might be violating norms of acceptable international conduct, it provides no legal precedents for how to tackle them under international law. Under domestic law, subversive activities might fall within the categories of espionage and collusion—with the latter being especially hard to prosecute, as the Mueller investigation into the collusion of the 2016 Trump campaign with Russia illustrated.

Hence, given that subversion may or may not be violent, and may or may not be illegal, it might be more useful to classify it as a means of warfare when it generates a significant effect in the physical domain of the information environment. This way, the debate can emerge from the narrow, dogmatic international legal norm of war to trigger a debate around the moral norms of war, including what is and what is not morally acceptable conduct in twenty-first-century global competition.[86] The Western-centric institutionalization of the norms of war have now been severely challenged by the evolution of the means of warfare as well as the consequent changes in at least the character of war. Looking at the information environment as a battlespace of its own, subversion should be considered a means of warfare as long as it is a continuation of "politics by other means" and has a significant physical effect in the shape of political, structural, or ultimately physical violence.

Subversion should be considered a means of warfare when it can mobilize people not just in the virtual space but also in the physical space, gearing up activism; potentially, in acts of dissidence; and, in the worst case, in empowering armed rebellion or insurgency. Weaponized narratives that remain entirely in the virtual domain without causing physical reaction or spillover have a low mobilization effect. For it to be a means of warfare, subversion needs to affect the decisions and actions of a significant group of people in the target audience who alter the structural context of sociopolitics. This altering effect can come in the form of a new civil-societal consensus and behavior or government policies—a causal relationship between subversive act and effect that is admittedly hard to prove and measure, as the next chapters will show.

Measuring the impact or effect of subversion operations is hardly a quantitative matter, because the quality of engagement is more important than the quantity of engagements. Subversion operations are based on network-centric, heterarchical engagements with target audiences, whereby operations happen simultaneously and, often in a nonsynchronized manner, across a range of different domains. The key indicator to assess the effectiveness of subversion operations should be the levels of mobilization or demobilization of target audiences, ranging from genuine social media users on one end of the spectrum to policymakers on the other end of the spectrum. The levels of mobilization and demobilization of target audiences reflect to what extent the attitudes, decisions, and behaviors of these audiences are affected by subversion operations. I suggest five levels of (de)mobilization—ranging from 1, low impact, to 5, high impact (see figure I.1)—that could be used to evaluate the impact of subversion operations:

1. Social media discourse among genuine social media users;
2. Offline civil-societal discourse involving conventional media;
3. Policy-relevant discourse between experts and policymakers;
4. Nonvirtual civil-societal (de)mobilization (e.g., protests or riots); and
5. A strategic shift in policymaking.

These effects might occur sequentially, simultaneously, or coincidentally, and therefore they are difficult to attribute to a particular perpetrator or singular operation. As the case studies will show, weaponized narratives are usually inserted on various levels simultaneously to generate maximum effect. The cumulative impact is then hard to measure, as it is likely going to be larger than the sum of its parts.

This leads to the next criterion: subversion needs to be political and instrumental. Though effects might only be measurable based on mobilization, it might be difficult to establish a causal relationship between the ultimate cumulative effect and a wider political strategy. As the perpetrator cannot know the exact effect of his or her subversion campaign beforehand, weaponized narratives rarely follow a clearly outlined political strategy, where ends, ways, and means are effectively lined up. Nonetheless, what is important here is that subversion serves as an instrument of political ends so as to differentiate between narratives shaped by social media influencers in a private capacity and an orchestrated strategic effort by an external political actor. Consider, too, that information networks combine a variety of direct, indirect, and coincidental surrogates. Some surrogates might be directly controlled by the subverting party, and others might work as autonomous entities voluntarily serving the cause and narratives of the subverting power.[87]

Third, subversion can only be means of warfare if it directly affects the will of people. Instead of purely looking at actions in the physical domain of the information environment, subversion must first affect the attitudes and decisions of people, both on collective and individual levels. Against the backdrop of the concept of "reflexive control," subversion needs to have an effect on the sociopsychological domain of the information environment first. It is here that narratives can shape the perception of individuals, groups, and communal influencers, particularly those on the strategic, policy level. In a clash of wills, reflexive control rests on the assumption that subversion can alter the will of individuals, which in a second step might generate an effect in the physical domain of the information space. If subversion campaigns merely trigger agents—such as bots, trolls, co-opted experts, and academics or co-opted policymakers—these campaigns hardly qualify as means of warfare. After all, even if administered or induced in the virtual space, subversion remains a distinctly human endeavor.

TOWARD A STRATEGY OF SUBVERSION

Freedman once said about strategy that "it is the art of creating power," by marrying political ends with military, economic, and political means.[88] In essence, the British strategist Liddell Hart states, "strategy depends for success, first and most, on a sound calculation and co-ordination of the ends and means."[89] And though Clausewitzians always invoke a reference to war, strategy more broadly is about the synchronized use of a variety of means in a number of ways to generate a political effect. Strategy, although rooted in the Greek word *strategos*, meaning "general," has long been detached from a narrow conceptualization of power in the military domain. Amid the era of subthreshold warfare, strategy today takes a whole-of-government approach to mobilizing all sources of power that can be employed to achieve particular political ends. Strategy is a "how to do it study" to find innovative ways to employ the means available to generate a desired effect— and a narrow focus on military means thereby limits the potential effects that can be generated. Thus, strategy is consequentialist, in that it is concerned with generating outcomes and effects; and it is instrumental, in that those effects should help a political actor to achieve the political endgame desired.

In the context of subversion as a source of subthreshold power, strategy provides the connection between the second aforementioned parameter of subversion: it needs to function as an instrument of political power because "strategy has just one function; to provide a secure connection between the worlds of purpose, which contestably is generally called policy, though politics may be more accurate, and its agents and instruments."[90]

Subversion therefore must serve a clearly defined political purpose. Strategy orchestrates the various means of subversion to achieve the desired objective of changing the attitudes, decisions, and ultimately behaviors of people in a clash of wills. The strategic employment of subversion means using the sources of information power in a way to achieve the desired ends of influence or information-psychological destabilization. As an instrument of power, subversion requires a sound strategy, which could involve coordinated employment of the means of an information network to unleash the power inherent in information.

In order to achieve the strategic effects of changing attitudes, decisions, and behaviors of people, subversion targets a variety of different audiences, ranging from the wider public to influencers in media and academia—all of which are ultimately supposed to affect policymaking.

Although it might be difficult to directly influence policymakers in office, information warriors have plenty of means available to indirectly influence policymakers by shaping media discourse, selecting the information policymakers are exposed to by staff members, and influencing the conversations policymakers are having with external experts. As the next chapters will show, even in a stable democracy like the United States, policymakers can be exposed to narratives in a way that alters their attitudes and decisions.

The means that can be used to achieve desired strategic effects through the information environment are very diverse. This book refers to the extensive assemblages of patrons and surrogates as information networks consisting of a range of virtual, human, and organizational surrogates that, with varying degrees of autonomy, directly or indirectly help the patron to disseminate, verify, and legitimize narratives amid civil society and policymaking. The three categories of surrogates that are integral in reshaping information environments are

- experts, consisting of academics, think tanks, and pseudoscientists who provide legitimacy and credibility to narratives;
- media, comprising both conventional media and social media outlets as well as public relations companies that help disseminate narratives; and
- practitioners, such as policymakers, politicians, civil servants, policy advisers, and lobbyists, who help translate narratives into policy agendas and potentially outcomes.

It is important to highlight that not all surrogates are directly paid and controlled by the patron. That is to say, in subversion, these information networks revolve around relatively flat hierarchies in which the patron directly engages crucial nodes in these networks but provides the rest of the network with relative autonomy to disseminate information as they see fit.[91] "Useful idiots" or coincidental surrogates are an integral part of every good subversion campaign. In the wake of Russia's invasion of Ukraine in February 2022, a generation of policymakers and pundits on the far right and far left in Europe and the United States rejected NATO's warning about Moscow's intentions in Ukraine as saber-rattling.[92] Attribution bias meant that the disinformation spread by the Kremlin was more readily believed by those "useful idiots" than the intelligence leaked by Western services.

Media outlets owned by patrons are directly controlled and enjoy little editorial freedom, such as Russia's RT Network, China's CGTN Network, and the Al Arabiya Network funded by Saudi Arabia and based in the United Arab Emirates (UAE). In the case of Taiwan, Chung T'ien News, owned by a local conglomerate with close business ties to China, had become an indirect surrogate to disseminate pro-China narratives in Taiwan before it was shut down in late 2020 by the Taiwanese government.[93]

Apart from that, attempts are being made by communication specialists to influence foreign journalists and affect their writing. This can come in the form of paid dinners and all-inclusive trips. Here, journalists can become coincidental and unconscious surrogates for the patron, as the case of *New York Times* op-ed columnist Thomas Friedman shows. After having been courted and chauffeured by Saudi crown prince Mohammed bin Salman, Friedman wrote a very flattering opinion piece on the crown prince, glossing over the extensive human rights violations committed under his watch.[94] The use of cyber surrogates in the social media sphere, such as trolls and bots, can take the form of both autonomous influencers paid for by patrons and digital armies following clear operational and tactical guidance of the patron,[95] as in the cases of the Russian Internet Research Agency and the Saudi troll farm in Riyadh.[96]

Funding for think tanks and academic research centers can be another way to build information networks in academia, in which researchers are either directly funded for research projects by patrons or receive donations for events and courses. Though the impact of think tank funding in established think tanks in the United States and Europe remains hard to measure, cases where think tanks are directly established by patrons often display more leniency toward official patron narratives. This is the case with the former Saudi-funded Arabia Foundation in Washington or the UAE-funded Bussola Institute in Brussels.[97] In other cases, surrogacy is again more coincidental when think tanks hire researchers based on their ideological compatibility with the patron's grand strategic narratives.

In the case of practitioners, surrogates tend to be more autonomous, as direct financial relationships in liberal democracies are impossible to hide. Lobbyists are the exception here, as they are directly paid to engage with policymakers to shape their decision-making through targeted briefings and hosting events, often in cooperation between think tanks and officials from patron countries. Members of parliament or members of congress, as well as their staffs, are being hosted by patron countries either locally or in the patron country. A case in point are the now infamous all-inclusive trips to Abu Dhabi for staff members on Capitol Hill organized and paid for by the UAE ambassador Yousef Otaiba.[98]

The means of the information networks can be employed in multiple ways to achieve the desired strategic effects. In a contestation over influence, surrogates can be used defensively to suppress and disrupt the subversion operations of adversaries. Having been subjected to weaponized narratives in the global public sphere by its neighbors since 2014, Qatar has responded with counter-narratives to disrupt defamation campaigns, especially from the UAE and Saudi Arabia.[99] When employed in a more offensive way, disruption can also be achieved by polluting the information environment with mis- and disinformation in an effort to polarize public debate and complicate consensus formation. Information and influence networks can also help to mobilize public opinion and activism in cyberspace as much as in the offline public sphere. Mobilization can also work in elite circles, where narratives enable the patron to directly mobilize elites in the policymaking nexus to act, especially if injected carefully through academic surrogates.

A Six-Step Approach to Subversion

Employed strategically, subversion tends to follow a six-step approach, starting from orientation and identification followed by formulation and dissemination to reach the final steps of verification and implementation.

In the first step, *orientation*, the subverting power determines the strategic end and effect it wants to achieve—even if the effect is merely disruption. The purpose of the operation has to be clearly laid out in order to determine what means and ways to employ to achieve the desired end state. In the orientation state, the subverting power needs to determine whose attitude, decision, or behavior it wants to change and how.

The second step, *identification*, might be the most crucial one for the success of the operation: identifying the vulnerabilities in the target audience's information environment and social fabric. Existing social, demographic, socioeconomic, and ethnic divisions can be targeted and exploited through carefully drafted and tailored narratives. The information-psychological center of gravity of the target audience needs to be properly analyzed in order to determine to what kind of narratives the audience is most likely to respond. Here, understanding societal grievances is essential as they provide inroads for external exploitation:

grievances are the root causes of mobilization and activism. Equally important is knowledge about existing biases in the target audience as well as understanding the infrastructural vulnerabilities of audiences, namely, how they process and consume information. Finally, subverting powers also need to identify physical vulnerabilities at the intersection between mobilization in the public sphere and policy-relevant debate. Only when information streams from the individual over the public sphere to policymaking circles are understood can subverting powers move to the next step.

During the next step, *formulation*, the subverting power needs to create narratives that would resonate well with the target audience, drawing on its existing biases and exploiting vulnerabilities in the infrastructural domain of the information environment.

The fourth step, *dissemination*, is about the cultivation and orchestration of the subverting power's own information and influence network. The orchestration of information power essentially revolves around nurturing or ripening decentralized networks, which heterarchically tie together different nodes of communication. These nodes operate as surrogates for the patron in the information environment, comprising (social) media elements, civil-societal and private sector agents, experts, and academics as well as in some cases policymakers. An inclusive subversion campaign involves a high level of orchestration of different, seemingly independent nodes in the information network that shape attitudes and behaviors of targeted audiences.

Verification, the fifth step, involves the subverting power predominantly relying on surrogates from the academic and expert level to provide legitimacy and credibility to narratives. Here, the subverting power needs to cultivate seemingly independent "experts" who act as authorities in the eyes of the public and policymakers. Though narratives that are only disseminated via the media and social media sphere might influence trends and shape what the public thinks about, it requires the "expert label" for it to become valid and relevant for policymakers. An expert publication or event can empower even disinformation-based narratives with a sense of credibility, as the case of experts who deny climate change illustrates.

Finally, *implementation* involves practitioners who can use established and verified trends in the public sphere and policy-relevant expert circles to engage policymakers. Former policymakers paid for by subverting powers are powerful tools to help feed narratives to relevant individuals in executive or legislative power. Such policymakers either directly or indirectly work for think tanks funded by subverting powers and bring their networks to the job. In the implementation phase, lobbyists also play a key role, as they can help the triangulation of narratives and information previously laid by other surrogates in the media or expert nexus. Lobbyists provide the important access points to policymakers to feed narratives to those ultimately deciding on policy.

CONCLUSION

Information has long been a source of power, but only more recently has information become a power in itself—a lever that, once manipulated, can help protagonists in the international system to achieve their political objectives. The concept of subversion, as used in this book, is a stand-alone lever of power that can achieve political outcomes that are highly disruptive and sometimes violent. The idea of subversion exploiting sociopsychological, infrastructural, and physical vulnerabilities in a target audience's information environment for the purpose of influence or destabilization allows protagonists to use information as power.

In this way, subversion in the information age exceeds the limited information capacities and capabilities of the analogue era. Digital technology allows subverting powers to multiply the potential of means and ways of information warfare conceived during the Cold War, such as political and psychological warfare, or "active measures." The potential of subversion to alter the opponent's will amid a polarized sociopolitical context and an unregulated information infrastructure has increased as narratives travel faster and deeper into the nexus of policy-relevant elites.

The next chapter examines the infrastructural developments in the information environment against the backdrop of a fundamental ideological narrative that divides the world into liberals and authoritarians. Before moving to the detailed case studies, where subverting powers use subversion as a means of "reflexive control" overseas, the next chapter looks at how subversion can be used domestically in authoritarian states to control the information-psychological center of gravity at home. The disruptive potential of weaponized narratives in the domestic context goes to show how far the effects of subversion can accumulate to generate death by a thousand cuts over time when employed as a means of warfare.

NOTES

1. Pincus, "Neutron Killer Warhead."
2. Ter Veer, "Struggle against the Deployment of Cruise Missiles," 213.
3. Rid, *Active Measures*, 256.
4. Rid, 258.
5. Jones and Kovacich, *Global Information Warfare*, 36.
6. Sun Tzu, *Art of War*, 40.

7. Von Clausewitz, *On War*, 13.
8. Jones and Kovacich, *Global Information Warfare*, 20.
9. Libicki, *What Is Information Warfare?*, 8.
10. Libicki, 32.
11. Giles and Hagestad, "Divided," 422.
12. Cheng, "Winning without Fighting," 2.
13. UK Ministry of Defence, "Allied Joint Doctrine," 1-1.
14. Fuller, *Tanks*, 320.
15. Taylor, *Global Communications*, 150.
16. Libicki, *What Is Information Warfare?*, 41.
17. Narula, "Psychological Operations," 179.
18. Cheng, "Winning without Fighting," 8.
19. See Manheim, *Strategic Public Diplomacy*.
20. Tuch, *Communicating with the World*, 3.
21. Olsson, "Public Diplomacy," 221.
22. Taylor, *Global Communications*, 162.
23. Robinson et al., *Modern Political Warfare*, xxiv.
24. Radvanyi, "Introduction to Psyops," 2.
25. Boot and Doran, "Political Warfare."
26. Kennan, *Inauguration*, 1.
27. Kennan, 3–7.
28. Smith, *On Political War*, 3.
29. Linebarger, *Psychological Warfare*, 15.
30. Taylor, *Munitions*, 38.
31. Linebarger, *Psychological Warfare*, 19.
32. Taylor, *Munitions*, 255.
33. Romerstein, "Disinformation," 57.
34. Pacepa and Rychlak, *Disinformation*, 3.
35. Pacepa and Rychlak, 54.
36. Dubov, *Active Measures*, 8.
37. President Truman's address during the opening of the US Information Agency in 1953, quoted by Taylor, *Global Communications*, 35.
38. Pacepa and Rychlak, *Disinformation*, 106.
39. Quoted by Waller, "American Way," 27.
40. Reilley, "Conducting a War," 127.
41. See Defty, *Britain*.
42. Lord, "Public Diplomacy," 68.
43. Schoultz, *That Infernal Little Cuban Republic*, 608.
44. Ross, "Honduras."
45. Kinzer, *All the Shah's Men*, 13.
46. Risen, "Secrets."
47. Taylor, *Global Communications*, 42.
48. Rid, *Active Measures*, 127.
49. Romerstein, "Disinformation," 60ff.
50. Giles, *Handbook*, 19–21.
51. Allenby and Garreau, "Weaponized Narrative."
52. Kramer et al., "From Prediction to Reflexive Control," 86.

53. Thomas, "Russia's Reflexive Control Theory."
54. Quoted by Giles, Sherr, and Seaboyer, *Russian Reflexive Control*, 6.
55. White, "Russian Disinformation."
56. Quoted by Warzel, "He Predicted the 2016 Fake News Crisis."
57. Schwartz, "You Thought Fake News Was Bad?"
58. Cheng, "Winning without Fighting," 3.
59. Helmus et al., *Russian Social Media Influence*, x.
60. Fridman, *Russian "Hybrid Warfare,"* 67.
61. Messner, *Vseminaya Myatezhevoyna*, 67.
62. Fridman, *Russian "Hybrid Warfare,"* 79.
63. For Meyer, see *SWR*, "Kritik an Mainzer Nahost-Experte Prof. Günter Meyer"; For Lüders, see Thöne, "Der Weiß-Schwarz-Denker."
64. Reuter, "Russlands perfider Feldzug gegen die Wahrheit."
65. Von Clausewitz, *On War*, 13.
66. Freedman, "Defining War," 20.
67. Deutsch and Senghaas, "Framework," 24.
68. Strachan and Scheipers, "Introduction," 7.
69. Paret, *Understanding War*, 10.
70. Wright, *Study of War*, 700.
71. Krieg and Rickli, "Surrogate Warfare," 47, 48.
72. Connable, Campbell, and Madden, *Stretching*.
73. Kennan, quoted by Harlow and Maerz, *Measures Short of War*, 3–14.
74. Connable, Campbell, and Madden, *Stretching*, ix.
75. Fridman, *Russian "Hybrid Warfare,"* 17.
76. Galtung, "Violence," 168.
77. Shaw, "Conceptual and Theoretical Frameworks," 102.
78. Jonsson, *Russian Understanding of War*, 123.
79. Deutsch and Senghaas, "Framework," 24.
80. Rettig, "Death Toll."
81. Rid, *Cyber War*, 37.
82. Kello, *Virtual Weapon*, 74.
83. Della Porta, *Social Movements*, 3.
84. Rid, *Cyber War*, 136.
85. Kitson, *Low-Intensity Operations*, 3.
86. Farrel, *Norms*, 6.
87. Krieg and Rickli, "Surrogate Warfare," 23.
88. Freedman, "Strategic Studies," 294.
89. Liddell Hart, *Strategy*, 336.
90. Grey, *Strategy Bridge*, 29.
91. Krieg and Rickli, "Surrogate Warfare," 11.
92. For Europe, see Karnitschnig, "Putin's Useful German Idiots"; for the United States, Graham, "Putin's Useful Idiots."
93. Wang and Ellis, "Taiwan Shuts Pro-China TV Channel."
94. Friedman, "Saudi Arabia's Arab Spring."
95. Krieg and Rickli, "Surrogate Warfare," 98.
96. For the Russian Internet Research Agency, see Seddon, "Documents"; for the Saudi troll farm in Riyadh, see Benner et al., "Saudis' Image Makers."

97. For the former Saudi-funded Arabia Foundation in Washington, see *Middle East Eye*, "Pro-Saudi Think Tank"; for the UAE-funded Bussola Institute in Brussels, see Krieg, "UAE's War."
98. Grim and Ahmed, "His Town."
99. See Krieg, "Weaponization of Narratives."

FOUR

....

Digital Authoritarians
and the Exploitation
of Liberation Technology

When twenty-six-year-old Mohamed Bouazizi left his house on Friday, December 17, 2010, with his vegetable cart on what was going to be a good day for business in the small Tunisian town of Sidi Bouzid, he had no idea how much this day would transform not just the lives of his family and his country but also the entire region. At about 10 a.m., a policewoman confiscated his unlicensed vegetable cart and imposed a fine of 10 dinars on him—a fine that would have been the equivalent of one good day's earning that would now threaten the very livelihood of Bouazizi as the only breadwinner in his family of eight. He pled for mercy, but the policewoman spat on him and insulted his family. Trying to complain at the local police headquarters, Bouazizi was dismissed and left humiliated.[1] Like so many young Tunisians of his generation, he had experienced countless episodes of arbitrary state power that had left the country on the brink of socioeconomic collapse while the political elite around the authoritarian ruler Ben Ali was living lavishly. Returning from the police, shamed Bouazizi poured petrol over himself and set himself on fire—a graphic act of desperation that caused nationwide outrage. Four weeks later, relentless mass protests in the face of police repression caused Ben Ali to step down after twenty-three years in office. The individual tragedy of Bouazizi had become the spark that set the region ablaze in what was later dubbed the "Arab Spring."

The story of the Arab Spring is a formidable demonstration of the link between communication power and political violence. The upward trajectory from Bouazizi's initial spark to protests and police repression and eventual revolution in the Arab world in 2010 and 2011 clearly shows the subversive potential of narratives that exploit existing socioeconomic and sociopolitical grievances.[2] This chapter does not argue that the Arab Spring was the result of a concerted effort by external protagonists to subvert authoritarian regimes. Thus, the Arab Spring does not serve as a case study of subversion but merely as an illustration of the potential for weaponized narratives to mobilize dissent that culminates in severe political violence. This chapter goes on to show how powerful narratives do not merely disrupt the sociopsychological and infrastructural domain of the information environment but also potentially can have far-reaching consequences in the physical domain.

Although the revolutions were started by brave dissidents breaking the barrier of fear from repression, it was the interconnectivity of different cells of dissidence across the region that were able to communicate and coordinate via social media that truly overwhelmed the security services of decades-old authoritarian regimes. The "Al Jazeera effect" implied that the revolutions were televised while social media provided influencers with an additional means to bypass regime censorship.[3] The narratives of social justice, political pluralism, and freedom were able to spread as quickly as they did from North Africa to the Levant and the Gulf because, unlike the revolutions that brought down the Eastern Bloc in the late 1980s, the uprisings that shook the Arab world in early 2011 took place in a highly mediatized environment. Satellite television and social media had undermined the monopoly of authoritarian regimes to shape "truth." Commentators were quick to praise the power of "liberation technology."[4]

For the authoritarians, however, especially in the Kremlin, the Arab Spring was perceived as a strategic shock, sparking fears over what was perceived as yet another episode of Western-led subversion.[5] The revolutions, especially in Libya, brought home the dangers of what Russian strategic analysts had already warned against for years: Western full-spectrum warfare relying on Western-centric networks mobilized through new technology in the information space.

This chapter examines the idea of "liberation technology" against the backdrop of the weaponization of narratives by both dissidents and authoritarians. The first half of the chapter sheds light on how weaponized narratives were able to not just galvanize and mobilize dissidence but also undermine the stability of political authority in Tunisia, Libya, Egypt, Syria, Bahrain, and Yemen. In all cases, weaponized narratives brought about regime change through a ripple effect. Although some would argue that Qatar and its Al Jazeera network carried out a strategic subversion campaign against the region's authoritarian regimes, this argument gives the small emirate on the Gulf too much credit. Though mobilization was high, the various activities that led to revolution were not orchestrated by Qatar in any strategic manner to serve a political objective that was clearly set out. There were genuine grievances and already-mobilized civil societies. Al Jazeera, together with social media, were important force multipliers for protesters facilitating the spread of narratives that helped mobilize dissidence across the region. The Arab Spring shows how the power of narratives can move dissent from the virtual to the physical space.

The second half of this chapter looks at the authoritarian learning curve in developing counternarratives to the revolutionary themes of social justice, political pluralism, and freedom. Digital authoritarians in Russia, China, and the Arab world have since been at war with any form of civil-societal activism. Making use of Internet 2.0 as a multichannel, participative platform, authoritarians have learned how to exploit "liberation technology" and to transform the Arab Spring into an "Arab Winter." The counterrevolutionaries understood the power of narratives to maintain information-psychological stability in their countries—at least for the short term.

UNDERMINING THE AUTHORITARIAN MONOPOLY ON TRUTH

The story of Mohamed Bouazizi in many ways represents the stories of millions of Arabs on the eve of the Arab Spring in 2010. The entire region had been severely hit by the global financial crisis of 2008 at a time when demographic pressures had already put strain on both public and private sector employment. Arguably the most educated generation of Arabs ever was confronted with one of the most contracted job markets in the region's history. The macroeconomic liberalization of Arab economies of the 1990s and 2000s, often in response to the pressures from both the World Bank and the International Monetary Fund, had left the traditionally socialist economies effectively exposed to the global economic downturn of markets after the most severe financial crisis since the Great Depression of the 1930s.[6] Foreign direct investment in the Arab world dropped after the market crash in late 2008. In parallel, the demand for manufacturing and agricultural products from the region also declined. The price of oil plunged in late 2008, particularly causing the oil-dependent rentier states of northern Africa to lose out on major sources of revenue. Because of lower investments and a sharp collapse in overall growth, people in the region were hit by relatively high inflation rates and unemployment.[7] Though the elites around the regimes had been able to bounce back from the effects of the macroeconomic crisis after 2008 fairly well, it was the middle class and the lower classes where poverty and economic despair were on the rise.

Rising food prices, declining wages, and unemployment, particularly among youth, created a dangerous cocktail for sociopolitical unrest in the region. Unlike their parents' generation, Arab youth had grown up under authoritarian regimes that since the late 1990s had struggled to cater to the needs of their people. Though the Arab nationalist narrative had still resonated with the previous generation, the regimes increasingly displayed a serious say/do gap between the sociopolitical and socioeconomic promises and their actual performance. Not only were regimes unable to secure a dignified standard of living for the majorities of their citizens, but on top, stories repeatedly leaked about the levels of lavish spending among those closely tied to the regime. Widespread nepotism and corruption had emboldened public sentiments of social injustice as the socioeconomic gap between regime elites and the public noticeably widened. For example, leaked reports on the lavish lifestyle of the Tunisian autocrat Ben Ali and his wife Leila Trabelsi in the aftermath of the financial crisis suggested to most Tunisians that their president had been out of touch with the people.[8]

The emerging fault line between the regime and the wider population could no longer be easily bridged by what had long been a policy of repression and accommodation. As Hanafi argues, "The authoritarian states have governed through their heavy 'right hand,' . . . using their security and repressive apparatus and . . . up to 2000, the population has 'borne' or tolerated this because the same state also has a 'left hand' which provides public goods to a large portion of the population, it being a remnant of the welfare state."[9]

A survey conducted in Egypt in the immediate aftermath of Mubarak's departure in April 2011 confirms that for Egyptians the three main concerns were unemployment, police repression, and corruption.[10] In the face of a retreating Arab welfare state and growing elite corruption, sentiments of alienation and public disenfranchisement with the antiquated narratives of "authoritarian stability" became widespread. The call for social justice—although initially only heard among liberal, tech-savvy youth—was one that potentially resonated deeply with large parts of an impoverished and aggrieved population. The seeds of dissidence had been sown in the Arab world by the 2000s but had grown into a seedling by 2008.

TOWARD AN ARAB PUBLIC SPHERE

A new generation of Arabs had been exposed to an information environment that in terms of infrastructure had been quite different from that of their parents. Though the notion of an Arab public sphere was certainly not new, the concept of Habermas's *Öffentlichkeit* had taken a different shape in the Arab world. First, the public and private spheres have never been effectively distinguished as it might have been in the Western concept of the word. The *majilis*, as the "assembly" or the "council," might exist within the private boundaries of the home, but it is open to the wider clan, neighbors, and visitors. It is here where social and political issues have been debated in the Arab world for centuries in a relatively inclusive, albeit gender-segregated, fashion. The *majilis* thereby exists both in the private space of the family and the space of civil society. In the same way, the *masjid*, the mosque, was always more than just a mere place of worship in the predominantly Muslim Arab world. This is where a local public sphere exists that is far from apolitical.

Second, the notions of the national and the transnational exist side by side in the Arab world. As a lingo-cultural community that transcends the boundaries of the state, publications in the Arab world immediately have a regional dimension, drawing in audiences that are transnational in nature. The same might be true for the Islamic public sphere, which often gets conflated with its Arab counterpart.[11] The transnational idea of the *umma*, as the community of Muslims, exists in parallel to the Arab public sphere as a transnational space of communal interaction and dialogue that transcends the authorities of individual states and governments.[12]

Hence, the Arab public sphere has its roots in the institutions of the *majlis* and the *masjid* and also exceeds the boundaries of state and nation. Nonetheless, the public sphere traditionally has rarely been able to act as a force of civil-societal mobilization, as it might have done in the Western world. Though the Arab nationalist and Arab socialist revolt against the monarchs and colonial powers of the 1950s and 1960s was accompanied by mass protests and dissidence, the regimes that followed consolidated their power by co-opting and subverting civil society. Nasser in Egypt, Assad in Syria, Gadhafi in Libya, and Saddam in Iraq had all made attempts to absorb public movements under the umbrella of the regime. As populist authoritarians, they widely exploited the revolutionary narratives that had toppled previous regimes, giving their rule a veneer of popular legitimacy.[13] The Arab public sphere had lost its intrinsic function as a public forum separate from the state and able to speak truth to power. The only exceptions to this rule in the Arab world were the Islamist movements that operated outside the co-option but often with the acquiescence of the state.[14] Consequently, at least since the late 1970s, the Arab public sphere had, unlike in the West, strong religious, Islamist connotations.

The revolution in the information environment that came with satellite and social media in the late 1990s and 2000s fundamentally reshaped the traditionally narrow, restricted, and co-opted Arab public sphere, moving discourse away from the control of the regime and beyond the boundaries of the *majlis* and the *masjid*. First, the emergence of satellite television in the 1990s challenged existing patterns of information consumption in the Arab world. It moved away from entertainment-based broadcasts to actual "news" reports that were no longer censored and filtered to comply with regime narratives and were now challenging them. A watershed moment in this development was the founding of Al Jazeera in Qatar in 1996—a satellite TV station funded by the Qatari government and equipped with levels of editorial freedom that were revolutionary for the region. Based on the slogan of providing the "voice to the voiceless," Al Jazeera attracted a range of talented dissident journalists who were now able to bring their political convictions to the studio without having to fear regime censorship. It was able to fill a void in an Arab public sphere that had long been successfully co-opted by the state, providing not just a channel for top-down communication but also a degree of reciprocity. It allowed viewers to actively take part in the news they were consuming and contributing to by giving them an opportunity to call in, offering a unique diversity of opinions to the networks. Al Jazeera became renowned for the spectrum of pundits it brought on giving a voice to Sunni Islamists, Shia clerics, and Israelis, among many others. Most infamously, Al Jazeera became the preferred outlet for Al Qaeda to release the video messages of Osama bin Laden. No other channel was able to so capture the consciousness of the Arab world.

Not only was the channel quickly becoming the first choice for news in the region,[15] it changed the viewing behavior of audiences in the Arab world— moving from entertainment and sports to news.[16] By the early 2000s, Al Jazeera's headlines shaped a pan-Arab consciousness.[17] Its coverage of the Second Intifada in Palestine and the burden of international sanctions on Iraq became regional agenda setters. For people in the Gulf, Al Jazeera provided a platform to dissidents from Qatar's neighboring countries, causing repeated diplomatic rifts, particularly between Doha and Riyadh. In many ways, Al Jazeera had become the thorn in the side of authoritarians in the region—a luxury Qatar's leadership could afford, owing to a homogeneous and extremely wealthy public at home with no real internal grievances.[18]

Serving as the spearhead of satellite television, Al Jazeera widened the Arab public sphere so that it became more inclusive and diverse, lowering the barriers for entry to a broader, even illiterate audience that could now be part of a transnational Arab debate on issues that mattered and were not prescribed by the regime.[19] Nonetheless, as Marc Lynch argues, while Al Jazeera was the driving force behind unscripted and unlimited controversial dialogue, it long remained disconnected from policymaking and shaping—something that would change with the emergence of social media.[20]

Although Al Jazeera had provided its audiences with an accessible forum for debate, interaction and reciprocity were still very limited. Al Jazeera's producers, although far more liberal than traditional regime gatekeepers, effectively still operated as gatekeepers, deciding whose voice was going to be heard. With the Internet advancing, Al Jazeera's website offered more opportunities for viewers to engage with the channel, leaving comments that would then stir up debate online in parallel to conventional broadcasts. In the late 2000s, Al Jazeera moved into the social media space, creating accounts on Twitter and Facebook that allowed an infant Arab social media sphere to more directly engage with the channel and its reporting. Most important, Al Jazeera moved into a space that was inhabited by tech-savvy, liberal Arab youngsters, who were disillusioned with the narratives of both authoritarians and antiauthoritarian Islamists and were trying to carve out their own public sphere. For the young, educated Arab intelligentsia, the Internet 2.0 and social media provided a unique tool to advance dissident ideas and mobilize support outside the control of the regime. Dissident narratives about social justice, political freedom, and civil liberties started to breed on social media, where, protected by relative anonymity, the young liberal elite started to express their grievances about macroeconomic mismanagement, corruption, and political repression. These were grievances that Al Jazeera did not shy away from addressing but was unable to translate into civil-societal mobilization.

Although the regimes were willing to tolerate expressions of sympathy with Palestinians during the Second Intifada after 2000 and with Iraqis after the United States–led intervention in 2003, they underestimated how this civil-societal activism could spread into other domains closer to home. The increased interconnectedness between the virtual and the physical information environment—that is, the cybersphere and the so-called Arab Street—meant that physical acts of dissidence on international issues could bounce back into the cybersphere, where it was amalgamated with domestic grievances.[21] Seemingly external issues such as "Palestine" or "Iraq" had repeatedly served as catalysts in the 2000s to galvanize protests that would spill over into domestic policy domains. For example, the Kefaya movement in Egypt that led to protests against the Mubarak regime in 2004 was a liberal civil society group that grew out of demonstrations in support of the Second Intifada and against the United States–led invasion of Iraq. It brought together a range of different opposition groups that eventually called for sociopolitical liberalization and change in Egypt.[22] Although the protests were small in size in comparison with the mass protests of 2011, the Mubarak regime in Cairo had completely underestimated the dissident potential of small pockets of political opposition once coordinated and properly mobilized. As Jon Alterman prophetically stated in 2001,

> Every authoritarian government in the region has to maintain a watchful eye on public sentiment, and it has to balance coercion and co-optation—albeit in different measures at different times in different places. Technological developments have made that balancing act more difficult because states have lost some of the tools that have helped them lead public opinion—and thus, co-opt their populations—in the past. While most states still maintain an overwhelming advantage over any possible opponent in the public sphere, their ability to control what happens in that sphere is waning.[23]

And it was social media that provided new tools to unite and coordinate voices of dissent across the borders of states in a pan-Arab, transnational public sphere. The sharing of grievances thereby went beyond the exchange of information. It helped consolidate dissent and empower others to express similar sentiments of political and economic disenfranchisement, social marginalization, and injustice. It also helped dissidents to coordinate activities across a wider geographic space below the radar of regime and intelligence surveillance. Social media would function as the interlocutor of grievances between the conventional media sphere and audiences on the ground, thereby creating an interactive, inclusive, and accessible public space for dissidents to use—yet with the caveat that, in the late 2000s, only a relatively small, mostly liberal Arab elite really had access to the Internet and social media.[24] The Internet 2.0 and social media really only became a tool of mass mobilization in the aftermath of the Arab Spring as Internet penetration in the region tripled.[25]

THE REVOLUTION WILL NOT JUST BE TELEVISED

The revolutions in the physical domain were possible only because of the revolutions in the infrastructural domain of the information environment. Still, the Arab Spring was caused neither by satellite television nor by social media—both merely provided means for dissidents who had found new ways to organize in the 2000s outside the private space of the house, the *majilis*, or the *masjid*. The new Arab public sphere was pivotal in collecting grievances and compounding grievers; building transnational communities of like-minded individuals—echo chambers of dissidence for those disenchanted with regime narratives; helping to consolidate causes and counternarratives to the regime; and serving as a tool of organizing and coordinating civil-societal activism in the virtual and physical space—outside the control of the regime and its security sector.[26] Hence, although it is not a case study of subversion because it was not instrumentalized by one adversary against another, it nonetheless shows the dynamics that weaponized narratives help to unfold if they are instrumentalized.

Narratives of self-victimization portraying the Arab as helpless at the hands of greater external powers and their proxies in the region had been fluctuating in the region before 2010.[27] The socioeconomic grievances that had been the actual root cause of regional dissidence had been debated online and on satellite TV for a decade before Bouazizi's self-immolation. Youth unemployment, rising food prices, and corruption were grievances that were not specific to any one country in the region but were existing transnational themes covered by Al Jazeera. After the 2008 financial crisis, the macroeconomic situation made life for ordinary people in the region unbearable, and Al Jazeera provided them with an outlet to make their grievances heard. The virtual community of viewers and callers was built around a common sense of grievance vis-à-vis regimes that appeared to be overwhelmed with managing the fallout of the economic downturn amid continuous elite largesse.

What the virtual community of grievers required was an initial spark to catalyze their fears and concerns and translate it into anger and rage—and Bouazizi provided exactly that. The story of the young, economically struggling street vendor from Tunisia humiliated by the power of the state while merely trying to make a living immediately fell on fertile ground in the Arab public sphere. Two decades earlier, the tragic story of Bouazizi might have remained local news containable by the regime. In late 2010, however, the individual tragedy of Bouazizi was instantly wrapped by Al Jazeera into a narrative of martyrdom symbolic for the individual struggle of the Arab youth for survival amid social injustice and regime repression.[28] The images of protests that unfolded in southern Tunisia were broadcast around the world by the Qatar-based channel. The immense communication power that Al Jazeera had acquired throughout the 2000s was now able to consolidate the narrative of "a fight for social justice" and deliver it to a pan-Arab audience of millions. Lower- and middle-class Egyptians and Libyans suddenly saw that they were not alone in their frustration and that others were doing something about it. The images of mass protests in Tunisia coupled with powerful narratives of martyrdom were able to create an echo chamber of dissidence where people felt empowered to act. The transnational diffusion of outrage over the individual fate of martyrs such as Bouazizi in Tunisia, Khaled Said in Egypt, Terbil in Libya, and Tawakkol Karman in Yemen was made possible only because of the symbiotic, reinforcing nexus between satellite television and social media reaching millions connected through uncontrolled, "liberal" channels of communication. Arabs across the region moved from being merely a lingo-cultural community to being a virtual community of grievers sharing not just the same values and culture but also the same frustration over social injustice and regime repression.[29]

The Arab public sphere was able to connect receptive and like-minded audiences that would now be able to mobilize each other through "learning by example." Emulation became a powerful dynamic of mass mobilization in an era defined by a new information infrastructure. As Eva Bellin observes, it "leads to the borrowing of 'mobilizational frames, repertoires, and modes of contention,' and it accounts for the fact that phenomena such as revolution, nationalism, and democratization tend to come in waves. By exercising the power of analogy, 'the seemingly impossible [becomes] possible,' and people are motivated to take action they might never have considered before."[30]

Revolutionary first movers, mostly from among liberal, media-savvy youth, were instrumental in emulating civil-societal activism from neighboring countries. The revolutionary wave from Tunisia reached Egypt next, where young liberals used Facebook groups to gain support for their causes, adopting similar narratives of social justice and martyrdom as activists in Tunisia. The Facebook group of the "April 6 Youth Movement" has been one of the most active online since after its inception in 2008. Its more than seventy thousand young and educated members saw the Tunisian protests as an opportunity to plug their narrative for more social justice and civil liberties into the emerging revolutionary narrative.[31] Equally active on social media was the Egyptian Facebook group "Kullena Khalid Said" that was formed in response to the fatal beating of liberal activist Khalid Said by Egyptian authorities in the summer of 2010. The Facebook group shared pictures of Said's abused body, using it as a vehicle to decry police violence and offering Egyptians an anonymous outlet to bond over their outrage, as the group administrator Ghonim writes in his book.[32] Through the use of "likes" and "comments," Facebook groups were able to interact with members helping to consolidate an online community of grievers.

The narrative of martyrdom was effectively transported to build a virtual place of belonging, demarcating between "us," the grievers, and "them," the perpetrators. Regime repression and the use of reactionary violence against protesters helped create more martyrs who increased emotional bonding between mourners and dissidents. With a rising death toll, the narrative of martyrdom in the region shifted increasingly from one of victimhood to one of empowerment and mobilization that was able to transcend the barrier of fear the authoritarian regimes had built up over several decades.[33] The collective struggle against repression helped foment a counternarrative to the regime, one that encouraged youth to become active even at the risk of their own lives. What started with expressions of solidarity on social media turned into an expression of solidarity with protesters on the street. Those who initially expressed their sympathy and empathy with martyrs online were motivated by images of protests flooding TVs and social media to take their solidarity to the street. The narrative of a collective Arab struggle against the "corrupt authoritarians" empowered many youngsters who felt, especially after the fall of the Ben Ali regime in Tunisia, that there was a window of opportunity for change to the sociopolitical constitution of the Arab world. The self-perpetuating dynamic of mobilization was helped by the erosion of fear of the regime, as authoritarians suddenly appeared unable to undermine online and offline activism. Thus, the sudden prospect of success further empowered activists to take risks in the face of offline repression. As Amira Mittermaier states, "Many young Egyptians described the willingness to sacrifice their lives as inseparable from the transformative experience of no longer feeling afraid"—a sentiment helped by a legitimizing narrative of fighting for the greater good.[34]

It is important to highlight that the Arab cybersphere at the height of the protests in 2011 was not as inclusive as it is today. For example, in Egypt, only between 20 and 30 percent of citizens had access to the Internet, limiting the reach of Facebook groups, YouTube videos, and tweets to a small group of tech-savvy youngsters.[35] Although first movers on social media played a crucial role in mobilizing the youth, the Arab Spring could grow into a mass phenomenon only because of the almost monopolistic position of Al Jazeera beaming images and commentary to the households of millions.[36] Social media was the critical force multiplier in the mobilization process of a new generation that went as far as printing Facebook pages and handing them out as hard copies to protesters on the street to fuel their resolve.[37] For the first time, social media showed its subversive potential. It helped break the barrier of fear by providing dissidents with safe places to organize, making it easy for them to forward messages inexpensively and under the radar of regime censorship. Social media became more than just a means to consolidate an Arab public sphere; it provided a way for relatively heterogeneous entities to assemble quickly. To borrow Rheingold's concept of smart mobs, social media and mobile communication technology provided heterarchically structured networks with means to communicate without clear command and control.[38] Anyone with Internet access and a social media account was able to participate in a decentralized mobilization effort. Using swarm tactics, "smart mobs" were able to organize quickly in a virtual safe place that at the time was impenetrable by regime authority. Once mobilized, the smart mob created an organic life of its own, producing dynamics that neither first movers nor security forces were able to control.[39]

It is important to highlight again that although the Arab Spring nicely illustrates the subversive potential of satellite and social media, it remained a leaderless revolution that did not serve any external political strategy. Allegations by Saudi and Emirati media that Qatar had instrumentalized the Arab Spring via Al Jazeera do not just inflate Doha's actual capacity to do so but, more important, belittle the narratives, ambitions, and activities of the first movers.[40] Though Al Jazeera did help create momentum, it was only when the revolutions were already in full swing that Qatar decided to exploit existing fault lines and grievances in the region to move against authoritarianism. And though Qatar eventually provided opposition groups with material support, Al Jazeera's role in the early months of the uprisings was not strategically linked to Qatar's foreign and security toolbox. Hence, although the narratives of social justice and liberalization helped shape the will of the people and mobilized millions to move against authoritarian power, the narratives were not orchestrated strategically by the Qatari government to change the regional status quo. For months, protests in the region remained decentralized, leaderless dynamics that would only later be co-opted by antiregime forces. Qatar's role was one of facilitation at best that lacked a clear strategy and understanding of how these dynamics could be effectively exploited.

"USURPING" THE ARAB PUBLIC SPHERE

In every country, the first movers of the Arab Spring were predominantly liberal and urban youth, despite coming from a variety of social, political, and economic backgrounds. In the beginning, religious symbols were absent from the protests as Islamists—the traditional opposition to authoritarianism—were initially hesitant to come out in support of the uprising.

Political Islam had mostly coexisted with the regimes they opposed in the lead-up to the Arab Spring, after severe crackdowns in the decades before. Both reformists and traditionalists had created a niche where they could work with the system rather than against it. The Muslim Brotherhood movement, via its many different local franchises and organizations, had been particularly active in the civil-societal space, complementing the services provided by the state rather than competing with it. As the Arab regimes were increasingly unable to cater to public needs inclusively, the Muslim Brotherhood provided education, humanitarian relief, and other charitable services to the growing number of disenfranchised people in Egypt, Jordan, and Palestine, among others.[41] The narratives of social justice wrapped in religious symbolism had been on the banners of many Islamist groups for decades, providing a religious counternarrative to the secular narrative propagated by the Arab nationalist regimes.[42] Islamist groups were operating with tacit regime consent, building extensive civil-societal networks among lower- and middle-class Arabs who had benefited from the many charitable activities Islamist organizations were offering. For the majority of Islamist groups, especially those affiliated with the Muslim Brotherhood, civil-societal activities were geared toward a slow, bottom-up approach to reform and not to revolution.[43]

With people taking to the streets in early 2011 in northern Africa, the old Islamist guard at first refused to publicly endorse the revolution. It was the younger echelons of Islamists engaged on social media who would reach out to other members of their generation to join the protests against the regime.[44] The first Islamist movers in Egypt were predominantly members of the Muslim Brotherhood and made an effort to portray their engagement as supporting the people's claims for more social justice, less repression, and more individual freedom.[45]

Yet, with the collapse of the regimes in Tunisia, Libya, and Egypt and the withdrawal of the regime in Syria, Islamist organizations had one competitive advantage over their secular, liberal comrades: they had more financial clout, had a deeper reach into large parts of Arab society, were better organized, and had networks in place that could sustain a political campaign on a large scale.[46] Islamist groups were able to mobilize huge numbers of people both online and offline to rally behind a candidate using narratives of social justice and democracy that resonated well with a majority of people who had protested for regime change. With a political race under way in Tunisia and Egypt, Islamists were able to draw on their legacy as the Arab world's only opposition that had championed the narratives being propagated by the revolutionaries. Their ability to mobilize their own people to vote resulted in a disproportionate Islamist voter turnout, slightly skewing the results during the first elections after the revolution.[47]

Islamists had used the Arab public sphere to speak directly to the Muslim *umma*, doing so with messages that already, before the eve of the revolutions, were not censored by the regime. Islamists had been at the forefront decrying public grievances publicly—an exemplary, charismatic Islamist leader, the Egyptian exile Yusuf Qaradawi, had his own show on Al Jazeera, where he directly spoke to an audience consisting of several million people across the region.[48] What Islamist preachers had understood early on was that new media would provide a powerful speaking tube for the messages and narratives of political Islam to fulfill an unforeseen potential of social mobilization in the region. In the aftermath of the Arab Spring, all generations and calibers of Islamists were present in the Arab public sphere via satellite TV and social media, providing seemingly simple answers to complex problems of how to restructure regional governance.

Although Islamists were competing in democratic elections in Tunisia and Egypt, the revolutions had degenerated into civil wars in Libya and Syria, where Islamist narratives provided legitimization and guidance for rebel groups taking up arms. Again, better-organized and better-funded Islamist rebel groups were able to mobilize more effective fighting forces whose morale and esprit de corps were strengthened through religious references and narratives. Rebel groups managed to create quasi-state entities to govern territory and provide security against regime forces. For instance, amid growing desperation in the face of relentless regime repression in Syria, Islamists were able to provide an alternative to the state using increasingly extreme Islamist narratives to gather public support on the ground while providing public goods relatively effectively.[49]

By early 2014, a new group appeared on the scene that had crossed the border from Iraq into war-torn Syria: the Islamic State in Syria and Iraq (ISIS). It had perfected the subversive use of social media to gather support and attract followership in the Salafi-jihadist spectrum. Bearing little resemblance to politically active Islamists in northern Africa, ISIS was the product of an unholy alliance forged in time of war between Iraqi tribal factions, remnants of Saddam's Baathist regime, and Salafi-jihadist ideologues.[50] Locally, ISIS drew on religious narratives that resonated with Sunni communities in both Iraq and Syria whose members had felt abandoned and disenfranchised by respective regimes in years of conflict. Globally, ISIS grew into a "cyber caliphate," merging seventh-century Islamic narratives with twenty-first-century pop culture. It was not only targeting existing grievances and fault lines in the region but also attracting and mobilizing thousands of youths in Europe to join its barbaric crusade to establish a new world order.[51] ISIS was no longer just utilizing narratives on social media; it mostly existed on social media as a transnational network of sympathizers and supporters who would provide ISIS with extensive depth in reach for their messages. Tens of thousands of followers became, willingly or unwillingly, surrogates of the ISIS franchise, spreading narratives that were tailored to the information consumption habits of the key target groups of youngsters.[52] ISIS was able to accompany its terror with messages of appeal, promising a utopian concept: a global Islamic caliphate whose members are distinct only in their degree of zealotry.[53]

The success of ISIS was not in its battlefield victories alone. It was also in its exploitation of the information environment, where the brand developed into a decentralized cult that would draw people into an exclusive organization that had total control over its members.[54] It was able to target the sociopsychological biases of target communities that felt disenfranchised without a clear sense of physical and ideological belonging. It provided vulnerable members of society with a victory narrative and a place within a well-organized hierarchy of terror removed not just from the conventional controls of states and regimes but also from the control of norms imposed by societies that seemingly rejected them. ISIS catered toward its target audiences' viewing behaviors, producing sophisticated audiovisual content that glorified its barbarism and promised power to the powerless. It was able to attract tens of thousands of followers—from the virtual space of the information environment to a physical space on the streets of London, Paris, and Brussels and the battlefields of Mesopotamia. The ISIS-inspired attacks in Europe in particular were the result of a highly sophisticated strategy of cyber subversion: attacks perpetrated by self-radicalized terrorists were the result of an instrumental political strategy of ISIS to change the will of the perpetrators to use physical violence against innocent victims. "Liberation technology" had become "terrorization technology."

As Larry Diamond highlights, "technology is merely a tool, open to both noble and nefarious purposes."[55] While "liberalization technology" might have enabled the mobilization of revolution 2.0, it has since also provided the tools to authoritarians and terrorists alike to demobilize the masses in an effort to establish a dictatorship 2.0.

DIGITAL AUTHORITARIANS: CONTROLLING THE PUBLIC SPHERE

Liberals might have initially appreciated the potential of the Internet to advocate for progressive change in an attempt to liberalize and empower civil society. Authoritarians and illiberals have both since closed the technology gap in order to use it for their own purposes. As Philipp Howard and colleagues state, "Social media have gone from being the natural infrastructure for sharing collective grievances and coordinating civic engagement to being a computational tool for social control, manipulated by canny political consultants, and available to politicians in democracies and dictatorships alike."[56]

The infrastructural revolutions in the information environment outlined in chapter 2 initially constituted a risk for authoritarian regime resilience. Now they offered a range of opportunities for civil-societal control and disruption. As Internet access and cyber infrastructure are often owned or co-owned by regimes in authoritarian countries, it is precisely these regimes that regulate access to this cyber public sphere by either throttling Internet speeds or cutting off the Internet all together—as was the case during the Arab Spring. These desperate moves cost authoritarian regimes hundreds of millions of dollars as the disruption of the cyber domain caused ripple effects for businesses and markets in an age of growing cyber dependence.[57] Attempts to create a "clean Internet" through censorship and self-censorship in countries such as North Korea, China, and Iran had only limited success. That is because such a move only responds to existing online content rather than offering proactive solutions for dealing with dissidence 2.0. Consequently, with a growing dependence on cyberspace, authoritarians had to become creative in finding proactive measures to turn the dynamics of civil-societal mobilization against itself in an effort to subvert the public sphere.

As a result of this arms race over "truth" between dissidents and authoritarians, the academic debate has become increasingly skeptical and cynical in its engagement with the romantic argument that revolutions in the information space are emancipatory for individuals and communities. Cyberskeptics such as Evgeny Morozov have called the premature euphoria about the emancipatory potential of social media and Internet 2.0 "cyber utopianism" that completely fails to appreciate how authoritarians could use the same infrastructure to monitor and control citizens.[58] The weaponization of narratives by authoritarians provides more subtle solutions to undermine civil society than the interference of Internet speeds. It allows for the manipulation of trends in the public sphere, injecting regime talking points into public debate and silencing those who deviate from the main regime narratives. With intimidation and repression working online and offline simultaneously, Peter Singer claims that the subversion of civil society by authoritarians has unleashed a spiral of silence, where intimidation and repression eventually lead to self-censorship until potential regime critics withhold their ideas.[59] Digital authoritarians understood that social media provides an opportunity for countermobilization and discourse framing that works in favor of the regime and its strategic narratives.[60]

Although domestic repression of civil society through information does not constitute subversion as a means of warfare, it nonetheless has provided authoritarians with a learning curve for how to reverse engineer "liberation technology" so that it can eventually be used as a means of subversion overseas.

China

China has been one of the pioneers of exploiting the information space to sustain regime security. Discussions about the Internet there have traditionally revolved around the so-called Great Firewall of China—a metaphor used for the Chinese state enforcement of regulations and technological restrictions on free flow of content on the Internet. Beijing has predominantly focused on the domestic realm of subverting civil society—providing lessons that China appears to increasingly apply overseas to become a "discourse power."[61] However, China's information operations are mostly defensive in nature, with the COVID-19 pandemic and protests in Hong Kong indicating how Beijing might apply subversion outside its borders more offensively.[62]

Since the early 2000s the Chinese state has invested heavily in means to control data flows by deleting unwanted content, blocking foreign websites, and slowing cross-border traffic, effectively creating an extensive intranet that exposes users to content that conforms to the narratives of Beijing.[63] Tens of thousands of cyber police patrol cyberspace, flagging content that would be considered harmful in an Orwellian police state. The result is a "cleaner" version of the Internet with a selective truth about history and current affairs. For example, the Chinese Wikipedia equivalent, Baidu Baike, features only a handful of events from 1989. It completely ignores the transformational events of the Spring of 1989 on Tiananmen Square that saw the Chinese state violently suppress and kill thousands of protesters and innocent bystanders.[64]

For China's leadership, the information environment, especially the perception of it becoming a "crypto-liberal Western paradise," has long been deemed a risk to regime security.[65] For Xi Jinping, the notion of a truly liberal public sphere where information flows freely has been anathema to Chinese values of harmony, unity, and stability.[66] Xi's vision of the "Chinanet" might run counter to the idea of a truly liberalizing tool for the public—for Xi, the Internet is supposed to reinforce rather than undermine the authority of the state and its monopoly on power. Values of sociopolitical harmony, unity, and stability take precedence in Beijing over liberal values of pluralism and civil liberties that are viewed as exposing the vulnerabilities of the sociopsychological and infrastructural domain of the information environment. In Xi's China, the destructive potential of an unregulated public sphere for social-political stability and harmony have caused the state to develop measures to increase the resilience of both the regime and the "public will." Mao's vision of the Cultural Revolution empowering the collective over the individual has now been digitized: Beijing strives for homogeneity in thought and discourse in a public sphere of hundreds of millions of citizens.

As the Internet 2.0 started to expand with the advent of social media, the Great Firewall of China was insufficient to keep up with public demands for socialization in cyberspace. Beijing had to allow users to spread information, engage in e-commerce, connect with like-minded people, and sustain intimate relationships.[67] China effectively created a parallel cyber universe where at least a low level of a public sphere was possible to emerge, albeit highly politically constrained and controlled. The Great Firewall was no longer able to cope with more than 800 million mobile Chinese on the intranet—a potentially powerful mass of online dissidents.[68] The state had to develop an additional tool to subvert an increasingly liberated community of users who, although unable to access potentially "harmful content" externally, was able to create and share content internally. Dubbed the "Great Cannon," it has the ability to arbitrarily replace and adjust unencrypted content as it travels through the Internet.[69] In addition, Beijing laid out clear guidelines for self-discipline for both Internet giants and users. The industry had to subscribe to a public pledge of self-discipline based on four principles of patriotic observance of law, uniformity, trustworthiness, and honesty. Though Yahoo! endorsed the pledge to retain its access to this lucrative market, Google decided to withdraw from China in protest.[70] Self-censorship has limited the flow of content that is deemed incompatible with the main strategic narratives of the Chinese state but was insufficient to effectively contain the drive of Chinese Internet users to create and share narratives.

More effective than manipulating content directly has been the cultivation of the *wu mao dang*, the "50-Cent Party," which are "crowdsourced propagandists . . . intended to merge the consciousness of 1.4 billion people with the consciousness of the state."[71] These more than 2 million cybersurrogates are paid a modest amount (explaining the nickname "50-Cent Party"), and they work either directly for the state or are outsourced to commercial companies to disrupt, co-opt, and subvert public discourse.[72] The *wu mao* might not be able to delete content, but they are able through sheer volume of engagement to silence content that might undermine the homogeneity and harmony the state envisages. These trolls directly engage with users who act outside the mainstream, questioning their patriotism or asking for more patience with China's government reform programs.[73] On the battlefield for narrative superiority, these cybersurrogates are able to create trends through phony comments, allowing content to go viral that makes the Chinese project appear in a positive light. Further engagement with such comments by genuine users increases the exposure of this content to other users even more. The result is a spiral of deafening and paralyzing positivity, whereby content that might only marginally go against the state-authorized mainstream gets swallowed up by the virality of positive content. Even more, China manages to mobilize users to cheer for the regime voluntarily, being trapped in an echo chamber of positivity. Aside from being confronted by an army of trolls, Chinese users are further discouraged from engaging in excessive social media commentary by draconian punishments for the spread of rumors.

Based on a 2013 Chinese Supreme Court ruling, any user posting a rumor that is seen by more than five thousand individuals and shared more than five hundred times could face defamation charges and up to three years in prison.[74]

Russia

Like China, Russia has recognized the disruptive potential of the public sphere and has actively tried to increase its resilience against civil-societal activism. Having classified information-psychological stability as of vital national interest, the Kremlin has proactively intervened in the public sphere first at home and then overseas. Russia sees itself on the forefront of a war over narratives under fire from a United States–led campaign to subvert the Russian public through the spread of liberal and human rights narratives.[75] Both the "Color Revolutions" and the Arab Spring shook the Kremlin to its core, making key decision-makers increasingly paranoid over what they saw as a Western campaign to "usurp" elites and mobilize the public. Russia's answer is populist authoritarianism, or illiberal democracy, which it presents as the counternarrative to the Western "liberal order." In so doing, Moscow provides one of the most appealing narratives to right-wing conservatives in the West who feel alienated by a perceived liberal elitist imposition of globalization and liberalization, as the next chapter details.

For Russia, the answer to openness and pluralism is a form of populist nationalism built around a charismatic and almost omnipotent leader—a personality cult that Vladimir Putin has been able to create around himself. For the Kremlin, information-psychological stability is most effectively achieved by instilling a sense of patriotism in the population, which provides resilience for both the social order and the regime.[76] The panacea to simmering dissent amid a struggling economy and political repression are narratives of "Making Russia Great Again" accompanied by the cult around a strong leader like Putin. The president's images as a B movie hunk in the wilderness, on the ice hockey rink, or on the hunt are meant to frame him as a superhero.[77] Russia frames the West's promotion of individual liberties and sociopolitical pluralism as narratives meant to emasculate a strong Russia—the disorderly years under former president Boris Yeltsin are presented as evidence of how liberalization has done little more than serve Western interests at the expense of Russia's greatness.

As Gunitsky argues, Russia has become very effective in employing its anti-Western, hypermasculine, and patriotic counternarratives as a means to mobilize its own constituency at home and frame public discourse so as to cater to the Kremlin's worldview.[78] Aside from the conventional media (which is almost entirely controlled by Kremlin affiliates), these narratives of strength are being disseminated on social media, where the very troll farms that Russia uses in its subversion campaigns overseas are employed, as the next chapter shows.[79]

The information network of the Kremlin thereby comprises a range of paid and unpaid surrogates, trolls, and bots that are able to outgun the potential collective communication power of dissidents within Russia. Patriotic netizens and hacktivists offer their support voluntarily, while others are being hired to do nothing else but troll the Russian-speaking Internet. The now-infamous troll farm Internet Research Agency (IRA) in Saint Petersburg has allegedly more than a thousand people working twelve-hour shifts to comment, share, like, and view content disseminated from within the IRA. They engage Internet users with positive messages about Russia and Putin while undermining narratives that might be seen as too pro-Western. Trolls work on assigned missions and subjects, and they follow clear performance indicators of eighty comments and twenty shares a day, creating artificial echo chambers that would suck in potential dissidents and their content. Those undeterred by repression and crackdowns are being swamped with Putin-friendly comments and engagements across social media, providing a force multiplication role to users who share narratives that endorse the position of the Kremlin.[80] Some of the statements made by both official state authority and its cyber surrogates might be entirely absurd from an objective examiner's point of view, "but it proves to the public that the Kremlin can reimagine reality at will, can say 'black is white' and 'white is black' with no one able to contradict."[81]

The United Arab Emirates

In the Middle East, authoritarians also learned their lessons from the Arab Spring. One wealthy tribal oil monarchy in the Gulf became the champion of the authoritarian counterrevolution: the United Arab Emirates (UAE). Under the direction of the ambitious leadership of Mohammad bin Zayed al Nahyan (MbZ), the crown prince of Abu Dhabi and de facto ruler of the country, the UAE rose from the Arab Spring as a powerful player in the region while the old powerhouses in Egypt, Libya, and Syria collapsed under the weight of protests. Financially well endowed, sociopolitically stable, and under the highly centralized command and control of Abu Dhabi and its crown prince, the UAE entered the postrevolutionary environment with less optimism than its neighbors in Qatar. For MbZ—a military leader who appreciates hierarchy, discipline, and order—the prospect of the old authoritarian structure collapsing under the weight of uncontrollable civil-societal activism was a nightmare. The reason for this was that unlike Qatar, the UAE presented internal socioeconomic and ideological fault lines between the seven emirates—some of whose leaders had themselves established relations with Al Islah, a group affiliated with the Muslim Brotherhood.[82] While both Qatar and the UAE entered the Arab Spring as force multipliers for NATO in Libya, both came out on two diametrically opposed ends of the spectrum: Doha viewing dissent, dissidence, and pluralism (including political Islam) as an opportunity, and Abu Dhabi viewing any form of uncontrolled civil-societal activism (especially if empowered through Islamist narratives) as a fundamental threat to the status quo of the region.[83]

The UAE's strategic approach to its narrative of "authoritarian stability" that demonized any form of activism as "terrorism" was first applied at home before it was weaponized in an extensive subversion campaign in the West, as chapter 6 shows. Since the early 2000s MbZ had been consumed by his fear of the rise of political Islam in the Arab world as the only potent opposition force able to mobilize and rally people against the existing political status quo.[84] For a man haunted by paranoias and described by his peers as a "control freak," the existence of civil-societal groups in his country was intolerable.[85] Like China, the UAE believes that in a truly harmonious society, only the central government should have the power to mobilize and inspire. Civil-societal activism and religious authority, conversely, are viewed as challenges to state authority. It was therefore not surprising that when political power in Abu Dhabi shifted to MbZ's court in 2007, one of his first moves was to purge educators in the UAE who had allegiances or connections with Al Islah, a prominent civil-societal group in the country.[86] The second, more serious purge started in 2011 after the protests across the region, at the end of which, two years later, ninety-four UAE citizens were tried as Islamist sympathizers for attempting to overthrow the government.[87]

Since then, Abu Dhabi has not only shown zero tolerance for any form of political Islam but also has actively worked to suppress any form of civil-societal activism that might not be in line with the country's metanarrative of "being the West's principal ally in the region." Linked to this metanarrative are the narratives of "stability," "tolerance," and "economic openness." Anyone with the potential ability to undermine these narratives has since come into the focus of a growing surveillance state.[88] Empowered by sophisticated tech companies employing American and Israeli cyber experts,[89] the UAE has created "transparent" citizens whose political views are under constant monitoring.[90] Those who resisted intimidation were either deported (like the antiauthoritarian activist and former UAE resident Iyad Baghdadi)[91] or were arrested and silenced (such as the UAE human rights activist Ahmed Mansoor).[92] The various cyber surveillance companies that have joined lucrative joint ventures with UAE companies have allowed the UAE to regain the monopoly over the public sphere as social media activity is no longer anonymous, and locations are being constantly tracked and bank accounts monitored, creating a sense of helplessness within any group of potential dissidents. As Mazzetti and others aptly stated, "You start to believe your every move is watched."[93] Mystery still surrounds the case of the UAE academic Abdulkhaleq Abdulla, who disappeared for ten days in January

2017, after which his social media activity, especially on Twitter, changed from balanced analysis to regime cheerleading. Suspicions among colleagues were that Abdulla had been arrested as a prisoner of conscience.[94]

In addition to overt repression, the UAE has invested in other measures to depoliticize the public sphere. First, Abu Dhabi has imposed stricter censorship and self-censorship laws that criminalize social media activity that could be viewed as defamatory. Content that runs counter to the regime's mainstream are blocked, such as news outlets tied to Qatar and promoting more pluralistic sociopolitical views in the Arab world.[95] At the same time, the UAE's Cyber Crimes Law and Penal Code imposes draconian sanctions on content shared that offends "religion," "public officers," and "the state." The combination of these measures makes political activity on social media highly risky.[96] After the blockade on Qatar was imposed in June 2017, the UAE severely tightened its Cyber Crimes Law, banning residents and nationals from sharing content that expressed sympathy with Qatar under threat of punishments of at least $150,000 and a jail term of up to fifteen years.[97]

The UAE has also used social media for countermobilization, inspiring patriotic netizens to take to the highly constrained cybersphere with social media licenses to spread positive content about the UAE and its leadership. Though some are paid to do so, others are volunteering to cheer for the political leadership in an increasingly apolitical public sphere. Contributing to the depoliticization of public discourse is the attempt to promote content that sells theater as news built on positive messages. Video bloggers such as Khalid al-Ameri have tens of thousands of followers. They generate views in the millions with "professionally curated messages [that appear] politically tame and shallow, trying to consolidate public debate around entertainment and lifestyle—away from a politically more active space."[98]

Yet, as apolitical as these messages appear, these bloggers use their seemingly neutral content to subtly sneak messages in that provide large audiences with easy-to-digest justifications for government policy. The result is a public sphere that no longer caters to the individual but to the state.

Saudi Arabia

Although not directly affected by large-scale protests during the Arab Spring, the Saudi kingdom invested into new communication technology as a means of countermobilization, discourse framing, and dissident repression. After the death of King Abdullah in 2015, the new King Salman elevated a new generation of royals from the family of Al Saud into key positions, first and foremost his son Mohammed (MbS), who became minister of defense and deputy crown prince. The new deputy crown prince—ambitious, eager, and impulsive—pursued a

vision that very closely resonated with his generation: steering the Saudi kingdom onto a path of modernization in a country where women were not allowed
to drive, public entertainment was banned, and the two genders existed in two
entirely separate parallel universes. Facing high unemployment in a widely
undiversified, hydrocarbon-dominated rentier economy, the young deputy
crown prince embarked on an overdue reform plan that envisaged the diversification and Saudization of the economy, generating more opportunities for an
alienated youth.

Although some were quick to label him a Saudi reformer, visionary, and
liberalizer,[99] the true colors of MbS came to the fore after he staged a "mini-
coup" inside the House of Al Saud in June 2017, during which he deposed the
crown prince and wrote himself down as the successor to the throne as his
father became increasingly unfit to rule.[100] After this, MbS launched a major
purge against key power brokers, kingmakers, and other influencers that cul-
minated in the mass incarceration of prominent Saudi decision-makers in the
Ritz Carlton in Riyadh—a move that was officially legitimized by a narrative
of "cracking down on corruption," which resonated with most analysts familiar
with the kingdom's affairs.[101] Less prominent influencers, religious leaders, and
activists were less lucky and were swallowed up by Saudi Arabia's massive political prison system.[102] The most tragic of these stories was the killing of Jamal
Khashoggi, a regime insider and journalist, who had been lured into the Saudi
consulate in Istanbul to be killed and dismembered in October 2018—on the
direct orders of MbS himself.[103]

Hence, under MbS, Saudi Arabia has become increasingly paranoid, as
social and economic liberalization have been married with political repression
in a move of authoritarian liberalization that caused crackdowns on Saudi's
infant civil society—crackdowns that have been unprecedented even by Saudi
standards.[104] For the new crown prince, modernization could only be driven
amid a context of a state monopolization of interpretative narratives, whereby
the regime drives the change and retains the authority over "truth." The absur-
dity of seeing women activists who had campaigned for the lifting of the women
driving ban for years being rounded up just after the ban was lifted can only be
explained by the inner circle's obsession with not giving civil society a precedent
to emulate. Change in Saudi Arabia is not driven by the people but by a shrink-
ing number of individuals around MbS.

The key player in the kingdom's internal and external communication strategy has long been Saud al Qahtani, a close friend and confidant of the crown
prince, who was tasked with cleansing the Saudi public sphere of all potential
dissent, in a country with some of the highest penetration of social media.[105]
Amid repression in the physical domain of the information space, Qahtani also
embarked on a campaign to subvert and co-opt the domestic public sphere in an

effort to unite the country behind the new crown prince. Though in the past, the Saudi state used to disrupt access to the Internet in large-scale shutdowns that cost the kingdom almost half a billion dollars in 2016, Qahtani's approach was more sophisticated, unleashing battalions of trolls and bots onto the Saudi social media sphere.[106] It earned him the name "Lord of the Flies." This was a reference to the term "electronic flies," which itself refers to the cyber surrogates that are known in Arabic as *dhabab iliktruniya*—very similar to the Chinese *wu mao dang*.[107] While involved in overseas subversion campaigns to tarnish the reputation of the kingdom's critics, Qahtani's cyber surrogates were also used internally to conduct strategic communication campaigns for the regime. Research by Owen-Jones on Twitter trends in Saudi Arabia suggests a very high degree of automation.[108] Trolls and bots, similar to those operated by Russia's IRA, are engaged in spreading positivity while out-trending potentially critical content. As Emilio Ferrrara explains, "These bots mislead, exploit, and manipulate social media discourse with rumours, spam, malware, misinformation, slander, or even just noise" to undermine any form of genuine public discourse.[109] Similar to China and Russia, these trolls propagate narratives of hypernationalism, portraying any repressive action as necessary evil in the fight against corrupt elites in the kingdom. They portray regime critics both domestically and overseas as "unpatriotic traitors," "spies," and "terrorists," mostly accused of working for external enemies.[110] Trolls assume fake online personas, whereby the same employee of Saudi Arabia's main troll farm can operate several accounts at the same time. Fake accounts that target social media trends domestically usually display a very strong pro-MbS nationalist biography; fake accounts that target critics in the West tend to feature biographies of seemingly Western expats who used to live in and have fallen in love with the Saudi kingdom; fake accounts that targeted Twitter trends in Qatar presented themselves as Qatari nationals alienated by the current emir.[111] The void in the Saudi public sphere created by regime repression has been filled by an automated pseudo–civil society consisting of bots and trolls who function as "cheerleaders" for the regime, trying to cater to the needs and sentiments of a Saudi youth that at least in urban areas feels socially and culturally liberated.[112] Qahtani's electronic flies have induced a rallying around the flag in a "spiral of silence" in which dissident voices feel suffocated by narratives of hypernationalism that are toxic to critical and reflective thinking.

Moreover, Qahtani's efforts to subvert public discourse in the kingdom have had an even more sinister side effect. The Saudi cybersurrogates were actively involved in sieving the social media space at home and abroad to identify and intimidate critical voices, particularly journalists and academics who could potentially give credence to anti-Saudi stories and narratives. Critical commentators on social media were flagged and referred to Spyware contractors, such as NSO Group working for Qahtani, who would then target these individuals trying to hack their personal devices.[113] Khashoggi was most likely targeted in the same way before he was killed in the Saudi consulate in Istanbul. In Saudi Arabia, the trending hashtag of his tragic death that made headlines across the world quickly disappeared—in its place came banal hashtags of "the kidnapping of ants and cockroaches," which was designed due to its spelling in Arabic to confuse the Twitter algorithm.[114]

Like China, Russia, and the UAE, the Saudi regime has created a public sphere that is widely depoliticized, where cheerleading for the regime runs in parallel to entertainment and lifestyle-consumed content, and where potential dissidents are too intimidated to voice any criticism.

CONCLUSION

This chapter has shown the potential of narratives to mobilize, counter-mobilize, and demobilize actors in the public sphere, illustrating how discourse in the virtual information space can spill over into the physical space, serving both noble and nefarious purposes. The public sphere, whether liberalized or constrained, provides individuals, communities, and states with a forum in which they can compete for power and authority. To be more precise, revolutions in the infrastructural domain of the information environment have functioned as an equalizer between state authority and dissident groups of all shapes and colors, creating a forum for constant competition between narratives and counternarratives. This competition may eventually change people's attitudes, decisions, and behaviors.

The largely leaderless revolutions of the Arab Spring would not have been possible without a previous liberalization of the media environment. Satellite and social media had removed the traditional gatekeepers to allow for dissident attitudes to grow amid a context of tangible public grievances that could be exploited by revolutionary narratives of "social justice," "pluralism," and "civil liberties." Though satellite media provided the infrastructure to disseminate narratives quickly to large audiences that contained both tech-savvy individuals and those who were not savvy, social media provided the tools for dissidents to organize and mobilize—taking the authoritarians by surprise. Being able to build collective sentiments and narratives of grievance and victimhood helped consolidate groups of first movers and imitators in a transnational space. Their narratives resonated with a generation of young Arabs who just waited to be mobilized in an effort to subvert the ancien régimes of the region.

The liberalization of Arab public sphere that preceded the revolutions of 2010 and 2011 had incrementally undermined the information-psychological stability of the authoritarian regimes in the Arab world. Mass mobilization and unfolding political violence saw authoritarians who had already lost the moral high ground in the public sphere capitulate. The Arab Spring shook authoritarianism to its core but at the same time illustrated the mobilizing potential of weaponized narratives that could be reverse engineered and redirected against dissidents at home and adversaries overseas.

What authoritarians have learned since is that the revolutions in the information environment could be instrumentalized to regain an advantage in a constant competition over narratives. Holding the ultimate control over telecommunication companies and cyberspace, authoritarians moved away from merely shutting down the Internet, which severely increased the costs of repression. They realized that the new means of technology could help mobilize loyalists and supporters behind their narratives without having to ban access to social media. In a carefully curated public sphere, authoritarians have found ways to create the illusion of public discourse that feeds regime narratives to millions of followers while silencing critical voices. Repression in the physical space empowered by new surveillance technology is accompanied by campaigns aimed at discourse framing and countermobilization.

Digital authoritarians accomplished intimidation and demobilization in the public sphere by tailoring narratives to key constituencies. Information-psychological stability is achieved by (1) depoliticizing the public sphere, (2) reframing political debates into positive cheerleading exercises, and (3) mobilizing netizens and loyalists who, supported by armies of paid bots and trolls, shame and demonize critics. China, Russia, the UAE, and Saudi Arabia have now extensive information networks at their disposal that initially worked to subtly remonopolize control over the public sphere at home but now can be redirected against adversaries overseas.

NOTES

1. Abouzeid, "Bouazizi."
2. Krieg, *Sociopolitical Order*, 138–48.
3. Seib, *Al Jazeera Effect.*
4. Diamond and Plattner, *Liberation Technology.*
5. Giles, *Handbook*, 41.
6. Noueihed and Warren, *Battle for the Arab Spring*, 101.
7. Ansani and Vittorio, "About a Revolution," 7.
8. Godeo, "Troubled Tunisia."
9. Hanafi, "Arab Revolutions," 49.
10. William & Associates, *Egyptian Public Opinion Survey.*
11. Kraidy and Krikorian, "Revolutionary Public Sphere," 114.
12. Krieg, *Sociopolitical Order*, 103–5.
13. Cavatorta and Durac, *Civil Society*, 22.
14. Owen, *State Power*, 25.
15. Noueihed and Warren, *Battle for the Arab Spring*, 49.

16. Seib, *Al Jazeera Effect*, 19.
17. Zayani, *Arab Satellite Television*, 17.
18. Krieg, "Weaponization of Narratives," 94.
19. Hanafi, "Arab Revolutions," 24.
20. Lynch, *Voices*, 247.
21. The term "Arab Street" has often been used in a derogative way to describe an emotionally charged and polarized Arab public sphere. It is used here to describe the physical domain of the information environment in the Arab world.
22. Wickham, *Muslim Brotherhood*, 154.
23. Alterman, "Mid-Tech Revolution."
24. Barrons, "Suleiman," 242.
25. Kader, "Internet Penetration."
26. Krieg, *Sociopolitical Order*, 118.
27. Kassir, *Being Arab*, 4.
28. Worth, "How a Single Match."
29. For a definition of the concept of diffusion, see McAdam and Rucht, "Cross-National Diffusion," 159.
30. Bellin, "Reconsidering the Robustness," 140.
31. Shapiro, "Revolution."
32. See Ghonim, *Revolution 2.0*.
33. Buckner and Khatib, "Martyrs' Revolutions."
34. Mittermaier, "Death," 3.
35. International Telecommunications Union, "Estimated Internet Users."
36. Ghonim, *Revolution 2.0*, 38.
37. Ghonim, 143.
38. Rheingold, *Smart Mobs*, 160.
39. Rid, *Cyber War*, 133.
40. Al Asoomi, "Qatar."
41. Soage and Granganillo, "Muslim Brothers," 40.
42. Anderson, "Fulfilling Prophecies," 29.
43. Hamid, McCants, and Dar, *Islamism*, 6.
44. Wickham, *Muslim Brotherhood*, 138.
45. El Errian, "What the Muslim Brothers Want."
46. Bradley, *After the Arab Spring*, 84.
47. Bradley, 64.
48. Mandaville, *Global Political Islam*, 314.
49. Holmes and Dziadosz, "Special Report"; Lister, "Dynamic Stalemate," 18.
50. Krieg, *Sociopolitical Order*, 215.
51. Singer and Brooking, *Like War*, 150.
52. Krieg and Rickli, *Surrogate Warfare*, 98.
53. Nissen, "Terror.com," 2.
54. Gaub, "Cult of ISIS," 114.
55. Diamond, "Liberation Technology," 72.
56. Howard, Ganesh, and Liotsiou, *IRA*, 40.
57. West, *Internet Shutdowns*.
58. Morozov, *Net Delusion*, 143.
59. Singer and Brooking, *Like War*, 95.
60. Gunitsky, "Corrupting the Cyber-Commons," 42.

61. Atlantic Council, *Chinese Discourse Power.*
62. Myers and Mozur, "China Is Waging a Disinformation War."
63. Chase and Mulvenon, *You've Got Dissent!*
64. Singer and Brooking, *Like War*, 98.
65. Bradley, *After the Arab Spring*, 96.
66. Economy, "Great Firewall of China."
67. Stockmann and Luo, "Which Social Media Facilitate Online Public Opinion in China?" 198.
68. McCarthy, "China Now Boasts More Than 800 Million Internet Users."
69. Marczak and Weaver, "China's Great Cannon."
70. Helft and Barboza, "Google Shuts China Site."
71. Singer and Brooking, *Like War*, 100.
72. Bennett and Livingston, "Disinformation Order," 132.
73. Anonymous, "How to Spot a State-Funded Chinese Internet Troll."
74. Kaiman, "China Cracks Down."
75. Robinson et al., *Modern Political Warfare*, 47.
76. Jones and Kovacich, *Global Information Warfare*, 36.
77. Pomerantsev, "Russia," 6.
78. Gunitsky, "Corrupting the Cyber-Commons," 45.
79. Jonsson and Seely, "Russian Full-Spectrum Conflict," 12.
80. MacFarquhar, "Inside the Russian Troll Factory."
81. Pomerantsev, "Russia," 7.
82. Krieg, "Weaponization of Narratives," 96.
83. Krieg, "Divided over Narratives."
84. Davidson, "UAE," 80.
85. Author's interview with UAE analyst I in London, December 11, 2019.
86. Davidson, "UAE," 79.
87. Ulrichsen, "Perceptions," 30.
88. Hedges, *Reinventing the Sheikhdom*, 81.
89. Ziv, "Mysterious UAE Cyber Firm."
90. Bing and Schectman, "Inside the UAE's Secret Hacking Team."
91. Hussain, "How the UAE Tried to Silence a Popular Arab Spring Activist."
92. Amnesty International, "UAE."
93. Mazzetti et al., "New Age of Warfare."
94. Middle East Eye, "Surprise Trip."
95. Freedom House, *Freedom on the Net 2018.*
96. Clyde & Co., *Defamation.*
97. Reuters, "UAE Bans Expressions."
98. Krieg, "How Saudi Arabia and the UAE Are Silencing Dissent."
99. Friedman, "Saudi Arabia's Arab Spring."
100. Reuters, "Addiction."
101. Kirkpatrick, "Saudi Arabia Arrests 11 Princes."
102. McKernan, 'Saudi Police Arrest Three"; Reuters, "Saudi Arabia Arrests Prominent Cleric."
103. Harris, Miller, and Dawsey, "CIA Concludes."
104. Khashoggi, "Saudi Arabia."
105. Ministry of Communication and Information Technology, "Saudi Arabia."
106. West, *Internet Shutdowns*, 7.

107. Benner et al., "Saudis' Image Makers."
108. Owen-Jones, "Propaganda," 1392.
109. Ferrara et al., "Rise of Social Bots," 2.
110. Owen-Jones, "Hacking."
111. Owen-Jones, "Propaganda," 1397.
112. Owen-Jones, *Digital Authoritarianism*, 119.
113. Mazzetti et al., "New Age of Warfare."
114. Trew, "Bee Stung."

FIVE

·········

Subversion and Russia's Concept of War in the Twenty-First Century

"This is the 21st-century equivalent of having the Russians landing Marines on the New Jersey shore. They invaded our country, they invaded our political system, . . . and they won," said Richard Clarke, former special adviser to the president on cybersecurity in the George W. Bush administration, in an interview with Bill Maher.[1] What Richard Clarke was referring to was Russia's cyber interference in the 2016 US presidential elections that saw outsider Donald Trump win the race against favored Hillary Clinton—allegations to which Russian president Vladimir Putin said in a 2018 interview with NBC, "Could anyone really believe that Russia, thousands of miles away, . . . influenced the outcome of the election? Doesn't that sound ridiculous even to you?"[2]

We begin by unpacking Russia's approach to warfare in the twenty-first century. During this period, Putin's Kremlin learned its lessons from the Soviet collapse in the 1980s and created a security apparatus that could provide the regime in Moscow with more resilience in the face of an expansive information environment. Since Putin's assumption of power two decades ago, the Russian state has created a more flexible approach to warfare in the traditional sense, going beyond a Clausewitzian interpretation of war as revolving around violence and the application of military force. Instead, subsequent national security advisers, white papers, and doctrines have outlined the intrinsic value of information as the source of power and the control of communication as the single most important lever of keeping power.[3] Consequently, amid a perceived onslaught by Western prodemocracy narratives and ideas, Putin's Russia, since the early 2010s, has not just prioritized the development of conventional military levers of power but has also heavily invested in weaponizing "counternarratives" to fight back. Putin's personal preoccupation with information and influence operations should not come as a surprise, considering that his former job as a lieutenant colonel in the KGB allegedly involved mastering what the

Soviet's called "active measures"—after all, in Putin's own words, "there is no such thing as a former KGB man."[4]

As this chapter intends to show, Russia provides the most sophisticated case study for how states weaponize narratives in an effort to subvert the opponent's information-psychological stability. In a synchronized effort, Russia has not simply viewed the information environment as a force-multiplier for other more conventional levers of power. It has refined twenty-first-century subversion as a stand-alone lever of power to be used to change the opponent's attitudes, decisions, and behaviors—hitting liberal democracies at their Achilles' heel. The targeted interference by Russia's information networks in the US presidential election in 2016 thereby might have just been the tip of the iceberg, with a range of other subversion campaigns ongoing in other Western countries. Thereby, Russia has been strategic in using information to achieve political effect following a clearly identifiable strategy.

We commence by outlining the historic legacy of information operations in the Soviet Union. It shows how strategic thinking in Russia since the collapse of the Soviet empire stimulated innovative thinking about the employment of information to gain both an operational and a strategic advantage. The chapter then breaks down the Kremlin's subversion strategy based on the six-step strategy introduced in chapter 3 to highlight how Russia has set the standard for subversion operations in the twenty-first century. Here, we take a more conceptual approach to the topic, referring to the various case studies of Russian subversion efforts to illustrate how this "neo-KGB state," as some have termed it, strategically employs narratives as politics by other means in a global clash of wills.[5]

"NEW GENERATION WARFARE" AND THE WAR OVER NARRATIVES

Russia's current obsession with the control of the information environment is rooted in a long history of harnessing the power of information in the Soviet Union. As outlined in chapter 3, "active measures," or *dezinformatsiya*, was a prominent tool in the KGB's repertoire during the Cold War, when subversion abroad was just as important to the Soviet secret service as intelligence collection. Amid a struggle over ideological narratives, the USSR assigned great importance to the effort to ideologically win over the hearts and minds of audiences in contested territories. Since the 1920s, the KGB had developed subversion programs relying on a range of surrogates—including "experts," media outlets, and front groups—with the objective of changing the attitudes, behaviors, and decisions of target audiences. Disinformation operations that featured prominently in what became known as "active measures" were assembly-line processes, whereby narratives were developed and disseminated almost permanently—throughout the Cold War, the KGB is believed to have conducted more than ten thousand disinformation campaigns.[6]

Oleg Kalugin, former head of KGB operations in the United States, described the KGB's subversion operations as follows:

> I would describe it as the heart and soul of the Soviet Intelligence—was subversion. Not intelligence collection, but subversion: active measures to weaken the West, to drive wedges in the Western community alliances of all sorts, particularly NATO, to sow discord among allies, to weaken the United States in the eyes of the people of Europe, Asia, Africa, Latin America, and thus to prepare ground in case the war really occurs. To make America more vulnerable to the anger and distrust of other peoples.[7]

More than fifteen thousand people are thought to have worked for the KGB on these operations at one time, a far greater number than the entire staff of the US State Department.[8] A KGB defector, Yuri Bezmenov, estimates that only 15 percent of KGB staff were actually involved in traditional intelligence operations, with the rest widely engaged in subversion operations. He explains in a lecture that for the Soviet intelligence apparatus, subversion, in theory, was an extensive, long-term effort attempting to "metaprogram" the target audience over decades, until at some point society in the target country no longer functioned consensually.[9] The ultimate goal was the disruption of civil-societal discourse.

However, within the context of an information environment that was less participatory and diverse than today, and where access was a lot more rigidly controlled and the number of contributors in the media sphere more manageable, the KGB's ability to effectively exploit what little sociopolitical fault lines might have existed at the time in the West was limited. The information operations against the neutron bomb, introduced in chapter 3, were arguably among the most successful KGB operations. Though most other operations might have been vaguely successful in tarnishing the reputation of the United States or its NATO allies, this operation was able to amplify dissident voices to an extent that Washington had to change its policy. In most other cases, the effects of "active measures" remained confined to a pro-Soviet echo chamber.

The dissolution of the Soviet Union in 1991 could be seen as a triumph of the Western, liberal metanarrative over that advanced by the KGB—a view that is widely shared among those elites behind a resurgent Russia since the early 2000s. Putin's Russia has been built around a deep state of Kremlin-friendly oligarchs and elites from the security sector, the so-called *siloviki*, who are tied to the charismatic, autocratic leadership of the Kremlin boss himself. Rather than being principally ideological, Russia's strongmen promote a pragmatist agenda focusing on a strong Russia, founded on authoritarian stability, and featuring patriotic-nationalist commitment to the state. This in many ways is a response to the widespread belief in Putin's deep state that Russia's liberalization and rapprochement with the West during the 1990s was the root cause of Russia's weakening. The economic crises of the Yeltsin era and the internal friction in the immediate post-Soviet era have been framed by the Kremlin as the result of a civilizational struggle between Russia and the West—a cultural and ideational struggle rather than a material and interest-based one. From this point of view, the liberalization of civil society in Russia exposed vulnerabilities the West was able to exploit through informational means. Russia's weakness amid the collapse of the Soviet empire is explained ontologically as Russia's surrender of information-psychological stability in the face of an onslaught of liberal narratives.[10] In this Kulturkampf, Russia has been able to successfully present itself as an alternative to the West—a powerful narrative that resonates well with and mobilizes anti-Western sentiments, as the global battle for the moral high ground during the war in Ukraine in 2022 demonstrated.[11]

Thus, the conceptualization of war (or "unpeace") in Putin's Russia begins with the premise that the country's greatest vulnerability lies not in the conventional military realm but in the information environment. And though Western scholars often securitize Russia's information operations as a cunning strategy used by the Kremlin to subvert Western sociopolitics, its exploitation of the information environment is rooted in the perception of being at the receiving end of a Western-led war over liberal political and human rights narratives.[12] Targeting Russia's information-psychological stability is seen today as a means by Western adversaries to exploit sociopolitical fault lines and vulnerabilities to drive a wedge between the political establishment and the population at large, eventually forcing the state to make decisions in favor of the adversarial side.[13]

Although the threat of "hostile content" to information-psychological stability had been recognized in Russian military circles throughout the twentieth century, it was only in the late 1990s and early 2000s that the importance of informational superiority found its way into mainstream Russian strategic thinking and doctrine. One military scholar reclaimed by Putin-era information warriors was Evgeny Messner, a Soviet exile who had fought for Tsarist Russia in World War I and, as some would argue, became somewhat of a spiritual "godfather" of Russian information operations in the late 1990s.[14] First in Yugoslavian and then in Argentinian exile, Messner predicted that future war would not be about the conquest of territory but the contest of souls in the enemy state.[15] For Messner, World War III would be fought as a "subversion war" or *myatezh evoyna*, in which the soul of the enemy's society would be the most important strategic objective to capture. The enemy would try to exploit existing sociopolitical fault lines in the enemy's society to stir up mass dissidence in an effort to drive a wedge between society and the political authority. Information operations could "create 'problems' and crises" that would "gradually estrange [the] masses from [their] government."[16] Messner anticipated that military operations in the future would be subordinate to the objective of creating a sociopsychological context conducive to the exploitation of operational and strategic objectives by one's own forces. Both military and popular movements were thereby only psychological organisms whose ability to feel, think, and act could be targeted by "subversion war" as an inherently psychological war.[17] According to Fridman, who extensively studied Messner's original texts, the writings of the Soviet exile remained virtually nonexistent in the USSR but were rediscovered in a resurgent Russia, where Messner's idea of outperforming a conventionally superior force through information was seen as an opportunity for the Kremlin to contain the West.[18] Though it may be overstated that Messner had a profound impact on the framing and definition of Russian concepts of information-psychological operations, the rediscovery of his idea of *myatezh evoyna* coincides with a resurgence of research on the information space in Russia in the late 1990s and early 2000s. In the early 2000s the idea of information-psychological warfare reappears in Russian military writing. It draws on the legacy of Soviet "active measures," defining it as a constant wartime and peacetime activity that affects all three elements of the information space: the sociopsychological, infrastructural, and physical domains.[19] Thereby, information-psychological warfare displays a great resemblance to Messner's notion of subversion war.

The 2000 National Security Concept, published by Putin's presidency, doctrinally outlined the importance of the information environment as the future battlefield for the first time. It stated, "There is an increasing threat to national security in the information sphere. The striving of a number of countries to dominate the global information space and oust Russia from the external and internal information market poses a serious danger."[20]

Putin's Russia defined its position on the receiving end of psychological operations over values conducted by the West with the purpose of undermining the sociopolitical stability of Russia. Russian strategic scholars would echo these observations, arguing, as Kazarin did, that the United States was behind an information campaign "to exert an all-round pressure on political and cultural life to undermine the society's national and state foundation and penetrate all level of state administration."[21] Jonsson, who has written widely on Russian military thinking, states that the military thinker Vladimir Slipchenko in particular defined the new Russian information-centric conceptualization of warfare.[22] For Slipchenko, the sixth-generation warfare that commenced with the 1991 Gulf War revolves around information—"a destructive weapon just like a bayonet, bullet or projectile."[23] As the deputy head of the Academy of Military Science, Slipchenko presented concepts of war based on the idea that information is a weapon on par with kinetic weapons that were immensely influential within the Russian military nexus.

In the context of a more holistic interpretation of the "information space" and "information operations" in Russian writing, which goes beyond technological infrastructure to incorporate sociopsychological domains,[24] Aleksandr Dugin's notion of net-centric warfare becomes equally important. For this ideologue and alleged Putin confidant, net-centric warfare is much broader than the Western concept of network-centric warfare, which mostly revolves around electronic computer networks. Dugin defines networks as social phenomena that tie communities to one another and to political authority. Net-centric warfare, then, is the mobilization of those social networks within an adversary's sociopolitical complex that are alienated or disenfranchised by the established political elite.[25] Dugin identifies pro-Western liberals, promoters of American interests, nongovernmental organizations, and liberal opposition as part of the "Atlantic networks" that are trying to subvert the integrity of Russian sociopolitics. In the same way, Dugin argues, Russia does not only need to maintain its information superiority domestically but also needs to find ways to cultivate its own networks in the West that are receptive to Russia's narratives.[26]

The influential military thinkers Chekinov and Bogdanov echo Dugin's notions of the West trying to achieve information superiority through the cultivation of extensive networks inside Russia. Both wrote in 2013 that

> with powerful information technologies at its disposal, the aggressor will make an effort to involve all public institutions in the country it intends to attack, primarily the mass media and religious organizations, cultural institutions, non-governmental organizations, public movements financed from abroad, and scholars engaged in research on foreign grants. All these institutions and individuals may be involved in a distributed attack and strike damaging point blows at the country's social system with the purported aims of promoting democracy and respect for human rights.[27]

Like other Russian strategic thinkers, Chekinov and Bogdanov conceptualize war in the twenty-first century not from an offensive point of view but primarily from a defensive one, linking Russia's perceived insecurity to the threat of Western information operations. Nonetheless, it is this realization that a vulnerability in the information environment exists at all that allows Russian strategists to turn this vulnerability into an offensive capability to be used against Western adversaries.

The experience of the Arab Spring in the aftermath of the "Color Revolutions" in Russia's traditional sphere of influence—in Georgia, Ukraine, and Kyrgyzstan—as well as protests in Russia during the elections of 2011 and 2012 fostered the securitization of sociopolitical dissent and civil-societal discourse in Russia. Information was viewed not just as the main driving force for mass mobilization in the Arab world but also, more importantly, as the driving force behind regime change in Libya. And for Russia, both the Arab Spring and the Color Revolutions were products of Western subversion campaigns compounding local grievances into revolutionary movements.[28]

It is against this backdrop that Russian chief of the General Staff Valery Gerasimov gave a speech in 2013 at the Academy of Military Science, which to Western observers was a watershed moment in Russian strategic thinking. Gerasimov's speech touched on the blurring of war and peace, and information operations being a constant part of a new generation of warfare, in which Arab Spring–type revolts could become the typical version of twenty-first-century confrontation.[29] The fact that the most senior Russian military officer openly prioritized nonmilitary means in twenty-first-century confrontations over the use of kinetic force led Western commentators to quickly speak of the "Gerasimov Doctrine," which is not so much a doctrine as a grand strategic vision and was based not on Gerasimov's thinking but on almost two decades of Russian strategic discourse on new-generation warfare.[30] The events in Ukraine that unfolded in 2014 seemed to confirm Gerasimov's remarks a year earlier: Russia had used a blend of military and nonmilitary means to mobilize networks in Eastern Ukraine and Crimea amid a widespread information offensive that Russian irregular troops exploited to make territorial gains. For Russia, the attempt to break the kill chain as far away from "pulling the trigger" as possible seemed to have paid off by taking the West by surprise.[31] Gerasimov's maxim to achieve political and strategic ends by nonmilitary means meant that subversive operations below the threshold of war would avoid the high risks and certain penalties arising from overt methods of war while still securing political objectives.[32]

Russia's Military Doctrine 2014 included the lessons learned from the Arab Spring. Domestically, it highlighted the threats from the information environment and civil-societal unrest. Under the headline "External Military Threats," it emphasized the dangers of "Color Revolutions" incited by external powers using information and communication technology to subvert state sovereignty, impairing a regime's political independence and territorial integrity.[33]

Hence, Russia's understanding of war today gravitates toward the blurred intersection between war and peace, whereby nonmilitary means of power are orchestrated to mobilize dissent and are supported by the media, civil-societal organizations, and community leaders. Dissent is induced by exploiting existing sociopolitical fault lines between communities and political authority, which could lead to protests in the best-case scenario and insurgency in the worst. Narratives are weaponized as means to mobilize or demobilize civil society either as a pretext for low-level military operations or as a means in itself to weaken the political authority structure in the target state. Though in Western military thinking such subversive measures might be considered nonmilitary means as ways to avoid war, for Russia these are means of war themselves, below the threshold of international legal norms of war.[34] Thereby, this new-generation war is not understood as a Russian innovation but as a Western, specifically American, style of warfare. Weaponized narratives feature prominently in what for Moscow is a new civilizational struggle between East and West.

RUSSIA'S SUBVERSION STRATEGY

As a leading information power, Russia understood how to effectively integrate its information networks into its overall global strategy. Unlike its competitors, Russia's subversion strategy showcases a high degree of integration, orchestration, and synchronization.

Step 1: Orientation

Russia's strategic decision-making regarding its subversion campaigns is still veiled in mystery, as it is unclear who gives strategic direction over objectives, targets, and means. Due to the complex nature of the Russian information network involving assemblages of state institutions, semiprivate organizations, and individual surrogates, the direct link between the information warriors and the center of power in the Kremlin is deliberately obscured. One name that often appears when investigating Russia's unconventional operations overseas is Yevgeny Prigozhin, often dubbed "Putin's Chef," who is an oligarch within the Kremlin nexus and is linked to both the infamous Russian troll farm Internet Research Agency (IRA) in Saint Petersburg and the Russian mercenary company Wagner.[35] Apart from that, the Kremlin's press secretary, Dimitry Peskov, and the first deputy chief of staff of the presidential administration, Vyacheslav Volodin, play key roles in formulating strategic narratives and disseminating them from the Kremlin to Russia's information networks.[36] The fact that Prigozhin, Peskov, and Volodin are close confidants of Putin means that the most important decision-makers and assets in the Russian information network are directly tied to the Russian president, making a dissociation between the Kremlin and IRA only nominal in character.

This suggests that though most of Russia's subversion campaign is delegated to a range of human and technological surrogates, financed via Putin confidants, the core decisions about where, when, and how to subvert are made at the highest level. Some even suggest that the decision to meddle in the US presidential elections in 2016 was made by Putin himself as an act of revenge against Clinton.[37] Amid protests after Russia's presidential election in 2011, then–US secretary of state Clinton came out publicly in support of the protesters and expressed her doubts about the legitimacy of the elections in Russia. Putin allegedly perceived this as a direct attempt to undermine his power as president—something some believe might have caused Russian interference in the US presidential elections in 2016 not so much in support of candidate Trump but against candidate Clinton.[38]

Russia's overall objectives in its subversion campaigns have been twofold. First, the more benign objective Russia pursues is attempting to exercise influence. Here, Moscow's objective is the pollution of the information space with weaponized narratives in an attempt to disrupt fact-finding or to relativize facts, making it harder for civil society, media, or policymakers to differentiate between fact and fiction. These influence campaigns create an enabling environment for Russia as the adversary's audience slides into a stage of paralysis or "infocalypse." It generates cynicism in the target audience, calling into question existing ontological assumptions about how the world works and potentially creating a void that Russia can fill with narratives that establish new "facts" on the ground.[39] Moreover, the resulting information paralysis can severely disrupt existing agendas for civil-societal debate that in a second step can be exploited for polarization.[40]

The more malignant objective of Russia's subversion campaigns is disrupting and undermining the sociopolitical consensus and status quo. Amid a created information paralysis, Russia finds it easier to polarize overwhelmed target audiences, drawing on narratives that feed on existing sociopsychological biases and grievances. The ultimate goal here is to undermine the sociopolitical status quo and mobilize activism against government authority by sowing discord and distrust between societal actors as well as between civil society and the state.[41] The interference in the 2016 and 2020 elections in the United States was aimed at undermining public confidence in American democracy, both vis-à-vis established political elites and the election process. President Trump's refusal to concede his electoral defeat and his attempts to cast doubt over the integrity of the election process made him and his campaign surrogates of Russia's information campaign.[42] Aside from possibly being able to mobilize or demobilize Americans to vote, Russia's gradual victory in the information space becomes more measurable in postelectoral polarization amid a growing rift between the political left and right—a sociopolitical polarization that will continue to undermine trust in the established governing elites both among liberals and conservatives.[43] Thus, as Russia approaches the issue of information-psychological instability with strategic patience, the process of eroding confidence in the political system is a gradual one, which only over time will present the full scale of the cumulative effect. Though some went as far as to argue that Trump was elected only because of Russian interference,[44] it was not so much the election results as it was the consequent widening of the sociopolitical rift that serves Russia's strategic objectives.[45]

Hence, Russia's strategic objectives in the information environment exceed the often-cited "4Ds" of Russia's information strategy: dismiss the critic, distort the facts, distract from the main issue, and dismay the audience.[46] Russia's strategic objective goes beyond influence and suppression to mobilization and countermobilization in an effort to undermine the existing sociopolitical status quo.

Step 2: Identification

Key to Russia's relatively successful subversion campaigns is its ability to identify, understand, and exploit key sociopsychological, infrastructural, and physical vulnerabilities in the adversary's information environment. Most importantly, to be successful in undermining information-psychological stability, Russia understands how to identify existing grievances in target audiences, deepen and widen them, and make them more receptive to mobilization. In line with Dugin's concept of "net-centric war," Russia actively tries to subvert the existing social networks or key constituencies of Western sociopolitical systems in a gradual attempt to erode the center of gravity on which Western sociopolitics rests. In its place, Moscow is trying to develop its own networks that exploit communal fault lines by providing disenfranchised communities with simple narratives of false hope that expectedly resonate widely.[47]

In the West, Russia has exploited existing antiestablishment and anti-Western sentiments in groups that feel disenfranchised by the existing sociopolitical system. Here, antiestablishment and dissident narratives based on grievances over socioeconomic issues, migration, globalization, and, more recently, pandemic control, have been used to plug narratives that exploit emotions of fear and hatred as well as cognitive dispositions, such as worldviews, biases, and ideologies.[48] In Europe, Russia especially targets audiences on both the extreme right and left wings of the political spectrum. Both these groups tend to feel alienated by the sociopolitical status quo that is predominantly perceived as a liberal mainstream; on the right, this is seen as incompatible with conservative social values, and on the left, it is perceived as incompatible with its socioeconomic objectives. However, despite engaging with socialists close to the German party Die Linke, Spain's Podemos, or Greece's Syriza, Putin's "New Russia" has predominantly forged ties with voters of populist movements and parties in Europe.[49] These parties and movements (e.g., the French Front National,[50] the German AfD,[51] the Dutch PVV,[52] British UKIP and its successor the Brexit Party,[53] and Italy's Lega Nord[54]) all take views that are critical of the liberal mainstream and oppose migration, EU-style supranationalism, global-ization, and social liberalization—an ideological and ontological overlap with Putin's deep state. Therefore, these politically, socially, and socioeconomically alienated audiences make for a highly receptive audience for narratives that oppose the current status quo. Russia's information networks particularly target followers of populist groups and movements who do not seek political change through the system but against the system. It is also among those audiences that confirmation biases, susceptibility to conspiracy theories, and cognitive dissonances vis-à-vis the political status quo are widespread.[55] Growing distrust of the "establishment" and sentiments of victimhood at the hands of "elites," especially during the heightened uncertainty brought about by COVID-19, have created fertile ground where Russia can plug narratives that do not only polarize but also widen the gap between sections of the public and the state.[56]

In the United States, Russia identified similar communities, predominantly in "Middle America," that are vulnerable for subversive narratives. Ahead of the 2016 and 2020 US presidential elections, Russia chose to activate conservatives based on grievances such as immigration, gun control, and social liberaliza-tion, while trying to demobilize left-leaning African American communities by undermining their faith in the elections and the establishment.[57] Both conser-vatives in "Middle America" and African American communities already dis-played socioeconomic and sociopolitical grievances, feeling alienated from and disenfranchised by an establishment unwilling or unable to cater to their needs. These grievances led to mass protests and riots after the killing of George Floyd by police officers in May 2020. Though Russia needed to activate conservative voters in key constituencies of America's southern and midwestern swing states in 2016, it was also trying to undermine the ability of liberals to rally around a single candidate. As in Europe, target audiences in the United States displayed similar degrees of distrust of the political establishment, democratic institu-tions, and elections amid widespread concerns that the American Dream no longer delivered for a growing number of Americans in the aftermath of the 2008 global financial crisis.[58]

In Eastern Europe, Russia has been even more effective at cultivating "natu-ral networks." Russophile or Russian-speaking minorities who either identify with their Slavic heritage, the Orthodox Christian faith, or the Russian language have traditionally been networks that display a stronger affinity toward Mos-cow. Even more, many of these minorities display sociopolitical grievances that Russia has actively sought to exploit. In Estonia in 2007, during protests over the removal of a bronze statue of a Soviet soldier, Russia was able to mobilize eth-nic Russians to rally around the cause to speak out against what was framed as the Estonian government disrespecting the country's Soviet past in favor of an approach hailing the legacy of Nazi collaborators—a narrative Russia recycled to justify the war in Ukraine in 2022. Of the approximately 25 percent ethnic Russians in Estonia at the time, almost half did not have Estonian citizenship. Throughout the 1990s and early 2000s, many of these Russian-speaking Estonians even suffered from an "undetermined" status, causing growing friction between the Estonian government and a Russian minority that felt politically and socially discriminated against. For Russia, these were fertile conditions to be exploited via weaponized narratives to sow seeds for riots and unrest.[59] The Russian strategy in 2007 thereby did not center on the bronze statue—it was a mere pretext that could be politicized in an information environment, which at least among ethnic Russians in Estonia was dominated by Kremlin-backed media outlets.[60] Russia has also tried to build "natural networks" with Polish minorities in Lithuania, presenting itself as a political sponsor for their cause as a discriminated cultural and religious minority—a narrative of victimhood that appears to resonate in times of identity politics.[61]

Most impressive has been Russia's mobilization of ethnic Russian minorities in eastern Ukraine during and since the Euromaidan protests in Kyiv. In a country divided along ethnic and ideological fault lines, particularly between Ukrainians who mostly look toward Europe and ethnic Russians who focus more on Eurasia, Russia found again fertile ground in public grievances that could be exploited by sociopolitical narratives. Ethnic Russians who viewed developments in Kyiv with suspicion were fed by Kremlin-linked media outlets with prominent narratives delegitimizing democratically elected actors in the capital. Liberal citizen movements were framed as neo-Nazi groups, and Nazi symbols were used to depict the Ukrainian state—images that resonated well with Russian speakers in the East who were steeped in the history of Ukrainian collaboration with the Nazis during World War II.[62] Russia's operations in the Donbas were supported by large-scale disinformation campaigns in an effort to mobilize grassroots movements to not only support unmarked Russian operatives but also to become active force multipliers in what developed into a secessionist insurgency against the Ukrainian state.[63]

Step 3: Formulation

A narrative campaign ought to begin with a grand strategic metanarrative, which provides the root from which all other narratives stem. Russia has been struggling in the post–Cold War era to define its metanarrative vis-à-vis its ideological adversaries in the West. Though the West has been able to instrumentalize liberalization and democratization as its metanarrative to make sense of its foreign and security policy decisions, Russia has no "ready-made" historical meta narrative. Russian "greatness" could either be tied to the prerevolutionary imperial or the postrevolutionary Soviet narrative, both of which fall short of providing an adequate foundation for the development of a new Russian identity.[64] The demarcation between Russia and the USSR has remained a difficult task for Putin's new Russia and its elites. Quite similar to China's attempt to build its grand strategic narrative around the idea of the civilization state, the Kremlin has tried to develop a metanarrative that revolves around the strength and resilience of the Russian state as an alternative pole in the Eurasian landscape.[65] Thereby, elements of imperial revivalism along the lines of "Making Russia Great Again" are compounded with the notion of *Russkii Mir*, the Russian world, the idea that Russia is the pole that holds a Russian-speaking and Eurasian community together. This idea transcends the boundaries of the Russian state. Under the umbrella of Russkii Mir, Russia is primarily providing a point of attraction to a Russian diaspora in post-Soviet countries that are yearning for social and humanitarian support.[66] Yet there appears to be intellectual friction in this narrative, as the Eurasian metanarrative could be potentially multiethnic and at odds with the patriotic, ethnic Russian metanarrative that calls for Russian ethnic homogeneity.[67]

For Western communities that lack any intellectual or identitarian parallel with the concept of Russkii Mir (or even Russia as a Eurasian power), Russia has tried to offer an insurgent metanarrative to that of the West—one that provides a populist alternative to the liberal order, progressive liberalism, and globalization. The Russian metanarrative of strength through homogeneity, patriotism, and hypernationalism, which are core features of the idea of Russkii Mir, resonates well with communities in the West that identify as socially conservative, are against a perceived liberal establishment, and see themselves through lenses of victimhood. To those groups, Russia offers a powerful alternative to the liberal order, its global governance complexes, its progressive values and norms, and even the capitalist system—a liberal capitalist system whose appeal is crumbling among disenfranchised and alienated communities.

Thereby, Russia has been fairly good at understanding the sociopsychology of the target audiences it is trying to influence and subvert. Its narratives followed the three rules for effectiveness Singer outlined in his book: simplicity, resonance, and novelty.[68] Russian narratives usually dilute the complexity of the world by providing target audiences with simple, black-and-white solutions to complicated problems, dividing the world in good and bad, winners and losers, and perpetrators and victims. Knowledge of the grievances of target audiences, especially in the West, allows Russian information surrogates to develop narratives that resonate with ontological and ideological predispositions—sometimes making them able to draw on very local grievances and biases. Combining simplicity with resonance, Russian "influencers" add novel, often outlandish claims to the mix, which breaks with the audience's expectation and helps content go viral.

Social conservative narratives merge anti-Western connotations with anti-LGBTQ sentiments that resonate well with evangelical communities in America's South and social conservatives in Eastern Europe. Themes of victimhood are constructed around narratives of "liberal imperialism" that promotes multicultural and multiethnic societies that leave "citizens as strangers in their country" and where migrants are stigmatized as scapegoats for individual loss of socioeconomic status. Themes of the Western, liberal mainstream defending migration, globalization, and (in Europe) supranationalism are juxtaposed with the values that Putin's Russia has branded for itself: nationalism, sovereignty, law and order, and patriotism.[69]

These narratives are spread via manufactured stories, social media memes, and micro blogging (the combination of which could be best described as infotainment), which allows for increased penetration as it touches on themes that resonate and present novel angles. Fake news stories dominated events in Ukraine in 2014, where Russian media outlets and social media surrogates were disseminating fabricated stories about how Ukrainian progovernment nationalists were lynching and crucifying an ethnic Russian boy from Solvyansk or how the Islamic State built up a training camp in Ukraine—all stories that resonated with eastern Ukrainians who already had vilified the central government in Kyiv.[70] The relative success of subversion activities in Ukraine after 2014 might be the root cause of hubris and overconfidence that the same narratives could be equally powerful to mobilize the rest of the Ukrainian public against the government in Kyiv in 2022. The opposite was the case: the all-but-ambiguous full-scale military invasion of Ukraine triggered a powerful anti-Russian counternarrative to be built inside Ukraine and the international community, which dominated the information environment.[71] In Germany, amid the polarization surrounding the migrant crisis, the Kremlin's media complex disseminated fabricated stories about girls and women being attacked and raped by refugees from the Middle East, creating hysteria among already-concerned Germans on the political right.[72] During the 2016 US presidential elections, Russian social media surrogates would disseminate false stories about the Ku Klux Klan infiltrating the American police force, which would be disseminated in African American echo chambers to further stir up outrage against American law enforcement. On the American right, Russia's cyber surrogates would help make stories and memes go viral that either portrayed Latin American migrants as ungrateful "freeloaders" or candidate Hilary Clinton as at the center of immoral or illegal activity.[73] In so doing, Russian messaging during the 2016 elections was partly consistent with messaging from the Trump campaign as well as with biases and predispositions on America's political right.

Russia's narratives flooding the adversary's information environment compete with factual stories and help blur the boundaries between fact and fiction.

Drawing on the sleeper effect, whereby audiences over time dissociate information from the source, Russia has been able to deeply penetrate public opinion in Western societies. Triangulation via an extensive information network creates a perception of truth through repetition—especially when narratives correlate with already-familiar biases. Usually rather sensationalist, Russian narratives are framed in a way that arouses negative emotions of anger, fear, and disgust, which are integral ingredients for information virality.[74]

Step 4: Dissemination

In the dissemination phase, Russia can rely on an extensive surrogate network of indirect and coincidental surrogates, including those that are only indirectly tied to the Russian state and those that coincidentally support Russian narratives. Not every event in the information environment that works in Russia's favor has necessarily been initiated by Russia directly—as is the case with many pro-Russian pundits who often voluntarily choose to take a pro-Kremlin line.[75] Indirect surrogates at times are directly financed through an extensive network of companies directly or indirectly tied to Kremlin-friendly oligarchs, creating levels of dissociation between surrogates and Putin's deep state that makes attribution impossible.[76] This multichannel approach might be inconsistent as each surrogate operates somewhat autonomously to further Russia's subversive cause. Though from a strategic point of view, inconsistency might appear as a challenge at first glance, in the information environment, the multipolarity of outlets and actors can both enhance the perception of triangulation as well as increase the effect of confusion over time.[77]

Russia's network of surrogates (comprised of social media and conventional media agents), experts, and policymakers tend to subvert the targeted information environment from the bottom up. They try to implant a narrative via smaller websites and social media outlets before creating a self-reinforcing triangulation effect that creates the illusion of a consensus that can be adopted by conventional media outlets. Though social media and conventional media agents often operate on separate narratives simultaneously, they are linked via key strategic narratives and stories. At the heart of the bottom-up approach stands the now-infamous Internet Research Agency—one of many so-called troll factories tied to Putin-confidant Yevgeny Prigozhin with a budget of $19 million, employing over 600 people in 2014, of whom each would administer six Facebook accounts, 10 Twitter accounts, and several Instagram accounts.[78] These cyber surrogates have designated performance indicators, engaging with news stories or posts as well as posting dozens of stories each day. During the Russian interference in the US election campaign in 2016, the IRA and other troll farms set up fake accounts that would mimic American voter stereotypes, with Facebook pages such as

"Army of Jesus," "Being Patriotic," and "Heart of Texas" engaging with tradition-ally conservative audiences. The 20 most popular Facebook pages managed by the IRA generated 39 million likes, 31 million shares, and 3.4 million comments and are estimated to have reached 126 million "real" voters on Facebook and 20 million more on Instagram.[79] "Blacktivist," a hipster troll also managed by the IRA, generated 103.8 million shares on his posts alone.[80] In some instances, Russian surrogates even operated as entirely fake freelance journalists, allegedly writing from Syria on the civil war there and presenting Russian talking points.[81]

Hence, although creating and fueling echo chambers, IRA-linked accounts with at times tens of thousands of genuine followers were able to single-handedly change patterns of discourse, using narratives and concepts that were novel and could manipulate the trajectory of civil-societal discourse in key constituen-cies. Setting the agenda, IRA-controlled bots and trolls boosted algorithmically curated trends. For example, the #basketofdeplorables, referring to a remark made by Clinton that many Republican voters found deeply offensive, became a Twitter trend because Russia's information network made it one through auto-mated amplification. Working in a symbiotic relationship with "true believers," meaning audiences cognitively vulnerable to Russian narratives, IRA-controlled accounts were able to exploit microtargeting to generate a force-multiplication effect.[82] America's Internet giants provided easy-to-use and entirely legal mecha-nisms for microtargeting: for example, a meme depicting Jesus wrestling Satan under the caption of "Satan: If Clinton wins I win" was an IRA-sponsored Face-book post that targeted Facebook users age eighteen to sixty-five years, whose profile suggested they were "interested in Christianity, Jesus, God, Ron Paul and media personalities such as Laura Ingraham, Rush Limbaugh, Bill O'Reilly and Mike Savage."[83]

In the run-up to the 2020 US presidential elections, Russia relied even more on coincidental surrogates, most often ordinary Americans who were paid to share their niche opinions on the periphery of the far left or far right. Run by the IRA, the fake news website Peace Data offered American freelancers the oppor-tunity to write commentaries and op-eds stigmatizing candidate Joe Biden and his running mate Kamala Harris as part of a "deep state establishment."[84] These genuine commentaries were complemented by pieces written by fake journal-ists.[85] The objective here was to draw in American progressives on the far left in an effort to curb their support for the Biden campaign.[86]

In Eastern Europe, where Russia is targeting Russian speakers, the Eur-asian ideologue Dugin himself is allegedly using a netwar portal rossia3.ru to feed netizens and true believers with ideology-heavy narratives that are com-pounded in powerful virtual echo chambers with the ability to mobilize.[87] As with the example of the IRA, the outcome is a mass mobilization of users for a cause in the virtual domain.

Russia's conventional media arm might be less subtle in its spread of weaponized narratives, but it has become a very potent actor in the global information environment. Under the umbrella of Russia's news agency Rossiya Segodya, headed by the ideologue and journalist Dimitry Kiselyov, who shares the Kremlin's main metanarratives,[88] Russia Today (RT) and Sputnik are the most famous Russian state-owned news outlets. As with other state-owned international broadcasters, RT's initial objective was to conduct defensive messaging, including public diplomacy to balance attitudes toward Russia. Yet, as the network expands its reach, defensive messaging has increasingly become offensive, directly targeting the "liberal mainstream" and undermining information streams that carry pro-Western messages.[89]

Measuring RT's global reach before it was banned in the European Union amid the war in Ukraine in 2022 remains difficult as RT tends to inflate its viewership based on reach estimates rather than other reliable data. While RT's website states that it has a viewership of 100 million in 47 countries,[90] data collected locally, both in Europe and the United States, suggests that its reach as a conventional news channel remains on the fringes despite an increase in market share.[91] More importantly, however, is RT's ability to attract viewers through its increased online exposure, where human interest stories have lured millions of viewers to their videos.[92] In France, RT's coverage of the mass protests by the Gilet Jaunes in late 2018 gave the channel an impressive boost in its online viewership as audiences were looking for "independent" coverage—allowing the Kremlin-affiliated network to disseminate narratives that would further fuel mobilization and unrest.[93]

Next to RT as Rossiya Segodya's flagship are websites such as Sputnik and Russia Beyond the Headlines, which are also used to triangulate narratives with mis- and disinformation. Like RT, they push conspiratorial narratives that are mostly absorbed on the extreme fringes of the political spectrum, mostly on the far right.[94] The outlets working under Rossiya Segodya's umbrella provide a platform as well for conspiracy theorists and "experts" who lend credibility to Russia's narratives. The British historian John Laughland and Andreas Rahr, a German political consultant, appear on RT to provide credence to Russian talking points, as the next section highlights.

Western influencers and executives become as much integral parts of the Russian information network as media outlets, trolls, and bots. Russia has invested in a range of institutes that are supposed to provide credibility and legitimacy to pro-Kremlin narratives. Front organizations like the Institute for Democracy and Cooperation, the Eurasian Institute, the Strategic Culture Foundation, Katehon, and Rusky Mir promote pro-Russian Eurasian narratives overseas and create a facade of independent institutes while disguising the true actor pulling the strings. These institutes have the ability to verify narratives by writing reports or organizing events that promote Russian talking points.[95] The Institute for Democracy and Cooperation is able to disseminate anti-Western narratives under the cloak of promoting "human rights based on traditional values."[96] Likewise, the Kremlin is also instrumentalizing the Russian Orthodox Church as a front group that can provide credibility and, most importantly, legitimacy to Russia's narratives in constituencies outside Russia's borders but who nonetheless share close religious ties to the heart of Russia's Orthodoxy.[97]

Front groups with links to policymaking circles are another part of Russia's information network. Most important, while the USSR's front groups were predominantly from the left-wing, socialist spectrum, Russia's patriotic-nationalist narrative predominantly finds a receptive audience among the far right on the political spectrum in the West. It is therefore not surprising that, though Russia still maintains ties to socialist groups, like those in Eastern Ukraine, it predominantly reaches out to ultraconservative and far-right groups in Europe and the United States.[98] In Latvia, Russia's governing party United Russia maintains political affiliations with the Centre Party.[99] In Austria, the Kremlin has spent considerable time since the early 2000s engaging with the right-wing FPÖ, hosting delegations in Moscow and setting up links between oligarchs and policymakers.[100] In Germany, the Kremlin has traditionally maintained links with the left-wing Die Linke but has more recently tried to build relations with members of parliament from the right-wing AfD, as a Russian strategy paper suggests.[101] In Belgium, Russia has engaged with right-wing secessionists from the Vlaams Belang.[102] In Italy, it has maintained connections with anti-EU, ultranationalist radical elements of Forza Italia and Lega Nord, whose electoral success made Matteo Salvini deputy prime minister between 2018 and 2019. Investigations revealed how far the Kremlin went to promise the investment of the equivalent of nearly $3.5 million into the party to build an anti-EU alliance.[103] Russia set up a complex financial mechanism to provide the French far-right party the Front National with an $11 million loan, which made headlines at the time in 2015.[104] Britain's UKIP and its successor the Brexit Party have also been accused of maintaining close relationships with Russia via its main donor, the businessman Aaron Banks.[105] And in the United States, a 2021 book drawing on former KGB sources claims that the KGB and its successor, the GRU, had been trying to actively turn real estate magnate Donald Trump into a politician for decades.[106]

Other key nodes in Russia's information networks are the "useful idiots"— namely, coincidental surrogates who are pulled into a Kremlin-curated debate and take a pro-Russian "alternative" position. Especially in the context of Russia's invasion of Ukraine in 2022, the self-proclaimed "lateral thinkers" took positions that were primarily countering the emerging consensus on Russian aggression, blaming NATO's eastern expansion and post–Cold War Western policies.[107] Anti-Western and anti-imperialist ideologues thereby presented a particularly receptive audience to Russian narratives about the "defensive character" of its actions. In Germany, not just voices on the far right and far left started to counter anti-Russian mainstream narratives but also members of the ruling social democratic party, SPD, whose worldview created a cognitive dissonance with the reality of Russian aggression inside Ukraine.[108] The effect of useful idiots on sociopolitical consensus in Germany in the run-up to the war in Ukraine in 2022 was immense, making it difficult for the German government to take a clear position against Russian aggression.

Regardless of whether the Kremlin provides financial or infrastructural support or merely maintains good personal or institutional relations with front groups, it becomes a direct or indirect surrogate for the promotion of Russian objectives and narratives. Russia has been able to ripen a united front of like-minded policymakers (and would-be policymakers), which not only disrupt the political discourse in their respective countries but also have more recently been able to take over political responsibility. Their populist antiestablishment, antimigration, and antiglobalization stance provides a natural ontological overlap with Russia's strategic narratives. Able to echo Russian talking points, they not only provide sociopolitical influence near the heart of policymaking in the West but they also have the potential to translate Russian narratives into political outcomes in the physical domain of the information environment: The German AfD has, since being elected to the Reichstag, pushed for the lifting of the EU's sanctions on Russia;[109] The Brexit Party voted against EU resolution to stop Russian interference in elections in the European Parliament;[110] Italy's Lega Nord openly campaigns for a lifting of EU sanctions on Russia;[111] and the French Front National has defended Russia's annexation of Crimea as a legitimate and legal act.[112] Reinforcing sociopolitical polarization, political deadlock, and shaping patterns of civil-societal discourse, Russia's front groups have become an effective lever of power for Moscow to undermine information-psychological stability in target countries.

Singer illustrates in his book *Like War* how Russia's bottom-up approach to disinformation works, based on an example taken from Ukraine. In a first instance, disinformation is released via Facebook pages and online news outlets such as "Donbass News International," controlled by the Kremlin; second, these stories are picked up by a Norwegian communist news aggregator that pitches it to far-left activist websites; third, seemingly reputable outlets, such as "Centre for Research on Globalization"—itself a pro-Russian online distribution point for conspiracy theories—try to give the narrative an appearance of credibility; fourth, conventional outlets such as Russia Today and Sputnik draw on the previous triangulation to "validate" the narrative; finally, IRA-linked bots and trolls share these stories via extensive botnet networks.[113] In the end, a self-contained circle of disinformation closes that at the very least provides those looking to confirm their biases a superficial illusion of an alternative truth.

Step 5: Verification

The verification element has become integral to the process of subversion in the twenty-first century. Though other subverting powers, such as the United Arab Emirates, invest more heavily in the verification element than Russia, the Kremlin has nonetheless understood how important the role of co-opted experts or fake experts at think tanks or in academia are to verifying and legitimizing its narratives. Implanting a favorable voice in a Western think tank, particularly in the United States, means Russia is placing a surrogate in the American policy-making ecosystem. Therefore, Russia has actively sought individuals at Western think tanks that are sympathetic to its narratives in an attempt to ripen potential surrogates that would help provide credence to Russia's talking points.[114]

So far, Russia's verification of narratives widely relies on quasi–think tanks directly tied to and financed by the Kremlin, undermining the verification status they intend to assume. For example, the self-styled think tank the Strategic Culture Foundation, financed and controlled by the Russian foreign intelligence service, developed into a hub for narrative verification publishing fringe thinkers and conspiracy theorists appearing as a legitimate academic outlet.[115] The same is true for the quasi–think tank Katehon based in Russia and the seemingly academic publication *New Eastern Outlook*, which publish supposedly independent, analytical material to lend credibility to disinformation-based narratives.[116]

The Centre for Research on Globalization, a website led by conspiracy theorist Michel Chossudovsky based in Canada, is among several institutes and pseudo-think tanks that serve as platforms for Russia to spread or "verify" disinformation by seemingly independent outlets based outside Russia.[117] In the case of the downed Malaysian Airlines Flight 17 over Ukraine in 2014—an attack most independent analysts attribute to pro-Russian separatists—Chossudovsky's self-publishing website provided "evidence" that would deflect the blame for the downing of the airliner away from Russia. In Germany, Russia's energy giant Gazprom provided 99 percent of funds to create a think tank Stiftung Klima- und Umweltschutz MV together with the regional state government of Mecklenburg-Vorpommern, with the intent to engage the public and increase approval for Russia's growing control of Germany's energy sector. With the regional state prime minister and other leading social democrats on its board, the quasi–think tank became a powerful vehicle of influence in the run-up to Russia's war in Ukraine in 2022.[118]

Equally important for Russia are a range of senior Western policymakers, businesspeople, political consultants, and journalists who provide direct and indirect means for the Kremlin to verify its narratives. One of Russia's key defenders in the West was the former German chancellor Gerhard Schröder, who served as chairman of the board of the German-Russian joint venture Nord Stream AG and the Russian energy giant Rosneft for years. Schröder repeatedly defended Putin as a "flawless democrat" and appeared in German media to take a view on Russian affairs that ran counter to the mainstream.[119] Alexander Rahr, another German, who has apparently worked as a paid communication consultant for Russian-owned energy companies, frequently appears on Russian media to provide a Western perspective endorsing Russian narratives.[120] Former Afghanistan correspondent of German public broadcaster ARD, Christoph Hörstel, also serves Russia Today as a pundit to provide an alternative perspective to Western narratives from an ostensibly Western point of view.[121] In the United States, the late university professor, columnist, and Russia expert Stephen F. Cohen was accused of being a "Putin apologist" before his death in 2020, blamed for recycling Russian disinformation and talking points.[122] Hence, without always directly providing remunerative incentives for "experts" and influencers, Russia can rely on its metanarratives to attract individuals who voluntarily and coincidentally verify Russia's talking points—not always with great concern for veracity.

Step 6: Implementation

The final step in Russia's subversion strategy is ensuring that mobilization and countermobilization in the virtual sphere of the information environment translate into physical effect. That is to say, information levers are orchestrated in a way so as to alter not just audiences' attitudes but also their decisions and behaviors.

As discussed previously, the most challenging part of subversion is finding an adequate metric to measure impact. The reason is that subversion deliberately takes a gradual approach, whereby effects become measurable only as they compound and accumulate. Particularly as the implementation of any subversion strategy relies heavily on an extensive network of direct, indirect, and coincidental surrogates, the effect as a whole is likely greater than the sum of its parts.

In the case of Russia's interference in the 2016 US presidential elections, a direct link can be established between IRA-sponsored activities in the virtual sphere and mobilization of target audiences in the offline world. The most influential social media accounts maintained by the IRA were able to solicit donations from real voters in the United States for the Trump campaign and organize rallies in the physical domain on both sides of the political aisle. As Special Counsel Robert Mueller writes in his 2019 report about Russian interference in the 2016 election,

First, the IRA used one of its preexisting social media personas (Facebook groups and Twitter accounts, for example) to announce and promote the event. The IRA then sent a large number of direct messages to followers of its social media account asking them to attend the event. From those who responded with interest in attending, the IRA then sought a US person to serve as the event's coordinator. In most cases, the IRA account operator would tell the US person that they personally could not attend the event due to some preexisting conflict or because they were somewhere else in the United States.[123]

In fact, there are extensive correlations between IRA-sponsored social media activity and rallies on both the right and left. Apart from pro-Trump or anti-Clinton rallies, IRA-linked fake accounts were also able to mobilize rallies and flash mobs under the banner of "Black Lives Matter."[124]

In Europe, IRA-affiliated trolls and bots have also tried to target election campaigns. In conjunction with Russian conventional media outlets, Russia's cyber surrogates might have also played a significant role in making an impact on trends in the run-up to the Brexit referendum in the United Kingdom in 2016.[125] In a 2018 working paper, Gorodnichenko and others argue that, because of the binary nature of the referendum, the widespread indecisiveness of voters, and the disproportionate ratio of human and bot tweets, the targeted engagement of Russian bots and trolls might have had an impact on overall voting behavior. According to Gorodnichenko and others, "the difference between actual and counterfactual traffic could translate into 1.76 percentage points of actual pro-Leave vote share."[126] Albeit not decisive for the outcome of the referendum, the effect was nonetheless measurable as it intensified sociopolitical polarization.

In Eastern Europe, Russian narrative campaigns have caused a spillover from the virtual domain to the physical. Whether in Estonia in 2007 or in eastern Ukraine in 2014, Russian disinformation led to a polarization and mobilization that shapes civil-societal activism in the physical space. Violent riots in Tallinn were as much an effect of Russian subversion as the mobilization of pro-Russian militia groups in the Donbas that are taking on the Ukrainian Armed Forces.[127]

Hence, although causal links between activities in the virtual sphere of the information environment and effects in the physical sphere are difficult to establish, actions by bots, trolls, conventional media outlets, and front groups can nonetheless be attributed to the Russian deep state. Though a change in social media trends might correlate with a change in civil-societal attitude toward politically relevant topics, it is equally difficult to measure to what extent a change in attitude potentially causes a change in voting behavior. As Jamieson writes, "Any case for influence will be like that in a legal trial in which the verdict is rendered not with the certainty that $e = mc^2$ but rather based on the preponderance of evidence. 'Beyond a doubt' is not a standard that works when as many different factors are simultaneously at play as they are here."[128]

Equally significant to voting behavior in the implementation phase is the impact that narratives directly or indirectly have on policymakers or on those practitioners with the influence and reach to affect policymaking. First, as Western policymakers with ties to or sympathies with the Kremlin assume positions with political responsibility, Russian narratives become part of the political mainstream.[129] A second, more subtle effect, policymakers and practitioners unwittingly help to propagate Russian narratives in civil-societal discourse as laymen. In liberal democracies, policymakers feel the urge to respond to discourse, even when those narratives (knowingly or unknowingly) develop on the backs of disinformation campaigns. The case of former FBI director James Comey is a case in point: exposed to a highly polarized public debate on Clinton's emails—shaped by IRA-affiliated trolls and bots—Comey admits in hindsight that his decision to investigate Clinton at a crucial time of the campaign was prompted by disinformation about President Obama's Justice Department potentially covering up Clinton's email affair.[130] Exposed to an agenda set in part by bots and trolls on social media, inflaming America's highly partisan conventional news media, Comey might have been persuaded to make one of the most consequential decisions in the 2016 US presidential campaign: he reopened an investigation into candidate Clinton days before the vote that severely undermined her reputation. This episode suggests that Russian subversion was able to generate the highest level of impact possible on the policymaking level.

Finally, as Rid argues, the very debate about Russia's meddling in the US presidential elections—which he considers to be inflated—generated a physical effect.[131] The more the media, academia, and policymakers were discussing Russia's interference in the electoral process, the more the interference became real, despite what was actually measurable. If the strategic end of Russia's campaign was to undermine confidence in the electoral process itself, then the public debate on the security of the electoral process, including the Mueller investigation, served Moscow's objectives.

CONCLUSION

The relative banality of means employed by Russia in its global contest of wills should not distract us from recognizing the severity of the effect of Russia's information network on sociopolitical discourse, civil-societal activity, and policymaking in the West. Unlike other players, Russia understands how to weaponize narratives to not only prepare the ground for conventional military operations but also, more importantly, to make it a stand-alone lever of power. In recent decades, Russia has purposefully directed its focus on the information environment, realizing that it is here that the diffusion of power is possible as Western military superiority in the conventional space appears, at least for Moscow, to be unchallengeable. For the Kremlin, subversion is politics by other means—a means of twenty-first-century warfare, albeit below the threshold of war, that exploits the vulnerabilities of Western adversaries more radically than any conventional, kinetic means of war.

Russia's subversion campaigns go beyond the defensive messaging that traditionally constitutes the core of public diplomacy. Although Russia perceives itself as being on the defensive against weaponized Western narratives, its approach to engineering narratives that strategically exploit the vulnerabilities of the sociopsychological domain, employing means that take advantage of the infrastructural revolutions of the information environment, makes Russian subversion as disruptive and instrumental as conventional means of warfare. The way that Russian narratives have spilled from the virtual to the physical world, while mobilizing hundreds of thousands of people both online and offline to gradually challenge the existing sociopolitical status quo in target countries, shows how violent subversion can actually be. Russian subversion campaigns have targeted the wills of people both on the grassroots level and in policymaking. Russia shapes the context in which policy decisions are being made. It does not just set the agenda or frame policy-relevant issues, but it also evidently manages to shape the attitudes, decisions, and behaviors of people in target audiences.

This takes place against the backdrop of growing sociopolitical polarization in the West, where narratives in support of a liberal political and economic order increasingly display a say/do gap. Therefore, Russian efforts to subvert information-psychological stability will not only increase but might even potentially be more successful. The revolution in the infrastructural domain of the information environment is ongoing against the backdrop of a laissez-faire approach by Western governments to making information environments more resilient. As existing patterns of information processing are changing radically, the liberal public spheres of the West appear to be most vulnerable to both influence campaigns and efforts to undermine the information-psychological stability of its civil society. Russia will play a key role in trying to further widen the gap between parts of the public and the existing political establishment, because subversion provides a cost-efficient lever of power to achieve a range of strategic objectives without ever crossing the threshold of war.

In the smart power confrontation between Moscow and those supporting a liberal world order, the Kremlin appears to have scored a range of short-term to midterm victories, which might not necessarily halt the macroeconomic decay of Russia—especially after the war in Ukraine—but at the very least paralyze the United States and its allies that have become increasingly preoccupied with addressing domestic over foreign policy crises. Plus, Moscow appears to have more strategic patience in letting subversion unfold its full potential, gradually, over time, to deliver an effect that is greater than the sum of its parts.

NOTES

1. CBS, "Richard A. Clarke."
2. NBC News, "Confronting Russian President Vladimir Putin."
3. Castells, *Communication Power*, 268.
4. Nemtsova, "Chill in the Moscow Air."
5. Abrams, "Beyond Propaganda," 18.
6. Singer and Brooking, *Like War*, 109.
7. CNN, "Inside the KGB."
8. Abrams, "Beyond Propaganda," 8.
9. Bezmenov, "Psychological Warfare Subversion."
10. Kello, *Virtual Weapon*, 218.
11. Al-Atrush, Parkin, and Cotterill, "Ukraine Conflict."
12. Robinson et al., *Modern Political Warfare*, 47.
13. Jones and Kovacich, *Global Information Warfare*, 34.
14. Klus, "Myatezh Voina."
15. Messner, *Myatezh*, 43.
16. Messner, *Vseminaya Myatezhevoyna*.
17. Fridman, *Russian "Hybrid Warfare,"* 66.
18. Fridman, 70.
19. Giles, *Handbook*, 9.
20. Russian Presidency, Указ Президента Российской Федерации.
21. Kazarin, "Nature of War," 21.
22. Jonsson, *Russian Understanding of War*, 12.
23. Jonsson, 48.
24. Thomas, "Information Security Thinking," 2.
25. Fridman, *Russian "Hybrid Warfare,"* 79.
26. Dugin, "Network-Centric Wars."
27. Chekinov and Bogdanov, "Nature and Content of a New-Generation War," 17.
28. Jonsson and Seely, "Russian Full-Spectrum Conflict," 8.
29. Gerasimov, "Value of Science."
30. Galeotti, "I'm Sorry for Creating the 'Gerasimov Doctrine.'"
31. McGeehan, "Countering Russian Disinformation," 50.
32. Kello, *Virtual Weapon*, 216.
33. Jonsson, *Russian Understanding of War*, 89.
34. Bartles, "Getting Gerasimov Right," 34.
35. MacFarquhar, "Yevgeny Prigozhin."
36. Lange-Ionatamišvili, *Analysis of Russia's Information Campaign*, 36.
37. *PBS Frontline*, "Putin's Revenge."
38. Jamieson, *Cyberwar*, 22.
39. Richey, "Contemporary Russian Revisionism," 109.
40. Jamieson, *Cyberwar*, 15.
41. Jones and Kovacich, *Global Information Warfare*, 204.
42. Shuster, "Why Russia Can Claim Victory."

43. Jamieson, *Cyberwar*, 15.
44. Holpuch, "Jimmy Carter."
45. Rid, *Active Measures*, 431.
46. White, "Dismiss."
47. Fridman, *Russian "Hybrid Warfare,"* 79.
48. Jamieson, *Cyberwar*, 77.
49. Wesslau, "Putin's Friends."
50. Bigg, "Crimea Visit."
51. Gebauer, "Aufklärung unerwünscht!"
52. *De Telegraaf*, "Wilders verrast met Rusland-reis."
53. Cadwalladr, "Arron Banks."
54. Nardelli, "Revealed."
55. Altemeyer, "Other 'Authoritarian Personality'"; Wilson, *Psychology of Conservatism*.
56. Pomerantsev and Weiss, "Menace."
57. Timberg, "New Report."
58. Jamieson, *Cyberwar*, 38.
59. Robinson et al., *Modern Political Warfare*, 47; Jones and Kovacich, *Global Information Warfare*, 95.
60. Maliukevičius, "Tools of Destabilization," 122.
61. Hågen Karlsen, *Divide and Rule*, 7.
62. Fitzgerald and Brantly, "Subverting Reality," 231.
63. International Crisis Group, "Rebels without a Cause," 2.
64. Malinova, "Constructing the 'Usable Past,'" 85.
65. Malinova, 94.
66. Pomerantsev and Weiss, "Menace," 19.
67. Torbakov, "Middle Continent," 38.
68. Singer and Brooking, *Like War*, 158.
69. Pomerantsev and Weiss, "Menace," 19.
70. Kramer, "To Battle Fake News."
71. Ali, "How the US, Ukraine and the Media Have Thrown a Wrench."
72. Giles, Sherr, and Seaboyer, *Russian Reflexive Control*, 25.
73. Jamieson, *Cyberwar*, 87.
74. Paul and Matthews, "Russian 'Firehose of Falsehood,'" 6.
75. Robinson et al., *Modern Political Warfare*, 56.
76. Beauchamp, "Meet the Shady Putin Crony."
77. Paul and Matthews, "Russian 'Firehose of Falsehood,'" 3.
78. Seddon, "Documents."
79. Timberg, "New Report."
80. Singer and Brooking, *Like War*, 113.
81. Toler, "Details."
82. Jamieson, *Cyberwar*, 122.
83. Paul and Matthews, "Russian 'Firehose of Falsehood,'" 140.
84. Dilanian and Ramgopal, "Facebook Blocks Russia-Backed Accounts."
85. Owen-Jones, *Digital Authoritarianism*, 181.
86. Kirby, "Yes, Russia Is Interfering."
87. Giles, Sherr, and Seaboyer, *Russian Reflexive Control*, 31.
88. Ennis, "Dmitry Kiselyov."
89. Robinson et al., *Modern Political Warfare*, 62.

90. RT, "RT Weekly TV Audience."
91. Erickson, "If Russia Today Is Moscow's Propaganda Arm."
92. Nelson, Orttung, and Livshen, "Measuring RT's Impact."
93. Agnew, "French 'Gilets Jaunes' Protests."
94. Pomerantsev and Weiss, "Menace," 15.
95. Jonsson and Seely, "Russian Full-Spectrum Conflict," 18.
96. Van Herpen, *Putin's Propaganda Machine*, 34.
97. Dubov, *Active Measures*, 29.
98. Giles, Sherr, and Seaboyer, *Russian Reflexive Control*, 18.
99. Robinson et al., *Modern Political Warfare*, 57.
100. Al-Serori, "Wie die FPÖ Russland lieben lernte."
101. Fiedler, "Russlands Spiel mit den Rechten."
102. Jonsson and Seely, "Russian Full-Spectrum Conflict," 18.
103. Nardelli, "Revealed."
104. Bigg, "Crimea Visit."
105. Cadwalladr, "Arron Banks."
106. Unger, *American Kompromat*.
107. Chotiner, "Why John Mearsheimer Blames the US."
108. Karnitschnig, "Putin's Useful German Idiots."
109. Fiedler, "Russlands Spiel mit den Rechten."
110. Stone, "Nigel Farage."
111. BBC News, "Russian Meeting."
112. Batchelor, "Marine Le Pen Insists."
113. Singer and Brooking, *Like War*, 108.
114. Tromblay, "Intelligence," 5.
115. Manson, Foy, and Murphy, "Biden."
116. US Department of State, "Pillars."
117. Fitzgerald and Brantly, "Subverting Reality," 233.
118. Mosebach, "Klimastiftung und Nord Stream 2."
119. *Frankfurter Allgemeine Zeitung*, "Schröder."
120. Banse, Flader, and Müller, "Deutscher Putin-Unterstützer."
121. Piatov, "Moskaus Propaganda."
122. Smith, "Is This Professor 'Putin's American Apologist'?"
123. Mueller, *Report*, 28.
124. Giles, Sherr, and Seaboyer, *Russian Reflexive Control*, 39.
125. Intelligence and Security Committee of Parliament, "Russia," 12.
126. Gorodnichenko, Pham, and Talavera, *Social Media*, 19.
127. Giles, Sherr, and Seaboyer, *Russian Reflexive Control*, 38.
128. Jamieson, *Cyberwar*, 14.
129. Polyakova, "Strange Bedfellows," 40.
130. Comey, *Higher Loyalty*, chap. 10.
131. Rid, *Active Measures*, 431.

SIX

······

Little Sparta's Counterrevolution, or How the United Arab Emirates Weaponizes Narratives

A Reuters article in 2018 ran with the headline, "Emerging Gulf State Cyber Security Powerhouse Growing Rapidly in Size, Revenue."[1] The article discussed the emerging cyber capability of the United Arab Emirates (UAE) and the growing assertiveness of the Middle East's "Little Sparta," as former US secretary of defense James Mattis once referred to the UAE.[2] For most observers of the Middle East and North Africa (MENA), the UAE's foreign policy has traditionally been quite reserved—at least in comparison with neighboring Iran, Saudi Arabia, and even Qatar. Recently, however, Abu Dhabi has become a more assertive player both in and outside the region, especially since the eruption of the Arab Spring in late 2010. It is increasingly using its growing conventional military muscle to advance its interests while developing new unconventional capabilities in the information environment. Yet, while the UAE's offensive use of information power for sabotage and espionage is widely documented,[3] few have looked at the UAE's more disruptive use of subversion.[4] Here, the UAE does not just influence public and policy debates in Western capitals. More importantly, it attempts to undermine the information-psychological stability of countries in their own region.

Abu Dhabi's rise as a cyberpower needs to be understood within the context of its ambition to become a "global soft superpower."[5] The country has gone beyond simply employing public diplomacy reactively to change its image overseas, and it now aims to more proactively dominate the information environment *in* the Middle East as well as the global discourse *on* the Middle East. The disintegration of the traditional regional powerhouses in Libya, Egypt, Syria, and Iraq in the aftermath of the Arab Spring created an opening for new rising powers such as the UAE to fill the void. These emerging powers used new methods to advance their objectives, couched in new narratives to frame them. "Emirati exceptionalism" meant propagating a new model for the region: one based on authoritarian stability with a twist of social and economic liberalization. Abu Dhabi's firm rejection of the Arab Spring as the root cause of regional disintegration, instability, and anarchy made the country the staunch-est counterrevolutionary force in the region in both the physical and virtual domains of the information environment. The UAE's paranoia about dynamics that could challenge or undermine the sociopolitical status quo of the region provided an incentive for it to go on the offensive to challenge how Western-ers think about the region and how Middle Easterners think about themselves. Amid the upheavals of postrevolutionary chaos, the UAE developed an exten-sive soft power apparatus to transcend domains of sociopolitics and security and involve religion and ideology. It also sought to appeal to media, academia, and policymakers both in the region and outside it.

This chapter sheds light on the rise of the UAE as an information power, which gave it the opportunity to learn how to mobilize and demobilize civil society and policymakers at home, in the region, and abroad, following a com-prehensive subversion strategy. It allowed this relatively small rentier state in the Arabian Gulf to punch well above its weight and become arguably the most dynamic and disruptive player in the Arab world. In so doing, Abu Dhabi has not shied away from subverting policy debates and processes in Western capi-tals by relying on an extensive information and influence network comprising media outlets, experts, lobbyists, and policymakers—all the while maintaining close working relationships with what are effectively its Western partners.

The chapter commences by outlining how the current regime in Abu Dhabi came into power and to what extent the ideas, values, and norms of its elites have shaped the narratives the country uses to legitimize its strategic objectives. We then look at how the Arab Spring has increased the urgency in Abu Dhabi to move from defensive messaging and public diplomacy to offensive messaging and subversion. Finally, we deconstruct the UAE's six-step subversion strategy, from orientation to implementation.

LITTLE SPARTA: SECURING A CITY-STATE

During the past two decades, the UAE, despite its relative "smallness," has emerged as one of the most influential countries in the region. The cultivation of diverse influence networks, allowing Abu Dhabi to delegate statecraft to sur-rogates, has been a key component of the UAE's ability to put its mark on the region. Information networks have thereby been instrumental in securing this city-state.

The Rise of MbZ

The story of "Little Sparta"—a benevolent business hub that has become a regional military power—begins with the rise of Mohammad bin Zayed al

Nahyan (MbZ), one of the children of the UAE's founding father, Zayed bin Sultan Al Nahyan. MbZ, to whom the *New York Times* referred in 2019 as "the most powerful man in the Arab world," was never even destined to become the UAE's first man.[6] As the second in line to the ruler of Abu Dhabi, the title of president of the UAE was supposed to rotate to Dubai's ruler, Mohammad bin Rashid al Maktoum (MbR), and MbZ was destined to live a relatively quiet life. But having been removed from the pampered environment of the royal court and educated in Morocco, MbZ learned how to fend for himself.[7] It was not surprising that he would join the military in 1979 after graduating from the Royal Military Academy of Sandhurst and eventually find himself working his way through the ranks. After the death of his father in 2004, his older brother assumed the leadership of the UAE, and MbZ became the crown prince of Abu Dhabi, catapulting him into the heart of political power in the UAE's capital.

Two events would change the trajectory of MbZ's career, from the military man in the background to becoming the omnipotent Svengali of the seven-emirate federation: first, the tumultuous regional turmoil of 1979, arguably the most consequential year for Islam in modern history, and second, the global financial crisis of 2008. The Islamic Revolution unfolded in Iran in 1979, the year his military career commenced. That same year, the Grand Mosque of Mecca was besieged by Sunni fundamentalists, while the Soviet Union's invasion of Afghanistan caused scores of young Muslim men joining the call for jihad. The eighteen-year-old MbZ was, for the first time, confronted with the transformational soft power of political Islam and its ability to challenge the status quo in the region—something that would shape his growing paranoia about Islamism.[8]

The second defining moment for MbZ, the global financial crisis of 2008, caused the glittering facade of Dubai to crumble after decades of uninterrupted growth. Between the poles of the two dominant emirates, Abu Dhabi and Dubai, the latter had widely outperformed the capital, becoming a global business hub based on a relatively well-diversified service economy. The two cities were not just competing for global soft power but also indirectly for sociopolitical power within the federation. Although both emirates were meant to be equal before the constitution, Abu Dhabi has incrementally seized key positions in the federation. Yet it was the near-financial collapse of Dubai amid the global financial crisis in 2008, along with the $10 billion bailout of oil-rich Abu Dhabi, that reshaped the balance of power between both royal families, the Al Nahyan of Abu Dhabi and the Al Maktoum of Dubai.[9]

When MbZ's older brother Khalifa suffered a severe stroke that incapacitated him in 2014, MbZ became the de facto leader of Abu Dhabi, plus the other six emirates that were now largely dependent on the security deep state that MbZ was building in Abu Dhabi. Driven by an obsession with discipline, centralized power, and hierarchical loyalty to the political leader, MbZ embarked on an ambitious reform project, first within the armed forces that he had led since 1994 as its chief of staff and later in the civilian realm.[10] "Little Sparta" was fast becoming a centralized security state, run by MbZ and a small circle of his most trusted men in Abu Dhabi. Centralization of power became more than a figure of speech; anyone willing to make a career in the security sector—including law enforcement, intelligence, or the armed forces—now had to physically move to Abu Dhabi and submit to the direct control of the omnipresent crown prince.[11]

Leading the UAE onto a path of political emancipation from its immediate Gulf neighborhood meant that the UAE would have to take over responsibility in the region as the region's emerging powerhouse—not least after the September 11, 2001, terrorist attacks on the United States were, among others, perpetrated by two UAE terrorists. The UAE was eager to present itself as an American partner, offering Washington not just a near-peer military but also a new model of statehood for the Middle East: one that would overcome both the shackles of Arab nationalism and political Islam to build a strong state where a military-based leadership controlled not just what people say but also what they think.[12] For MbZ, military hard power had to be complemented by a soft power appeal. People required an alternative to the existing prevalent ideologies in the region, of which especially political Islam was framed as a challenge to the very existence of the UAE's tribal-based monarchy.[13]

The idea of a "secular state in the Middle East" was born after the 9/11 attacks, when MbZ, then in charge of the security sector, engaged in a relentless crackdown on Islamism at home. Like other Gulf states, the UAE had witnessed the arrival of Islamists in the 1950s and 1960s to staff the administration of its fast-growing hydrocarbon rentier state.[14] By the 1990s, the local Islamist group, al-Islah, had an extensive following among civil servants, especially in the education and cultural sectors, while also attracting considerable appeal among UAE residents in the more deprived northern regions of the country.[15] MbZ was personally alienated from political Islam, considering it both a powerful counternarrative to the UAE's political system and a potential rallying point for popular mobilization outside the control of the state. Thus, he engaged in a zero-tolerance campaign to wipe out al-Islah in the federation—a policy that would culminate in the country's counterrevolutionary stance during the Arab Spring.[16] As a man driven by security paranoia, MbZ's angst about political Islam is rooted in his fear of heterarchical power structures, which are common to the Arabian Gulf, whereby power is shared among certain elites and where any sultan, king, or emir can only act as a primus inter pares. More than that, political Islam could empower a nascent civil society in the region that might call for more dilution of power away from the tribal power centers. It is therefore not surprising that over the past decade, MbZ's deep state has increasingly consumed religious elites in the country, going as far as dictating the sermons given in mosques on Fridays.[17]

The Arab Spring and Regime Insecurity

The images of millions of Arabs taking to the streets in early 2011 exacerbated existing paranoia in Abu Dhabi. MbZ's state revealed itself to be increasingly hostile to any form of political dissent. As a military man who believed that statecraft was the prerogative of an autocratic, transactional leader, MbZ would not perceive calls for more political pluralism in the region as an opportunity but instead viewed them as a threat. Much more, MbZ would over time become the spearhead of a regional counterrevolution advancing a narrative of "authoritarian stability" as opposed to "pluralistic chaos."

For "Little Sparta," the mass protests in late 2010 came as a surprise, overwhelming Abu Dhabi just as much as other regimes in the region. Within weeks, some of the protests had escalated into revolution, pushing Libya and Syria to the brink of insurgency and civil war while toppling old powerhouses in Tunisia and Egypt. Civil society had demonstrated that benign calls for social justice and individual liberty could escalate into highly disruptive currents with the ability to topple the authoritarian guard of the region. The UAE's response was cautious to start, while its neighbor Qatar went all out to throw its financial weight and information power behind the calls for sociopolitical liberalization at all costs—an idealistic approach with little consideration for the aftermath. The fact that Qatar tapped into the region's most resilient opposition network—the Islamist Muslim Brotherhood—alarmed MbZ's deep state to the potential of a civil society empowered by Islamist narratives. Islamist mobilization could solidify a regional dynamic that might even sweep the tribal monarchies of the Gulf off their feet. With a homegrown Muslim Brotherhood–affiliated group with ties to royal families of some of the northern emirates, the UAE saw itself on the receiving end of regional upheaval that could undermine regime security at home.[18]

MbZ's personal alienation from political Islam, and his belief in strong, state-centric institutions controlling both political and civil-societal affairs, meant that the UAE could not afford to look at the Arab Spring as an opportunity. The antidote to "pluralistic chaos" was the orientalist myth of "authoritarian stability," based on the assumption that the Middle East would be best governed by authoritarian autocrats as opposed to pluralistic systems that would provide platforms for Islamists to "usurp" civil society.[19] Centralized power legitimized through the support of the security sector were promoted as guarantees of security and stability, necessary to fight "terrorism" in the region.

The terrorism label has since been the centerpiece for the UAE's counterrevolutionary narrative justifying the crackdown on any form of political Islam and non-state-sanctioned civil society in Egypt, Libya, and Yemen. MbZ's fierce state would not only move against Islamists at home but also provide counterrevolutionaries in the region with the financial means, military support, and narratives to securitize Islamism. Political Islam and its supporters were dubbed enemies of the state who were engaged in either direct or indirect support for what was framed as "terrorism." Based on a simplistic neoconservative "conveyer belt theory," which suggests that moderate Islamists move along a conveyer belt to eventually become jihadists, even moderate forms of Islamism are framed by Abu Dhabi as "entry drugs to jihadism."[20] Hence, following this logic, the UAE's broad definition of terrorism encompassed any form of religiously inspired civil-societal activism and its support networks. In many ways, Abu Dhabi emulated the American approach to "terrorism" in the aftermath of 9/11: a neoconservative narrative playing on the fear of the unknown used as a political instrument to override liberal and humanitarian norms.[21] More important, the UAE employs the terrorism label to create a false dichotomy in the information environment between "authoritarian stability" and "terrorism." It confronts liberal Western audiences with an illusory choice between regional liberalization, which could lead to "terrorism," and the region's old political status quo of authoritarian stability.

From Public Diplomacy to Offensive Messaging

Abu Dhabi's information operations, which have relied on a complex information and influence network across a wide geographic and media spectrum, date back to a controversy in the United States in 2006. The UAE's flagship company, Dubai Ports World, one of the world's leading port terminal operators, was about to take over the management of six strategically important ports on the US East Coast. At the height of America's war on terrorism, a company owned by a Middle Eastern state was set to manage entries in the United States—an unthinkable notion for leading policymakers on both sides of the aisle. In the end, despite US president Bush's intervention, Dubai Ports World dropped the deal. As one security official said to the *Washington Times* in 2006, "letting a Middle Eastern company manage key ports would be like putting the fox in charge of the henhouse."[22] For Abu Dhabi, this episode painfully demonstrated how vital strategic communication was in Washington to prepare the ground for effective foreign, security, and trade policymaking. The perception in Washington that the UAE were "just another Middle Eastern state" had to be challenged, opening up opportunities to do business, plug foreign policy initiatives, and ultimately secure America's support as the region's protector.

As a small state, the UAE's rise to regional prominence commenced with the realization in the early 2000s that the UAE required the backing of a great power to protect itself from the uncertainties and vulnerabilities of a volatile region. Sandwiched between Saudi Arabia and Iran, the UAE was eager to break the vicious circle of bandwagoning and hedging in its foreign policy by becoming an independent pole that would not have to cater to either Riyadh or Tehran—an objective that could be achieved only if the United States would accept the UAE as a state of its own right rather than just an adjunct in the Saudi sphere of influence. This is where MbZ's vision for "Emirati exceptionalism" comes in: the vision for a progressive Middle Eastern country where state and mosque are separated and where relative social liberalization sets the country apart from the ultraconservative theocracies in the neighborhood.[23] The target audience for this metanarrative has been Washington's policy nexus.

A new UAE ambassador in Washington, Yousef Otaiba, a socialite with an American accent and a Western lifestyle, was supposed to embody the narrative that the UAE was indeed different from its Gulf peers. Otaiba arrived in Washington in 2006 with a blank check and would soon become the center of gravity for social events in the US capital's foreign policy community. Otaiba was able to spend tens of millions of dollars for outreach campaigns, gala dinners, luncheons, and events while donating generously to think tanks, research centers, and lobbying firms. Although Otaiba predominantly focused on neoconservative policy circles, he was not overly selective in his engagement of policymakers, media representatives, academics, and think tankers on both sides of the aisle.[24] On the eve of the Arab Spring, Otaiba had single-handedly turned the UAE's image in Washington around from being just another Middle Eastern state to being America's desired partner in providing stability in the region. This was crucial at a time when the new Obama administration was looking for local allies that would help share the burden in the region. Yet, while many in Washington felt that Otaiba's donations and support came with no strings attached, for Otaiba's direct boss, MbZ, the networks that his ambassador built could be used to disseminate narratives that would shape policy discourse and eventually policymaking in Washington.[25]

What started as a defensive network of influence in Washington quickly turned into an offensive influence campaign targeting the UAE's perceived adversaries in an attempt to undermine their standing vis-à-vis the policymaking community on Capitol Hill and in the White House. Amid the collapse of the old powerhouses of the Middle East in 2011, the fears and paranoia of Abu Dhabi's elite of a resurgent "Islamist menace" were wrapped in narratives and plugged predominantly in conservative circles in Washington. While neighboring Qatar threw its weight behind revolutionaries, opposition forces, and rebel groups of all shapes and colors—often with the direct or tacit support of the Obama administration—the UAE was lobbying for a more reactionary Middle

East policy.[26] In the early months of revolutionary enthusiasm in Western capitals, when policymakers, the media, and academia were endorsing idealist narratives of liberalization and democratization in the Arab world, Abu Dhabi's pessimistic and dark vision for the region did not gain traction.

Yet, by late 2012 and early 2013, with revolutions getting bogged down in insurgency and civil war in Libya and Syria, with Morsi struggling economically to keep the promises of 2011 in Egypt, audiences on the political right became more receptive to the idea of an "Arab Winter"[27] and an Islamist "hijacking" of the revolutions.[28] It was against this backdrop that the UAE's information networks became more active in Washington and regional capitals alike to shape hearts and minds about the perception of political Islam along with the role Qatar and Turkey played in stoking regional instability. The idea put forward by Abu Dhabi was that the only way out of the morass was through authoritarianism, providing certainty in the midst of postrevolutionary chaos. The model to emulate for MbZ and Abu Dhabi elites was that of the American Israel Public Affairs Committee, which has been at the forefront of building resilient networks in Washington's Middle East policy community to not only promote Israeli interests but also to directly attack the reputation and standing of actors it deems as antagonistic to Israel—all based on narratives and frames built around Judeo-Christian values and insecurity paranoia.[29]

For the UAE, the comeback from the Dubai Ports World controversy through effective public diplomacy and lobbying alone provided an immense lesson learned. It illustrated the importance of effective policy engagement in Washington while showing the ability of weaponized narratives to change how policy elites think about the Middle East as a whole. The bottom-up approach of plugging narratives with media influencers, think tanks, and academics promised to shape debates in Washington's policymaking nexus, where a revolving door between policy advisers and think tankers would ensure that narratives would find their way into reports, communiqués, and eventually policy documents. Based on its experience of public diplomacy and lobbying in the late 2000s, Abu Dhabi has since elevated the information environment to a key domain of foreign policy contestation and warfare. MbZ and his deep state have understood the immense potential of weaponized narratives in achieving strategic objectives in a broad, multilever policy approach.

UNDERSTANDING THE UAE'S
SUBVERSION STRATEGY

Unlike its regional competitor, Qatar, the UAE learned how to integrate its information networks into its overall grand strategy, making its activities in the information environment far less coincidental than those executed by Qatar. Equally,

Abu Dhabi understood how to strategically orchestrate the various activities in an effort to achieve its objectives beyond the information environment.

Step 1: Orientation

The different strands of the UAE's subversion operations all come together in Abu Dhabi in the hands of Crown Prince MbZ and his brother and national security adviser Tahnoon bin Zayed Al Nahyan (TbZ). Dominating the information environment has become a matter of national security not just domestically but also regionally, which remains under the tight control of MbZ's direct nexus in the capital. An integral part of this inner circle is Simon Pearce, an Australian public relations specialist who has acted as Abu Dhabi's de facto head of strategic communications since the late 2000s. Pearce has been instrumental in brokering deals between Abu Dhabi's leadership and the Manchester City football club as well as business and political leaders in the United Kingdom.[30] Under his leadership, the UAE's strategic communication's portfolio has moved from defensive, reactive messaging aimed at protecting the reputation of Abu Dhabi to much broader, proactive, and offensive subversion operations. Another strategic decision-maker and key interlocutor is Hamad Al Mazrouei, a senior figure in the UAE's intelligence services, who reports directly to TbZ and runs social media campaigns in both English and Arabic via the network of troll farms he commands across the region.[31] Al Mazrouei acts also as a bridge between Abu Dhabi and Riyadh, where he coordinates information operations with the two most important advisers to Saudi crown prince Mohammed bin Salman (MbS), Turki al-Sheikh, and Saud al Qahtani—the latter being instrumental in the targeting and killing of Saudi dissident journalist Khashoggi (as outlined in chapter 4).

The strategic objectives for the United Arab Emirates in the information environment are twofold: it is about, first, influencing civil-societal and policy-relevant discourse, domestically, regionally, and globally in Western capitals, and second, disrupting information-psychological stability in vulnerable communities and countries in the Middle East through mobilization and demobilization of civil society and key actors in the policy domain. Thereby, both influence and information-psychological destabilization are often accompanied by a range of other levers of UAE power to move from disruption to destabilization. In the countries primarily targeted by the UAE's destabilization operations—such as Egypt, Libya, Tunisia, and Qatar—other levers of financial and military power were used in an attempt to undermine the sociopolitical status quo through the information environment. Nonetheless, activities in the virtual domain dominate and precede activities in the physical domain of the information environment.

First, in terms of influence, Abu Dhabi has activated its information network to alter civil-societal and policy discourse in both the Middle East and in the West to change the perception of Islam in general and political Islam in particular. The securitization of political Islam as a strategic threat in the post-9/11 context was an attempt by Abu Dhabi elites to tap into the existing fears of terrorism in Western capitals. Linked to this strategic objective is the UAE's attempt to change the perception and discourse on governance in the Middle East post–Arab Spring, rallying support for its vision of strong, autocratic, and often security-sector-based leadership as opposed to sociopolitical pluralism. Further, the UAE's influence operations aim at isolating proclaimed antagonists in the information environment, primarily the global network of the Muslim Brotherhood, Qatar, and Turkey. Influence campaigns aimed at tarnishing the reputation of these antagonists and affiliates serve to isolate these actors politically—especially in the West.

Second, the UAE's subversion strategy targets information-psychological stability in key communities and countries. In Egypt since 2013, in Libya since 2014, and increasingly also in Tunisia in recent years, Abu Dhabi has skillfully tried to implant narratives in an effort to undermine the sociopolitical status quo and mobilize forces against political authority by sowing discord and distrust between different societal actors and between civil society and the state. As in Russia, weaponized narratives are tools for mobilizing vulnerable communities with grievances against the existing sociopolitical status quo. In Egypt in 2013, the UAE was instrumental in mobilizing dissent against the country's first democratically elected president, Mohamed Morsi, who himself was a member of the Muslim Brotherhood.[32] In Libya, the UAE has built an entire alternative governance structure around the warlord Khalifa Haftar, mobilizing and consolidating followers behind him in his campaign since 2014 to seize political power in the country.[33] In Qatar, Abu Dhabi unsuccessfully tried to mobilize domestic outrage against the political leadership in May and June 2017 by disseminating false statements by Qatar's emir on the website of the local news agency—an outrage that some argue was meant to be a pretext for military action.[34] Meanwhile, in Tunisia, the UAE has tried for years to ripen dissent against the Islamist Ennahda movement, which might have played into the hands of Tunisian president Kais Saied's ability to dissolve parliament in July 2021.[35]

Step 2: Identification

Abu Dhabi's information operations have undergone a transformation since the early days of public diplomacy campaigns in Washington in response to the Dubai Ports World controversy. Its influence campaigns in the global West have thereby become somewhat separate from its regional campaigns to undermine information-psychological stability in an effort to reshape the sociopolitical trajectory of the Arab world. Both campaigns are interlinked via the same metanarratives: One campaign focuses on audiences in the West, while the other focuses on local audiences in the Arab world.

At the onset of the UAE's defensive messaging campaign in Washington in the second half of the 2000s, Abu Dhabi identified the neoconservative policymaking nexus around the Bush administration as a key audience for the UAE narrative of a "strong bilateral partnership to fight terrorism." This target audience in the United States had a clear ontological predisposition toward the Middle East as a region torn apart by conflict, where authoritarian regimes were harboring or supporting terrorist organizations while merging Islam with politics to counter American influence. In essence, neoconservatism prescribed a more assertive US foreign policy to maintain American hegemony in the world by bringing regional players into a "Western orbit." In the context of the Middle East, that meant turning regional states into pro-Western entities that endorse liberal values and advocate for the separation of religion and the state.[36] This, in turn, would help build the foundation to eradicate what was securitized to be an existential threat to US interests in the region and the world: global Islamic terrorism.[37] Hence, Abu Dhabi found an audience on the conservative and neoconservative spectrum of Washington's policy debate that was susceptible to the securitization of both Islam and terrorism. The aftermath of 9/11 created an opening in America's conservative civil society for fear-based frames and narratives, to which the United Arab Emirates was able to provide a panacea: a Middle Eastern state that was not just tough on "terrorism" but was also eager to help the United States drive a wedge between Islamism and politics.[38]

Although a fear-based approach worked on conservative audiences, the UAE identified a slightly different ontological predisposition among liberals during the Obama years, which served as a sociopsychological vulnerability to exploit. Those who hoped the Arab Spring would liberalize and democratize the region from the bottom up became increasingly concerned about the so-called Islamist hijacking of the revolutions. By the end of 2011, the rise of Islamist opposition and rebel groups across the Arab world caused more and more liberal voices in the United States to start speaking of an "Arab Winter."[39] Those who had called for the liberalization of sociopolitics in the Arab world at the beginning of the Arab Spring were now concerned that Arabs might choose a form of Islamist democracy that could undermine the project of creating a Western, liberal Middle East. "Illiberal liberals" have come to particularly shun political Islam as a threat to liberal values, thereby undermining the very inclusive and tolerant premise inherent in liberal thought.[40] What for conservatives and neoconservatives was a security fear of terrorism was a philosophical and sociopolitical fear among liberals that the project of the Arab Spring could develop into one that might end up being nonliberal. Here, Abu Dhabi found an intellectual vulnerability to plug the metanarratives of tolerance and secularism as a response to the rise of political Islam.

Within the region itself, fault lines were not just intellectual but also sociopolitical in nature, bringing severe grievances to the forefront that provided a fertile ground for the UAE's narratives. For the few liberal first movers of the Arab Spring, the fear of political Islam was also mostly intellectual.[41] Yet, for the millions of Arabs who lived through the chaotic aftermath of revolution and civil war, sociopsychological vulnerabilities emerged in hope for stability and quick fixes. Especially as socioeconomic grievances and perceptions of insecurity and injustice grew, the unfulfilled promises of the revolution made millions susceptible to counterrevolutionary narratives. Especially in Egypt, where the Muslim Brotherhood had been voted into power, rifts between President Morsi and civil society started to emerge in late 2012. The promises of social justice were not realizable at the necessary pace while the Brotherhood started to coup-proof Morsi's presidency out of a deep-seated paranoia about the omnipotent Egyptian military-industrial complex behind the throne.[42] Discontent over political gridlock, the lack of reforms, and prevailing insecurity also became widespread among Libyans in 2013, opening tribal and geographic rifts between the National Transitional Council along with both revolutionary factions and the wider public, especially in the eastern part of the country.[43]

Amid a prevalent sentiment of uncertainty and a quickly deteriorating macroeconomic and security context, the Arab world in 2013 presented an information environment that was disillusioned with the narratives and promises of revolutionaries. Abu Dhabi saw a sociopsychological vulnerability that could be exploited to spread counterrevolutionary narratives that not only challenged the fragile postrevolutionary political status quo but also improved the future trajectory the region was about to embark on: a trajectory that moved from revolution to counterrevolution. What Qatar tried to nurture through the instrumentalization of "liberation technology" in 2011 was now ripe for an assertive and strategic mobilization of information power from Abu Dhabi. Mobilizing civil society in the region parallel to policy-relevant elites in Washington and other Western capitals against the sobering experience of the Arab Spring was a deliberate attempt by the UAE to redraw the map of the Middle East.

Step 3: Formulation

Abu Dhabi's deep state has invested in one overarching metanarrative that would encompass aspects of religion, sociopolitics, and civil society and rebrand the United Arab Emirates under its own umbrella of regional exceptionalism: moderation and tolerance. These were two concepts that most Americans or

Europeans would not associate with the Middle East post-9/11. UAE exceptionalism is founded on three main themes that stem from the metanarrative of moderation and tolerance: secularism, counterterrorism, and authoritarian stability.

"Secularism" has been a defining part of the UAE brand in Washington since the late 2000s. Abu Dhabi invested heavily to present itself as a secular Middle Eastern state and, more importantly, to push for a narrative that would associate progress in the region with the separation of state and mosque—a narrative that resonated with conservatives and liberals alike.[44] What some came to cherish as a Jeffersonian model of statehood in a region prone to extremism and radicalization represents the idea that the problem is religion rather than sociopolitical and economic grievances.[45] This notion might very well emanate from MbZ's personal disenfranchisement and disillusionment with political Islam in the aftermath of 9/11. It targets one of Abu Dhabi's most deep-seated fears of political Islam as an anti–status quo power that could challenge regime legitimacy in the region.[46] Under the pretext of secularization, the UAE has itself not just tried to counter Islamism but has also actively sought to find religious alternatives to the more activist forms of political Islam. Aside from occupying the religious space domestically with ecumenical tolerance and interfaith initiatives—itself a means to sideline more politically active forms of Islam—the UAE has deliberately invested in breeding its own brand of Islam around the theological premises of Sufism.[47]

Sufism has therefore been used as a strategic vehicle to depoliticize Islam and fill the religious space with political quietism. By prescribing loyalty to the political establishment and outlawing rebellion, this creates both an Islamic narrative that is more palatable in the West and one that is political in itself.[48] The reason is that while traditionally Sufism has focused more on the intrinsic virtues of Islam as an almost esoteric means of self-advancement removed from the communal domain, Abu Dhabi has instrumentalized Sufism for political ends to consume religious space held by political Islam that could be a threat to regime security.

Although the engagement of Abu Dhabi's elites with Sufi scholars started already in the early 2000s, it was only after the Arab Spring in the 2010s that the UAE made an overt effort to promote its form of quietist Islam. Through "tolerance," it aimed to reject any form of civil-societal activism against the political establishment. Watching fearfully from the sidelines as the old regimes of the Middle East disintegrated in 2011, the UAE required an alternative religious narrative to those of the Salafists, like those in the Muslim Brotherhood. In 2016, Egypt (the UAE's closest ideological ally since 2013) and Abu Dhabi jointly financed a conference in Grozny, Chechnya, that was supposed to develop a religious alternative to confront Salafism and Wahabism in the region—a direct challenge to Saudi Arabia's ambitions for Islamic leadership.[49] The choice of Chechnya as the venue was not a coincidence; it points to the important link between Russia and the UAE in their shared attempts to promote quietist versions of Islam. The Caucasian creed of Sufism has been a powerful soft power tool for Chechnyan president Kadyrov—a close adviser to Russian president Putin and confidant of MbZ whose "reformed" version of Islam helped justify the authoritarian rebuilding of Chechnya after the wars there in the 1990s.[50] Sufi scholars such as Sheikh bin Bayyah who call for the separation of state and mosque and reject civil society's right to rebellion have been courted in the UAE, which provides them with the financial means and information tools to shape religious narratives.[51]

A network of Sufi scholars has thereby been fully integrated into the country's information and influence network to propagate religious narratives of tolerance to the West while building a religious complex that could rationalize depoliticizing civil society, undermine the legitimacy of political opposition, and provide the religious justification for the moral equivalence between Islamism and terrorism—an integral part of the UAE's narratives.

The second theme at the core of the UAE's exceptionalism is "counterterrorism." "Counterterrorism" proceeds logically from the first theme of "secularism" and has been formulated deliberately in view of the identified sociopsychological vulnerabilities in the post-9/11 environment. Amid the securitization of "global Islamic terrorism" as an omnipresent and unpredictable threat, the "terrorism" frame had been used extensively in the early 2000s to justify the curtailment of civil liberties and freedoms in the name of security. As Gearty writes, "Governments will often attempt to condemn their opponents as terrorists, since the public relations victory achieved by this linguistic sleight of hand can be crucial in any ensuing struggle for popular support," making "terrorism" both a normative and a political term.[52] The potential for abuse that comes with the politicization of the concept of terrorism is particularly great among populist authoritarians who instrumentalize the term in order to delegitimize and sometimes even dehumanize a political opponent.[53]

The UAE has invested heavily in a strand of academic scholarship on radicalization and terrorism—the conveyer belt theory—to advance a narrative that would create a moral equivalent between any form of political Islam and terrorism.[54] The conveyer belt theory is a simplistic conceptual construct that suggests that radicalization is purely an issue of ideology, whereby religiously conservative individuals move up a gradual ladder of radicalization until they become violent religious individuals. In other words, any form of political Islam, usually tied to social conservatism, is viewed as an "entry drug" on an individual's automated journey through religious radicalization until they become ready to endorse violent means of terrorism. The academic mainstream has meanwhile abandoned this theory as overly simplistic. Most scholars today would argue that by putting too much emphasis on ideological factors of radicalization, the theory entirely neglects important sociopolitical and socioeconomic factors and grievances that feed into the radicalization process.[55] Yet Abu Dhabi's simplistic reading of terrorism provides an easily digestible concept of radicalization based on a linear process that entirely revolves around Islamic ideology—giving way to a narrative of terrorism that resonates especially with concerns among conservatives in the West.[56] The UAE narrative of "terrorism" divides the ideological spectrum of Islam into those Islamic creeds with political ambitions and those without, the former being labeled as "terrorist" ideologies—a narrative that resonates among audiences with clear Islamophobic tendencies.[57]

In the post–Arab Spring world, the securitization of political Islam by the UAE has particularly centered on the Muslim Brotherhood, the oldest Islamist movement in the Arab world, with its roots in the anticolonial struggle of the 1920s in Egypt. Over the past century, the Brotherhood has grown into a highly diverse movement with local chapters across the region that incorporate charities, religious institutions, and political parties.[58] Nonetheless, despite the intangible nature of the Brotherhood as an intellectually and ideologically diverse movement, the UAE's messaging has taken a broad-brush approach to outlaw and vilify all elements of it. It therefore should not be surprising that Abu Dhabi prides itself on being "tougher on terrorism" than its Western partners, presenting a list of "terrorist organizations" that encompass a range of regular Islamic charities and nongovernmental organizations in the United States and Europe.[59]

Apart from designating individuals and organizations as terrorists who display views opposing those of MbZ, Abu Dhabi has used its "terrorism label" broadly to attack external affiliates or sponsors of such organizations or individuals as sponsors of terrorism. At the heart of the Gulf dispute between Qatar and the UAE stands the contentious issue of the Muslim Brotherhood.[60] Qatar's harboring of exiled dissidents from the Brotherhood in parallel to providing financial and informational support to Brotherhood-affiliated groups during the Arab Spring led the UAE to securitize Qatar and its partner Turkey as a fundamental threat to national security—a narrative that has not only been used domestically but has also been exported through an extensive information network to Western capitals since 2014.[61]

The third theme, "authoritarian stability," builds on the theme of "terrorism" as it is based on the premise that stability in the Middle East can only be provided by means of secular, security-sector-based strong states that can contain civil society in a way that prevents the chaos of the Arab Spring. Instead of acknowledging the empirical evidence for sociopolitical and socioeconomic grievances driving radicalization, the remedy to "terrorism" is authoritarian control and state-regulated civil society, according to the UAE's state ontology.

This narrative not only feeds Orientalism in the West but also adds to unnuanced, largely uninformed debates on the Middle East by providing simple solutions that have a wide appeal as a convenient "truth" vis-à-vis more complex and difficult debates on finding more inclusive sociopolitical solutions to the issue of governance in the Middle East. At the same time, "authoritarian stability" grants these regimes with legitimacy both regionally and globally—justifying the UAE's expansion of its surveillance state at home.

Step 4: Dissemination

Like Russia, the United Arab Emirates can draw on an extensive surrogate network to orchestrate its subversion strategy. The multichannel approach that the UAE is pursuing taps into a variety of audiences, allowing surrogates to autonomously advance subversive UAE talking points, messages, and narratives. Some of the coincidental surrogates comprise scholars and experts whose ontological view of the world coincides with the UAE's metanarrative. As with Russia in this case, inconsistency in the diversified messaging approach is not a challenge for the UAE but an asset. The information network curated over more than a decade has been able to generate perceptions of triangulation, reinforcing subversive messaging across a spectrum of media outlets, trolls, academia, think tanks, and policymakers—all tied to a comprehensive dissemination strategy that takes a bottom-up approach. Hence, the UAE's subversion strategy relies on the quantity of outlets, not always necessarily on quality.

Trying to emulate Qatar's investment in Al Jazeera, the United Arab Emirates has invested in conventional media outlets as well. English-language daily newspapers such as *The National* have a moderate reach beyond Emirati borders. Yet, in the broadcasting domain, channels such as Al Arabiya and Sky News Arabic have been able to reach a greater regional audience and serve as outlets for UAE narratives. Here, the partnership with Saudi financiers has become quite important. Al Arabiya is owned by Saudi-based Middle East Broadcasting Centre but is based in and run out of the UAE. In print, the UAE can tap into media joint ventures between the Saudi Research and Marketing Group based in Riyadh and run by Sultan Abuljadayel, who has close ties to King Salman, and international brands such as *Bloomberg* and *The Independent.*[62] The Arabic-language outlet *Bloomberg Asharq* is entirely run from offices in Dubai, while the joint venture *Independent Arabia* is managed from London.[63] While the strategic investments by the Saudi Research and Marketing Group have been critically eyed as Saudi soft power efforts, few have looked at links to the UAE that widely rely on Saudi surrogates in their information operations.

More intriguing were the UAE's efforts to cultivate fake personas who would not just act as bots and trolls on social media but develop profiles of journalists or analysts who would go on to publish op-eds on online platforms created by UAE-affiliated public relations firms.[64] In some instances, these fake journalists, complete with fake biographies and false academic credentials, even published commentaries in fairly credible outlets, such as the *Jerusalem Post*, spreading Abu Dhabi talking points on Qatar, Turkey, or Iran, while praising the United Arab Emirates.[65]

On social media, UAE narratives are often disseminated by joint Saudi-UAE operations. Few trolls and bots are commanded by companies inside the UAE, such as Charles Communications or DotDev.[66] For the most part, however, Hamad Al Mazrouei, Abu Dhabi's man for information ops, works with surrogate outfits in Egypt and Saudi Arabia. Al Mazrouei has allegedly liaised with the now infamous right-hand man of Saudi crown prince MbS, Saud Al Qahtani, to coordinate messaging campaigns against designated targets in the Gulf, the wider region, and even the West.[67] Looking at social media accounts linked to the Saudi information network, their messaging has been consistent with UAE narratives on a variety of issues, providing Abu Dhabi with a powerful messaging tool with plausible deniability.[68] Elsewhere, Abu Dhabi has relied on social media bots and trolls to not just distribute its metanarratives but also to target key audiences in regional theaters. For example, in Libya, many social media accounts that are cheerleading for the warlord Haftar—himself heavily supported by Abu Dhabi with arms, equipment, and capacity—have been consistent in their narratives with pro-UAE, anti-Islamist, or anti-Qatar narratives, suggesting that they are linked to entities in Abu Dhabi, although direct attribution remains difficult.[69]

In Egypt, Al Mazrouei has procured smaller troll farms that work jointly for UAE client President Sisi and his regime domestically and for the wider UAE information operation across the region. An Egyptian troll farm called New Waves is operated by a former member of the Egyptian military whose accounts on Facebook, Twitter, and Instagram do not only cheerlead for the regime in Cairo but also for Haftar and other protagonists in the UAE counter-revolution.[70] New Waves is paid via a UAE-based company with the same name. As a 2019 *New York Times* article states, "Its messages are a mirror image of the foreign policy objectives of Egypt, the United Arab Emirates and Saudi Arabia—a powerful axis that has wielded immense influence across the Middle East since 2011, bolstering authoritarian allies or intervening in regional wars."[71]

The UAE's bottom-up approach relies on a fusion of conventional media and social media outlets. To increase its triangulation and amplification effect, Abu Dhabi increasingly moves away from feeding a few conventional media operations such as *The National* or Al Arabiya to nurturing networks of websites that spread weaponized narratives and conspiracy theories in the Arab world, where the nature of media consumption has shifted to online sources, not least since the Arab Spring. In Libya, for example, websites financed by a media empire under the alleged control of former Libyan ambassador to the UAE and the Sufi scholar Aref Al Nayed have complemented the already dominant position of the UAE in the Libyan media space.[72] Several news channels—such as Libya HD, Libya 24, and Libya al Hadath—have alleged financial ties to the UAE, either directly or indirectly via interlocutors.[73] In the West, the UAE has also engaged in supporting websites such as the European Eye on Radicalisation and the rather wordy European Centre for Counterterrorism and Intelligence Studies, Germany & Netherlands. Both operate as hubs to spread "terrorism"-based narratives that are closely aligned with UAE talking points and are linked to a former UAE intelligence officer and CEO of the Abu Dhabi–based Hedaya Forum.[74] When directly integrated into a network of social media accounts, these websites help plug narratives via seemingly objective outlets that are then disseminated via affiliated social media surrogates.

Furthermore, the UAE has understood the value of validation, as the next section shows, investing heavily in think tanks and academic centers as means to give their narratives credibility. While the Arab Gulf State Institute in Washington is a UAE creation, the UAE's lobbying in Washington is mostly operated through existing think tank brands. With consistent two-digit, multimillion-dollar investments each year, the UAE has set a precedent for think tank–based lobbying in the United States that other Gulf states have come to emulate. But even regional competitor Qatar barely has half the budget that Abu Dhabi has for these activities.[75] Particularly on the fringes of the policy debate in America's capital, the UAE has been able to plug its narratives into neoconservative and at times Islamophobic outfits such as the Foundation for the Defense of Democracies[76] and the Middle East Forum,[77] which have been allegedly funded via interlocutors such as the conservative businessman Elliot Broidy, according to press reports.[78] The overarching purpose here is to lend credibility to UAE narratives on "terrorism" and political Islam. The use of public relations companies, such as Bluelight Strategies run by Steve Rabinowitz[79] and a network of coincidental surrogates like Broidy, who share the UAE's ontological predispositions on political Islam and the Arab world, creates levels of dissociation and anonymity, which make it difficult to trace the sources of financial support provided to events that are obviously built around UAE talking points.

The UAE's multidomain approach to influence operations thereby also relies increasingly on seemingly coincidental surrogates from the business sector who either have commercial interests in the UAE and/or agree with the UAE's strategic narratives. Three businessmen who repeatedly feature in US federal investigations for their alleged role as unregistered agents of Abu Dhabi are Elliot Broidy, George Nader, and Thomas Barrack.[80] With close personal ties to Abu Dhabi's leadership and considerable business interests in the UAE, they were instrumentalized as unregistered channels of influence, able to develop direct access to the White House during the Trump administration,[81] while procuring financial networks that allowed the UAE to pay surrogates in their information network.[82]

For Abu Dhabi's army of public relations companies, think tanks and seemingly independent research centers are strategic means to fill the gap between communication and policymaking.[83] Their links to predominantly conservative media outlets and journalists in the West require complementary academic platforms that not only help verify narratives but can help transport narratives from the public sphere directly to policymakers. Conferences provide opportunities for engagement between policymakers and like-minded scholars and experts whose conceptual support for theories such as the "conveyor belt" and "authoritarian stability" provide accessible and easily digestible solutions for policymakers. A conference hosted by the Hudson Institute in Washington in October 2017 titled "Countering Violent Extremism: Qatar, Iran, and the Muslim Brotherhood," directly targeted the new Trump administration, providing a platform for senior officials and policymakers to engage with UAE narratives.[84] Former defense secretary Leon Panetta, then White House adviser Steve Bannon, and former head of the US Central Intelligence Agency David Petraeus and a range of congresspeople featured in a conference that singled out Qatar, Iran, and the Muslim Brotherhood as the most threatening menaces in the region.[85] The overlap with UAE talking points was not coincidental: the conference was paid for by the two above-mentioned businessmen, George Nader and Elliot Broidy—both with links to the Republican Party and the Trump White House.[86]

Beyond helping to disseminate narratives and building networks between like-minded academics, journalists, and policymakers, public relations and lobbying companies help Abu Dhabi silence critical voices in the West. A London-based consultancy, Cornerstone Global Associates—according to the *New York Times* a part of the UAE's information network in Europe—closely works with a British libel lawyer to send aggressive cease-and-desist letters to academic publishers, universities, and social media companies in an effort to target individuals critical of the UAE and its regional policy.[87] The libel lawyer thereby targets not just references to Cornerstone and its director but also mentions of other individuals closely aligned with Abu Dhabi's information nexus—most notably Mohammad Dahlan, allegedly a key interlocutor for Abu Dhabi's Crown Prince MbZ.[88] This type of lawfare is meant to intimidate critics and provides the UAE's information network with ammunition to attack such critics.[89]

In addition, former policymakers and officials are being accommodated through all-inclusive trips to Abu Dhabi with full luxury hospitality or advisory positions in Abu Dhabi–financed organizations.[90] The UAE-funded think tank Bussola Institute in Brussels provided board positions to former

Irish president Mary McAleese and former NATO secretary general Anders Rasmussen.[91] Former British minister for the Middle East Alistair Burt—himself a close acquaintance of the former UAE minister of state for foreign affairs Anwar Gargash—was appointed honorary chair of the Emirates Society by the UAE embassy in London at the end of his political career.[92]

The highly diversified information network of the UAE covers the domains of media, academia, and policymaking and is able to construct narratives from the ground up. Although most media campaigns cater to existing biases of target audiences, for years the UAE's information operations remained unopposed, allowing Abu Dhabi to fill a void in Middle East discourse in the West and political discourse in the Middle East. Until the Gulf Crisis in 2017, Abu Dhabi has been able to plug its counterrevolutionary narratives without being confronted directly by its ideological antagonist Qatar, which has had to play catch-up in the information environment ever since.

Step 5: Verification

Academia and think tanks form an integral part of the UAE's information and influence network. A 2020 report highlights that the UAE made $15.4 million in regular donations to think tanks in the United States between 2014 and 2018.[93] This figure, however, does not include irregular payments or donations made to think tanks in Washington, such as a $20 million donation to the Middle East Institute in 2016,[94] or payments made via interlocutors for events such as the $2.7 million given to the Hudson Institute and the Federation for the Defence of Democracies (FDD) for hosting an anti-Qatar conference in 2017.[95]

Abu Dhabi has invested in the creation of a range of seemingly neutral outfits, such as the Arab Gulf State Institute in Washington (AGSIW) and the Bussola Institute in Brussels, which, although generating academically solid research, also provide platforms for niche opinion pieces and events to further UAE narratives on the Arab world. The legitimacy and credibility generated from employing or collaborating with internationally acclaimed experts on a range of issues allows the AGSIW and the Bussola Institute to subtly plug narratives with distinguished audiences.[96] A selective research agenda that is both conducive and complementary to the UAE's messaging ensures that UAE interests are not harmed, and it guarantees that academic freedom does not become a liability.

Much more important than the AGSIW in the verification stage of UAE narratives has been a neoconservative nexus of institutes in Washington that are not only accommodated to support UAE narratives but also have an ideological predisposition that is conducive to the UAE's metanarrative. Especially with regard to the securitization of political Islam and its sponsors, neoconservative and right-wing institutes share Abu Dhabi's concern about the rise of political Islam after the Arab Spring and are more inclined to accommodate the UAE's narrative of "authoritarian stability." In Washington, the UAE's ambassador Otaiba has been instrumental in liaising with individuals and institutes on the conservative end of the spectrum to rally support for military authoritarians labeling themselves "counterterrorists," such as Haftar in Libya or Sisi in Egypt.[97] The previously discussed conferences held by the Hudson Institute[98] and the Middle East Forum, which singled out the Muslim Brotherhood and Qatar as the most significant threats to regional stability, did not just try to validate UAE talking points.[99] They were tied to public relations companies and interlocutors working for Abu Dhabi in Washington. Both conferences vilified political Islam as a source for instability in the region by trying to establish a moral equivalence between Islamism and terrorism. As part of this conservative nexus in Washington's think tank world, the growing rapprochement between UAE ambassador Otaiba and the pro-Israel think tank FDD is noteworthy, which, apart from securitizing Iran, has strongly echoed UAE narratives against the Muslim Brotherhood and Qatar as its sponsor.[100] Commentaries and analyses written by individual FDD fellows attack both the Muslim Brotherhood as a "gateway to terrorism"[101] and Qatar as a supporter of "terrorism."[102] It remains difficult to ascertain to what extent UAE support to the FDD—channeled with plausible deniability by interlocutors Broidy and Nader—paid for events, programs, or publications.[103] Yet the FDD's publications and talking points provided references for newspaper articles and media narratives aiming at discrediting the Muslim Brotherhood and Qatar in Washington. More important, with the FDD's conservatism broadly in line with the Republican Party, the organization's analysis and lobbying found an audience in policymaking circles around the Trump administration.[104]

In the Middle East, the UAE has also boosted think tanks to lend legitimacy and credibility to their metanarrative of "tolerance and moderation." Research centers, such as Kalam Research & Media based in Dubai and the Forum for Promoting Peace in Muslim Societies in Abu Dhabi, are means for the UAE to add a layer of legitimacy to its use of Sufism as a soft power tool. Under the pretext of the noble cause of encouraging religious coexistence, these research centers have provided theological justification for the depoliticization of not just Islam but also civil society as a whole, linking postrevolutionary anarchy in the region to Islam being used to justify revolt. Think tanks such as the Libyan Institute for Advanced Studies, with offices in Dubai and founded by former Libyan ambassador to the UAE Aref al Nayed, provide local platforms to engage with audiences on the ground about how to manage the postrevolutionary chaos in Libya.[105] As a scholar, Nayed allegedly feeds a network of media outlets, websites, and seemingly academic centers tied to both LIAS and Kalam Research & Media. They help advance UAE talking points about the menace of

"Qatar-sponsored terrorism" in Libya, while promoting the warlord Haftar as an anchor of stability in the fight against terror.[106]

Thus, in the UAE's information network, think tanks fulfill three functions: (1) they secure access to strategically important policymaking circles;[107] (2) they help verify narratives with a semblance of academic objectivity and neutrality; and (3) they can prompt and shift policy debate through events, commentaries, and publications.

Step 6: Implementation

Establishing a clear causal relationship between media campaigns, think tank engagement, and policymaking is often difficult. As with Russia, the nature of the UAE's information network is such that, despite following a clear strategy, a variety of direct, indirect, and coincidental surrogates feed into a campaign whose success often depends on deliberate dissociation and the illusion of triangulation. However, looking at the prevalence of UAE narratives among its Western target audiences, it seems that the UAE has been fairly successful at promoting its ideological predispositions. UAE-sponsored programs at research centers and think tanks have shaped debates about the postrevolutionary future of the Arab world, the role of political Islam in the region, and Qatar's and Turkey's roles in shaping the Arab Spring. Although unable to dominate in what is a highly diverse academic and policy debate in Western capitals, the UAE was at least able to cast doubt over the revolutionary enthusiasm of 2011, riding a wave of analyses and concerns in the West that the transition from authoritarianism to democracy might not be as smooth as initially hoped. Coincidental surrogates, including experts and academics whose ontological predispositions widely overlap with those of Abu Dhabi, have played an important role in the UAE's counterrevolutionary campaign since 2011. Supporting their research and providing them with a platform to make their voices heard allowed for the shifting of the intellectual balance in both academic and policymaking debates. This was often owed to the fact that Abu Dhabi's main ideological competitor, Qatar, entered the information space proactively only after the Gulf Crisis in 2017.

Of the various case studies, three represent how the UAE has been able to translate narratives from the virtual into the physical domain: (1) the mobilization of Tamarod, a small liberal opposition group, in Egypt in 2013; (2) the UAE's impact on the United Kingdom's decision to review the Muslim Brotherhood in 2014; and (3) the mobilization of support by the Trump White House for the blockading of Qatar by the UAE, Saudi Arabia, and their partners in 2017.

As with many subversion campaigns that the UAE conducts in the region, a central player in its counterrevolutionary campaign in Egypt in 2013 was Mohammad Dahlan, a Palestinian based in Abu Dhabi who controls an extensive surrogate network across the region. Dahlan has been one of the most important conduits for UAE outreach to Libya, Russia, Turkey, the United States, and Palestine.[108] Determined to overthrow President Morsi, the UAE was eager to find an opening to form an opposition that could provide a pretext for the UAE-aligned military to step in. Amid widespread sociopolitical and socioeconomic grievances in postrevolutionary Egypt, Abu Dhabi found a receptive audience for anti-Morsi narratives. Although Dahlan is believed to have channeled funds to the Egyptian military around then–defense minister General Sisi, he also helped establish a link to the Tamarod.[109] Tamarod, meaning "rebellion," had emerged out of the liberal, secular opposition to Mubarak in the late 2000s but by early 2013 had shrunk to a few hundred grassroots activists who opposed the increasingly erratic policy decisions of the Morsi government. Through the first half of 2013, the UAE systematically transformed the group into a potent front group.[110] Apart from collecting signatures against President Morsi, the Tamarod was instrumental in mobilizing dissent and organizing protests against the president across the country. Apart from direct financial support, the Tamarod could rely on the UAE's information support. This included money from Abu Dhabi to Mohamad El Amin, the owner of Egypt's CBC cable network, which was turned into preferential coverage of the Tamarod.[111] This happened while liberal, Christian billionaire Naguib Sawiris—a coincidental surrogate for the UAE's campaign against Qatar and the Muslim Brotherhood—used his media networks to boost the Tamarod and its narratives.[112] By June 2013, the Tamarod was able to mobilize hundreds of thousands to join in nationwide protests against Morsi—a pretext the Egyptian military exploited to stage its coup on July 3.[113] Abu Dhabi's financial support for the Tamarod, and its collusion with the Egyptian military and intelligence, as well as its liaising with an overtly anti–Muslim Brotherhood media landscape, created a momentum of dissidence in Egypt. Although this mobilization of dissent was inflated in the UAE-sponsored media campaign, it provided a pretext for the Egyptian military to intervene to "restore order"—a watershed moment that set a counterrevolutionary precedent for the UAE in North Africa. Events in Tunisia in July 2021, which saw the president dissolving parliament amid a campaign against the Islamist Ennahda Party, also feature the hallmark of the UAE.[114] As in Egypt in 2013, the UAE had been involved for years in ripening civil society and policymakers through extensive subversion campaigns to mobilize against Islamist politicians who were framed as scapegoats for political crisis in the country.[115]

The UAE's campaign to get the Muslim Brotherhood designated as a terrorist organization in the United Kingdom is another example of how the UAE has been able to mobilize media, academia, and policymaking through the use of narratives and political leverage. In a widespread campaign using public relations companies, conservative journalists, and commentators, and its financial leverage over several UK companies, Abu Dhabi had been able to push the narrative in policy-relevant circles that the Muslim Brotherhood was a threat to British interests.[116] On top of a narrative campaign demonizing the Muslim Brotherhood in British media, the UAE openly used its economic leverage to put pressure on the Cameron government to launch an inquiry into the Muslim Brotherhood. This was run by Sir John Jenkins, who in 2014 was still Britain's ambassador to Saudi Arabia and shared the UAE's securitization of the group.[117] Although the final report of the Jenkins commission was never made public, the review came to the conclusion that the Brotherhood could not be designated a terrorist organization. This episode demonstrates that the UAE's access to media, academia, and policymaking has been instrumentalized by Abu Dhabi to shape British policy elites' thinking about political Islam and the need for authoritarian measures to contain it.[118]

President Trump's initial endorsement of the UAE and Saudi-led campaign to blockade Qatar for its alleged support of "terrorism" is another case study of how UAE narratives can shape policy overseas when combined with access to policymaking. Since at least 2013, the UAE has used its information network to attack Qatar and its support for revolutionaries during the Arab Spring, framing its Gulf neighbor as a sponsor of "terrorism." Among conservatives, the UAE's conveyer belt theory and moral equivalence between political Islam and terrorism was well received, cultivating a receptive audience for Abu Dhabi's claim that Qatar was a threat to US interests.[119] The UAE's collaboration with conservative think tanks such as the Hudson Institute and the FDD was instrumental in ensuring that Middle East experts around the Trump administration were exposed to narratives that heavily securitized Qatar's foreign and security policy.[120] Both think tanks hosted a UAE-sponsored anti-Qatar conference just weeks before the UAE-led campaign to isolate Doha in June 2017. In addition to framing the debate around Qatar in policy-relevant circles in Washington, Abu Dhabi actively engaged with the Trump campaign in late 2016. MbZ's unannounced visit to Trump's transitional team in New York in December 2016 not only touched on establishing relations with Russia and countering Iran but it also started problematizing Qatar as a sponsor of "terrorism"—a narrative that resonated well with Trump's son-in-law, Jared Kushner.[121] In the months that followed, Abu Dhabi aggressively pushed for Kushner's endorsement of MbZ's protégé, Crown Prince MbS, in Saudi Arabia. In the same breath, it also pushed the Trump administration to adopt a more hardline stance on Qatar, using interlocutors Barrack,[122] Broidy, and Nader to achieve this aim.[123] When a coalition of Saudi Arabia and UAE imposed the blockade on Qatar on June 5, 2017, Trump initially endorsed the step, despite the fact that more than ten thousand US CENTCOM troops were based in the country.[124] The president's tweets appeared to echo UAE narratives, while his Rose Garden speech on June 9 clearly pointed toward conversations Trump had had with "Arab leaders" in Riyadh: "So, we had a decision to make: do we take the easy road, or do we finally take a hard but necessary action? We have to stop the funding of terrorism; . . . the nation of Qatar, unfortunately, has historically been a funder of terrorism at a very high level."[125]

After the intervention by both Secretary of State Rex Tillerson and Secretary of Defense James Mattis, Trump eventually distanced himself from these comments. According to a federal investigation into Barrack's unregistered lobby work for the UAE, Abu Dhabi continuously used Barrack in an attempt to subvert any measures by the Trump administration to reconcile the Gulf Crisis.[126] Abu Dhabi's narratives had clearly found their way into the Oval Office.[127]

In the end, coupled with an assertive foreign and security policy, the impact of the UAE's weaponized narratives on both regional politics and regional policy has been measurable on the highest level on the continuum. The narratives that the UAE has promoted did not remain in the virtual domain of the information environment but were translated into a change of attitude, decisions, and behavior of policymakers at the highest levels. Policymakers and practitioners alike have been targeted by a variety of different outlets in Abu Dhabi's information network to change both their attitudes and their behavior toward relevant issues in the region. Taking a gradual approach, the cumulative effect of UAE subversion might not yet have come to the surface.

CONCLUSION

"Little Sparta" has become increasingly assertive in the Middle East and beyond. As a city-state with its own space program, it punches above its weight. Its strategic development of alternative levers of power allows the financially well-endowed small state to translate economic power into instruments of political power. The UAE's inherent capacity issue of a small indigenous population has been solved by Abu Dhabi through the externalization of the burden of conflict and foreign policy to surrogates, who operate not only in the military space but also increasingly in the information domain. Abu Dhabi's extensive information network enabled it to plug narratives strategically to shape discourse in the media, in academia, and in policymaking circles. It is doing so assertively not just for purposes of defensive messaging but also offensive messaging with the aim to both influence and subvert information-psychological stability.

The experience of the coup in Egypt was a watershed moment in the UAE's self-perception and information power projection. While, in the second half of the 2000s, the UAE built up channels to shape the perception of itself in the

West, the Arab Spring triggered regime security paranoia about MbZ's deep state, which caused a strategic rethinking of the use of information power to undo the revolutionary developments in the region. The UAE's ability to successfully exploit existing socioeconomic and sociopolitical grievances in Egypt against Islamist president Morsi signaled to Abu Dhabi that the battle of post-revolutionary narratives had not been decided. Tens of millions of dollars carefully invested to curate an information network comprising media, academia, and policymaking have since meant that Abu Dhabi could shape how people think and feel about regional developments. In some cases, the UAE was able affect the decisions and behaviors of policymakers in the West.

While the Middle East remains in a state of highly contested transition a decade after the outbreak of the Arab Spring, Abu Dhabi appears to be in a much more secure position at the helm of regional affairs. Unlike Russia or Saudi Arabia, the United Arab Emirates does not register on Western radars as an antagonist but rather as an important regional partner. As a consequence, the UAE's "lobbying," which exceeds the overt and benign engagement of policymakers by registered agents, has never been put into question. The attempt to shape how the United States and Europe look at the various issues in the region comes at a time when both Washington and European allies have very little appetite to approach issues proactively and strategically. Catering to ontological and ideological biases among key audiences in the policymaking nexus in Western capitals means that in the 2020s, the UAE has a lot more freedom to maneuver when selling repression and authoritarianism with the narrative of "stability"—and all this when audiences in the region, tired from protracted transition processes, are being bombarded with narratives that provide simple solutions to complex problems.

NOTES

1. Cornwell, "Emerging Gulf State Cyber Security Powerhouse."
2. *Economist*, "Gulf's Little Sparta."
3. DeYoung and Nakashima, "UAE Orchestrated Hacking."
4. Mazzetti, Perlroth, and Bergman, "It Seemed like a Popular Chat App."
5. Aldroubi, "UAE to Take International Lead."
6. Kirkpatrick, "Most Powerful Arab Ruler."
7. Worth, "Mohammed bin Zayed's Dark Vision."
8. Worth.
9. Davidson, "Tale of Two Desert Dynasties."
10. Young, *Political Economy of Energy*.
11. Author's interview with UAE analyst I in London, December 11, 2019.
12. Krieg, "Weaponization of Narratives," 96.
13. Worth, "Mohammed bin Zayed's Dark Vision."
14. Davidson, "Arab Nationalism," 885.

15. Bayoumi, "UAE Islamist Group."
16. Herb, "Kuwait," 359.
17. Author's interview with UAE analyst I in London.
18. Bloghardt, "Muslim Brotherhood."
19. Krieg, "Divided over Narratives."
20. Trager, "Muslim Brotherhood."
21. Rosenau, *Subversion and Insurgency*, 3.
22. Gertz, "Security Fears."
23. Qassemi, "UAE's Reformed Foreign Ministry."
24. Grim, "Diplomatic Underground."
25. Grim and Ahmed, "His Town."
26. Krieg, "Weaponization of Narratives," 105.
27. *Haaretz*, "Arab Spring"; Smith, "Coming Arab Winter?"
28. Bradley, *After the Arab Spring*; Gerges, "Irresistible Rise of the Muslim Brothers";
    Joscelyn, "Osama Bin Laden's Files"; Rosen, "Arab Spring Optimism."
29. Grim and Zaid, "Hacked Emails"; Krieg, "Never Mind Russia."
30. McGeehan, "Men behind Man City."
31. Author's interview with UAE analyst II over Skype, December 14, 2019.
32. Ketchley, *Egypt*, 104.
33. El Gomati, "Libyan Revolution Undone," 187.
34. Oliphant, "Trump Offers to Mediate Talks."
35. Fabiani, "Tunisia's Leap."
36. Schmidt and Williams, "Bush Doctrine," 196.
37. Marshall, "Remaking the World."
38. Castells, *Communication Power*, 169.
39. *Haaretz*, "Arab Spring"; Smith, "Coming Arab Winter?"
40. Hamid, "Rise of Anti-Liberalism."
41. Hamzawy, "Egyptian Liberals."
42. Trager, *Arab Fall*, 204.
43. Kane, "Barqa Reborn?" 215.
44. Krieg, "On the Sinister Objectives."
45. Roberts, "Mosque and State."
46. Worth, "Mohammed bin Zayed's Dark Vision."
47. Al-Azami, *Islam*, 99.
48. Krieg, "On the Sinister Objectives."
49. Diwan, "Who Is Sunni?"
50. Walker, "'We Can Find You Anywhere.'"
51. FPPMS, *Pursuit of Peace*, 23.
52. Gearty, *Terror*, 15.
53. Lewandowsky et. al. "Misinformation."
54. Roberts, "Mosque and State."
55. Lynch, "Neo-Weberian Approach."
56. Powell, "Counter-Productive Counterterrorism," 52.
57. Salem and Hassan, "Arab Regimes."
58. Wickham, *Muslim Brotherhood*, introduction.
59. Kerr, "UAE Blacklists 83 Groups."
60. Trager, "Muslim Brotherhood."

61. See Krieg, "Weaponization of Narratives."
62. Waterson and Deghan, "Independent's Deal."
63. Walker, "Mandrake."
64. Rawnsley, "Right-Wing Media Outlets."
65. Farhad, "Has Iran's Presence in Iraq Marginalized Sunnis?"
66. Huang, "Facebook Removes 'Coordinated' Fake Accounts"; Dogantekin, "Twitter Shuts Down Troll Armies."
67. Author's interview with UAE analyst II over Skype.
68. Owen-Jones, "Propaganda," 1396.
69. DFRLab, "Libyan Hashtag Campaign"; Grossmann et al., "Blame It on Iran."
70. Walsh and Rashwan, "'We're at War.'"
71. Walsh and Rashwan.
72. Barnard, "Man of God."
73. Author's interview with a senior Libya analyst in London, February 11, 2020.
74. Krieg, "Laying the 'Islamist' Bogeyman to Rest."
75. Freeman, *Foreign Funding of Think Tanks*.
76. Grim and Zaid, "Hacked Emails."
77. Selliaas and Ødegård, "Mr Fuller."
78. Associated Press, "How the UAE's Effort."
79. Merill, "Qatari Exile."
80. *United States of America v. Al Malik Alshahhi et al.*, 1.
81. DeYoung, "How Thomas Barrack's Alleged Illegal Lobbying Shaped Trump's Policies."
82. Akkad, "Revealed."
83. Khatib, *Arab Lobby*, 68.
84. Asher-Schapiro and Emmons, "At Neocon Think Tank."
85. Hudson, "Countering Violent Extremism."
86. Kirkpatrick and Mazzetti, "How 2 Gulf Monarchies Sought to Influence."
87. Montague and Panja, "Ahead of Qatar World Cup."
88. Archer, "Exiled Palestinian Politician Mohammed Dahlan."
89. Nuseibah, "Fighting Jew Hate."
90. Grim and Ahmed, "His Town."
91. Bussola Institute, "Bussola Institute Honorary Board."
92. Scott-Geddes, "UAE Embassy."
93. Freeman, *Foreign Funding of Think Tanks*.
94. Grim, "Gulf Government."
95. Kirkpatrick and Mazzetti, "How 2 Gulf Monarchies Sought to Influence."
96. Krieg, "UAE's War."
97. Grim and Zaid, "Hacked Emails."
98. Asher-Schapiro and Emmons, "At Neocon Think Tank."
99. Selliaas and Ødegård, "Mr Fuller."
100. Grim and Zaid, "Hacked Emails."
101. Schantzer, *Muslim Brotherhood's Global Threat*.
102. Schantzer and Havard, "By Hosting Hamas"; Weinberg, *Qatar*.
103. Kirkpatrick and Mazzetti, "How 2 Gulf Monarchies Sought to Influence."
104. US Government Publication Office, *Muslim Brotherhood's Global Threat*.
105. LIAS, "Dr. Aref Nayed."
106. Al Saeedi, "سياسي ليبي: قطر وتركيا تواصلان دعم الإرهاب.. والإخوان تعرقل الانتخابات"

107. Khatib, *Arab Lobby*, 68.
108. Abramson, *Proof of Conspiracy*, chap. 10; Hearst, "Exclusive"; Parry, "Top Arab Spy"; Reuters, "Turkey Adds former Palestinian Politician Dahlan."
109. Filkins, "Saudi Prince's Quest."
110. Kirkpatrick, "Recordings."
111. Holmes, *Coups*, 252.
112. Na'eem, "Egyptian Crisis," 51.
113. Ketchley, *Egypt*, 104.
114. Parker, "Influential voices."
115. Spencer, "UAE."
116. Delmar-Morgan and Miller, *UAE Lobby*.
117. Ramesh, "UAE Told UK."
118. Mason, "Egypt Crisis."
119. Krieg, "Weaponization of Narratives," 96.
120. Kirkpatrick and Mazzetti, "How 2 Gulf Monarchies Sought to Influence."
121. Butler and LoBianco, "Princes."
122. *United States of America v. Al Malik Alshahhi et al.*
123. Kianpour, "Emails."
124. Wintour, "Donald Trump."
125. Smith and Siddiqui, "Gulf Crisis."
126. DeYoung, "How Thomas Barrack's Alleged Illegal Lobbying Shaped Trump's Policies."
127. Baker, "Trump Now Sees Qatar as an Ally."

SEVEN

Toward Information
Resilience

The problem with dis- and misinformation wrapped in weaponized narratives has been widely acknowledged. However, the question of how to defend against it is mostly underresearched. Subversion does not even feature in the *Tallinn Manual*, a nonbinding study on how cyber operations fit into the international legal framework, produced by the NATO Cyber Defense Centre.

The reasons are manifold. Subversion, as it is introduced in this book, neither neatly sits in the cyber domain nor fits nicely into more analogue modes of malicious activities below the threshold of war. As Thomas Rid observes, "Subversion, in contrast to what some security scholars seem to think, is not principally illegal and it is not even principally illegitimate—only the most extreme forms of subversion are."[1] Especially in liberal, open democracies where civil liberties are protected and the public sphere is an integral element of political discourse and accountability, subversion appears to be entirely within the boundaries of law.

Hence, Western liberal democracies appear to be particularly vulnerable to weaponized narratives. Actors such as Russia and the United Arab Emirates (UAE) seem to exploit the protection of speech, press, and civil liberties in liberal democracies. The unwillingness to regulate the freedom of speech and channels of political communication make it hard, yet not impossible, to adequately distinguish between subversion and legitimate expressions of political dissent—the reason being that subversion relies heavily on legitimate civil-societal activism.[2] For authoritarians on the other side, any form of civil-societal activism is inherently subversive.[3] Thus, liberal democracies have a greater challenge when trying to balance civil liberties with countersubversion, specifically when faced with civil-societal actors that do not play by the rules.

Consequently, establishing effective deterrence against weaponized narratives might be the greatest challenge to liberal democracies. In light of the challenges that emerge from attribution, the absence of political will to act, and the lack of understanding around the threat posed by subversion, deterrence can have only a limited role when trying to contain weaponized narratives. This chapter looks at how to counter subversion through the prism of resilience, namely, the "ability of the community, services, areas or infrastructure to detect, prevent, and, if necessary, to withstand, handle and recover from disruptive challenges."[4]

Unlike deterrence, resilience acknowledges the possibility that some challenges cannot be effectively deterred either by denial or punishment, necessitating the targeted subject or object to be able to withstand these challenges without critically failing. In the context of subversion, we look at what will be necessary to achieve information resilience, including creating communities that are able to sustain weaponized narratives without losing their information-psychological stability.

We start this chapter by addressing the importance of understanding and acknowledging the challenge of subversion before outlining how both authoritarians and liberals confront the sociopsychological, infrastructural, and physical vulnerabilities of the information environment. The final question to be asked in this chapter is whether offensive capability in the information environment can help deter potential antagonists.

ADDRESSING KEY VULNERABILITIES OF THE INFORMATION ENVIRONMENT

The first and arguably most important step in countering subversion activities is understanding one's own vulnerabilities in the information environment, while acknowledging that rivals and opponents might use seemingly benevolent activities to disrupt and undermine information-psychological stability. The politicization of the debate on information operations, "fake news," and disinformation itself is thereby highly counterproductive because it does not only relativize hostile subversive acts but also weakens the readiness of government agencies to respond.[5] Policymakers need to be vigilant and aware of the potential dangers of weaponized narratives in the rapidly expanding and democratizing information environment, which is far broader than the issue of disinformation. Just because some policymakers might directly or indirectly benefit from weaponized narratives that intend to undermine the sociopolitical status quo, there needs to be an acknowledgment that such operations must not be part of the regular civil-societal and political discourse because they call into question the very integrity of a political system. The fact that the Trump administration in the United States did not acknowledge that Russia interfered in the 2016 presidential elections, let alone take action against the perpetrators, severely challenged the ability of the United States to establish credible deterrence.[6]

More so, while the weaponization of narratives by Russia and China appears to register as potentially hostile operations, activities conducted by the UAE are not considered potentially harmful or hostile—at least in Western capitals. The fact that the UAE and Russia coordinate heavily on strategic narratives and Western engagement over issues that concern the Middle East and North Africa (MENA) region is often left in the dark.[7] In the MENA region itself, the UAE's information operations have already made elites and policymakers more vigilant, especially in Qatar and Oman.[8] Identifying the perpetrator of subversive operations remains the most difficult task, making it ever more imperative for policymakers, government agencies, and the public to stay aware and alert.

In order to achieve resilience in the face of weaponized narratives, the three key vulnerabilities in the twenty-first-century information environment need to be addressed: the sociopsychological, infrastructural, and physical vulnerabilities. Unlike authoritarians, liberal states find it harder to put measures in place to address these vulnerabilities without changing the very character of their sociopolitical system.

Sociopsychological Vulnerabilities

The greatest vulnerability in any information environment is cognition, including the processing, storage, and filtering of information in the human mind. The sociopsychology behind the way we perceive the world, interpret and analyze facts, and make sense of ourselves in a wider societal context is exceptionally vulnerable to exploitation and manipulation through subversive operations. Weaponized narratives are means of gradual erosion of how audiences perceive the world around them, especially on questions of judgment relating to "right" and "wrong," "friend" and "foe," "risk" or "threat," and "just" and "unjust." The assertion that there is nothing more dangerous in sociopolitics than the human mind certainly holds in the context of subversion, where weaponized narratives try to exploit our biases.[9]

Thus, resilience in the information environment has to start with the most difficult of tasks: making sure that we do not become victims of our cognitive shortcuts when processing information. Education is key here to ensure that the public is aware of how narratives can be weaponized to target the human mind. Understanding the threat, the instrumentalization of information and the price at stake becomes a matter of national security. Civic and media education is required to create audiences that are better able to think critically and are first and foremost aware of their own biases before being able to assess the biases of others.[10] In a highly mediatized, digital environment, citizens need to learn how to navigate information, misinformation, and disinformation when assessing different sources. Education curricula were often conceived in an analogue context and are ill equipped to prepare citizens for a digital information environment.[11] Scientific method and argument need to be understood more thoroughly by the next generation to help them distinguish facts from "alternative facts."[12] In Britain, the Ministry of Education started a campaign in 2019 to ensure that school curricula prepare children adequately to understand biases, disinformation, and conspiracy theories when reading information online.[13] In Finland, the government has taken a multipronged, cross-sector approach to educate citizens of all ages in media literacy, with a clear focus on countering Russian subversion.[14]

Pluralism of thought and information might thereby make it more difficult for liberal states and societies to confront sociopsychological vulnerabilities, as compared with authoritarians, who find it easier to control all dimensions of the information environment. Authoritarians found that the most effective remedy to weaponized narratives in the sociopsychological realm was the creation of strong, patriotic counternarratives of nationalism that instill a sense of loyalty and devotion to the regime and what it stands for. The logic is to induce a sense of belonging and collective identity that streamlines and monopolizes civil-societal discourse to the extent that alternative narratives that negate or undermine regime-instilled narratives are automatically rejected as false. Russia, for example, has identified patriotism and nationalism as natural remedies to external narratives that can make its own population more immune to liberal narratives from the West.[15] Maintaining national harmony built around one-dimensional narratives rather than discursive pluralism has been used by Russia to create sociopsychological resilience to alternative views, talking points, and ideologies. In Saudi Arabia, hypernationalism has been an important tool of social mobilization as well, which, although initially implanted from the top down, has led to grassroots cheerleading for the Saudi nation (and, by extension, the regime).[16] Hypernationalism has allowed Crown Prince Mohammed bin Salman to rally the support of youth for highly disruptive policies while creating resistance in parts of the population to critical voices from outside. Although those who cheerlead for the nation in defense of the crown prince are often supported by bots and paid cyber surrogates, the framing of critical journalists, activists, and politicians as enemies of the state is often the result of genuine bottom-up resistance against narratives that run counter to the regime's prescribed mainstream. Though patriotism and nationalism might be effective transformational means for authoritarians to create sociopsychological resilience in the public, much of this effect is owed to transactional, coercive measures by authoritarians sanctioning critical voices and narratives.

For liberals, the establishment of counternarratives by the state as a direct intervention in civil society does not come naturally. Yet sociopsychological resilience in a liberal context depends just as much on the ability of communities to call out disruptive narratives as it does on governments to fill the say/do gap when addressing the fault lines within society. Instead of merely glossing over existing grievances in society—which through polarization, disenfranchisement, and alienation provide fertile ground for disruptive narratives—liberal governments have to fill the cracks in the societal fabric.[17] It is the social, demographic, ethnic, and economic divisions in society that cause audiences to embrace disruptive narratives that create insiders and outsiders as well as frame individuals or groups as victims and perpetrators. Returning to the source of disenfranchisement, alienation, and polarization means that liberal states need to develop better metrics to measure societal grievances across communities and develop awareness of potential sociopsychological vulnerabilities.

Unlike authoritarians, liberal governments cannot rely on a synchronized media apparatus to communicate policies coherently and effectively without public pushbacks. Therefore, an essential element of filling the cracks in the societal fabric for liberals is actually filling the say/do gap and ensuring that policies are implemented coherently rather than merely communicated effectively. If policies are enacted with inclusive societal benefit and geared toward the many and not the few, liberal governments have an advantage of creating greater buy-ins through accommodation rather than coercion.[18] "Liberal authoritarian" populists of the caliber of former US president Trump, Brazilian president Jair Bolsonaro, Hungarian prime minister Victor Orban, and Turkish president Erdogan all operate as authoritarians within the boundaries of a liberal democratic system. Their ability to manipulate the say/do gap to distract from their own shortcomings in addressing public grievances can be undermined by addressing existing societal grievances. In the case of Ukraine, where local Russian-speaking communities became susceptible audiences for Russian subversion operations, the key vulnerability of the Ukrainian military was not so much its inability to militarily defend against unmarked Russian soldiers but mistrust toward it within local populations. As an extension of a Kyiv government that had lost local buy-in in the Donbas, the Ukrainian military found it hard to defend its operations. For many locals, years of disenfranchisement in the eastern parts of the country had created deep-seated alienation that rendered any attempt by Kyiv of a positive engagement in 2014 ineffective.[19] The opposite was true when Russia invaded the country in 2022, as President Zelensky impressively demonstrated how narratives of unity, defiance, and resilience could mobilize Ukrainians to rally around the flag.[20]

In a next step, liberal governments and societies should embrace many of the lessons learned from counterinsurgency operations, which again rely on effectively closing the say/do gap in building trust with civil society. Though subversion is an attack on the apparent vulnerabilities of liberal society, liberal states and societies need to display a coherence with their core values rather than abandoning them under pressure. The commitment of open societies to transparency, civil liberties, and the rule of law all need to be highlighted in the response to weaponized narratives. Only in this way can liberal narratives build up the resilience that is needed when dealing with disinformation.[21] Before being able to adequately rebut the onslaught of weaponized narratives, liberal societies need to ensure the commitment to their own narratives that draw on the liberal values and norms they are trying to defend.

Only once say/do gaps are narrowed can liberal societies think about developing counternarratives that are in sync with core norms and values. The case of the anti-ISIS operation is one of the few instances where liberal states have instrumentalized counternarratives effectively, targeting the cyber caliphate in support of a military operation against the physical caliphate. Though counternarratives were unable to improve the physical needs and grievances of vulnerable communities, they were successful in showcasing "incongruities and contradictions in the terrorist narratives and how terrorists act, disrupting analogies between the target narrative and real-world events, disrupting binary themes of the group's ideology, and advocating an alternative view of the terrorist narrative's target."[22]

In the end, supported by ISIS's diminished success on the physical battlefield, Western counternarratives were able to negate ISIS's ability to create effect in the information environment. It was arguably here that the group had the biggest impact initially.[23] To what extent this counternarrative operation would have been successful without degrading ISIS's physical capability on the ground is questionable. Plus, against a near-peer adversary in the information environment that disseminates weaponized narratives that appear more benign and less radical than that of the jihadists, developing counternarratives might be a more difficult task. In the case of ISIS, it appeared relatively simple, at least from a Western point of view, to identify say/do gaps as inconsistencies between ISIS actions and narratives became increasingly obvious, at least for indigenous Western audiences.

Instead of merely building counternarratives around dry facts, liberal information warriors need to connect with target audiences on an emotional level, wrapping facts in novel narratives that allow for them to achieve virality. Here, veracity does not necessarily have to undermine virality as long as the sociocultural context of target audiences is understood and facts are transported creatively to account for the intended recipients' information processing behavior. To borrow from Aristotle's three modes of persuasion, effective counternarratives require a healthy balance of logos, pathos, and ethos (reason, emotion, and moral appeal). The attribution bias thereby needs to be broken to allow the penetration of so-called antiestablishment communities. For example, white supremacists on the political right would be highly suspicious of narratives being disseminated by government authorities, in the same way that jihadists might trust a seemingly like-minded religious authority more than a moderate religious authority.[24]

Infrastructural Vulnerabilities

As outlined in chapter 4, authoritarians who regard any form of civil-societal activism as subversive have taken a range of measures to undermine the proper functioning of the public sphere, thereby minimizing infrastructural vulnerabilities. Trying to subvert civil-societal discourse through bots and trolls, narrative campaigns, or draconian punishments for spreading "fake news" and "rumors," authoritarians have found means to undermine and demobilize civil society. The technological gap that was created by the infrastructural revolution through liberation technology was quickly closed by digital authoritarians, who have found ways to reverse engineer information technology from a tool of potential civil-societal control to one used to control civil society. Commanding large information networks, authoritarians have been able to exploit the infrastructural vulnerabilities in a constant competition over narratives with "subversive" dissident discourse. Social media has become their tool to impose information-psychological stability by depoliticizing the public sphere, installing cheerleaders for the regime, and mobilizing netizens, bots, and trolls to shame and intimidate critical voices.

Liberals tend to be torn between self-regulatory regimes and government regulation of the media, including social media. One proactive measure that liberal governments can take is to support public broadcasting to provide a viable alternative to a highly commercialized market for media, where veracity is often trumped by virality and the need to generate profit.[25] Instead of creating state-owned propaganda channels, public broadcasting in liberal societies has an important function to play in providing programs that speak to audiences more inclusively. Public broadcasters—such as the German ARD, the British BBC, or the French Télévision—can become democratic and inclusive platforms to reach out to disenfranchised communities and represent their interests, concerns, and grievances—an ambition of which most public broadcasters still fall short. A public broadcasting network that enjoys high credibility and trust from the public could help rally the audiences around the flag, while providing balanced reporting based on sober analysis and critical reflection in an effort to counter polarization and marginalization. Public broadcasters also possess the funds needed to employ professional journalists, who are provided with appropriate time and resources to develop in-depth stories without unnecessary time pressure or the need for a commercial spin.

Self-Regulation

The most common approach liberal governments have taken to counter the infrastructural vulnerabilities is self-regulation, encouraging multistakeholder initiatives that include government, social media providers, media corporations, journalists, and other members of civil society. Since subversion targets the human mind, an inclusive approach beyond the state and its institutions is required to counter any such efforts. Like other subthreshold threats in the twenty-first century, weaponized narratives require a "whole nation" approach to construct a multiagency information capability that flags up and rebuts disinformation and weaponized narratives. It is important that the state remains in the background so as to prevent such initiatives from losing trust and buy-in from audiences alienated by government and state institutions.[26]

Such multistakeholder initiatives should also comprise content developers and bloggers, who themselves have a responsibility for veracity and not to be instrumentalized for political purposes by foreign powers.[27] The UN Special Rapporteur on Freedom of Expression issued a report in 2018 calling for the establishment of so-called Social Media Councils that were supposed to act as open, transparent, and participatory multistakeholder forums for content moderation on social media.[28] These councils bring together social media companies and users to establish basic codes of conduct based on human rights standards for signatories who voluntarily agree to respect and execute the developed principles.

Establishing voluntary codes of conduct and standards for acceptable use of information are multidimensional means by state and civil society to establish a commitment to facts-based reporting and civil behavior between social media users. The EU Commission sponsored a Code of Practice on Disinformation in 2018, whereby social media giants like Google, Twitter, and Facebook agreed on a voluntary basis to self-regulatory standards to fight disinformation in the context of electoral campaigns. Together with advertisers, social media companies committed to transparency in political advertising and the closing of fake accounts and demonetization of accounts spreading disinformation.[29] Lacking an enforcement mechanism, EU Commission reports in 2019 suggest that more needs to be done by the industry against disinformation.[30] In particular, social media companies should be more vigilant about bots, trolls, and fake accounts who are being abused by authoritarians to skew algorithm-curated trends. The narrative propagated by social media giants such as Facebook claiming to be "bastions of the freedom of speech" thereby have to be rejected on grounds of how liberation technology has enabled digital authoritarians.[31] Initiatives by Twitter to remove fake accounts tied to the UAE and Saudi-led information networks in this regard were a mere drop in the bucket. The move was in response to civil-societal criticism about the dubious role played by social media giants in indirectly assisting the Saudi government to silence dissident and regime insider Khashoggi.[32] With thousands of fake accounts being created every day, social media giants should more assertively rely on machine learning to sieve through cybersphere to detect and disable these surrogates.

Moreover, social media giants have a responsibility to ensure that the algorithms they rely on to curate information on their platforms allow for more diversity of opinion. To be exact, algorithms should be redeveloped to allow for more heterogeneous relationships between information and consumers. This means breaking the toxic echo-chambering by linking users with information that might be incoherent with previous consumption.[33] Only in this way can social media help support critical thinking and break the vicious circle of the echo chamber that is often an integral part of polarization and mobilization. Borrowing from epidemiology, inoculation theory predicts an immunization effort when media users and consumers are forcefully and repeatedly confronted with counterarguments and counternarratives. Algorithms would have to be changed in a way to ensure that this form of triangulation happens repeatedly and coherently to fight the uphill battle against ingrained beliefs.[34]

Linked to the aspect of algorithm-induced triangulation is the aspect of fact-checking and the flagging of disinformation as recommended by most self-regulatory regimes. Social media companies need to invest in fact-checking through reverse image searches, geolocation, and speaking to experts or primary sources.[35] Facebook has introduced the label "disputed" for mis- or disinformation, which can bring down readership by 80 percent but is still unable to discourage sufficient numbers of consumers to read what confirms their biases. Research shows that articles that are labeled "disputed" still invite debates over opinion and interpretation, which allow deep-seated biases and the illusionary truth effect to persist.[36] Instead, articles should be labeled "false" to bring down readership and feed its algorithms with data from its fact-checker to make less accurate articles less prominent.[37]

Actions by Twitter to label comments by former president Trump over alleged voter fraud as false following the 2020 US presidential elections were important steps to counter potentially mobilizing disinformation.[38] Only after the US Capitol riots on January 6, 2021, did social media companies take serious action against false and weaponized narratives on its platforms. In an unprecedented move, Twitter suspended the outgoing president's account @realDonaldTrump for inciting violence—a move some argue came too little too late for Trump, who had generated hundreds of millions of engagements on Twitter over the years and was then on his way out anyway.[39] Moves by Facebook and Twitter to ban accounts linked to the QAnon conspiracy theory—falsely claiming that a satanic and pedophile network of liberals runs the world—shows the difficulty of fighting ideas through the closing of accounts. Though superspreader accounts can be identified and banned, deeply embedded networks still remain that allow QAnon content to continue to spread.[40]

These interventions by social media companies, albeit late in the process, constitute a break from their previous policies. As some would argue, they constitute an attack on civil liberties as these companies effectively act as gate-keepers and mediators. Apart from this being potentially bad for business—as new platforms are being created outside the social media mainstream—these actions might only ever be taken in extreme circumstances when conspiracy theories or deliberately false information is being spread. Weaponized narratives, however, might be more persistent because they involve judgment calls based on degrees of veracity wrapped in palatable storylines. Here, account closures or fact-checking work only when narratives can be identified as deliberate and direct attempts to incite violence or spread false information. In most circumstances, narratives are more subtle and display varying degrees of veracity that only indirectly cause a mobilization effect that could turn violent.

Government Regulation

The more drastic approach taken by liberal governments to contain weaponized narratives in the infrastructural domain is relying on top-down regulation. Looking at the information networks of antagonists, some have suggested outlawing and banning media outlets that are known for spreading disinformation and/or acting as agents of foreign governments. Though such measures might not be easily reconcilable with civil liberties, they also often backfire without actually delivering the desired outcomes. Not to mention, they rarely work against weaponized narratives that are not based on disinformation. In March 2016, the Latvian government banned a local version of Russia's *Sputnik* online magazine, after the EU's sanctioning of the head of *Sputnik* in Russia. The Latvian government did not allow *Sputnik* to register its site under an .lv address. *Sputnik* bypassed this sanction by reregistering as a .com site—providing Russia with a propaganda pretext claiming that Latvia was trying to limit freedom of speech for its Russian-speaking minority.[41]

In the United States, the government designated Chinese media companies as foreign agents, treating state-broadcaster CGTN, China's International Radio broadcaster, and three other outlets as extensions of Beijing's foreign policy arm.[42] This designation hampers these companies' freedom of movement as the State Department retains control over these companies' ability to buy or rent property and hire staff. This move sets a precedent for how the US government might deal with other foreign news outlets. Russia Today, meanwhile, was only taken off air in the United States due to technology companies and television providers dropping RT America during Russia's invasion of Ukraine.[43]

More controversial, however, have been actions taken by liberal governments in an effort to outlaw "fake news"—actions whereby governments would assume the role of the arbiter deciding what is and what is not truthful. In France, Parliament passed a law in 2018 that allowed courts to rule whether news reports in election times are credible. If necessary, the law provides courts with the power to order these reports to be taken down.[44] This law would also force social media platforms to disclose the source of funding of sponsored content—something Twitter disagreed with, closing its platform for social media campaigns from the French government.[45] In Germany, the government has taken a more expansive approach to contain hate speech, agitation, and disinformation. The so-called Facebook Act passed in 2017 was primarily motivated by a desire to contain right-wing extremists in Germany but provided a blueprint to be "copied by authoritarian governments eager to curb political dissent."[46] Based on this law, social media companies can be fined up to €50 million for certain content that is not deleted from their platform, such as Nazi symbols, Holocaust denial, or language classified as hate speech.[47] The issue arising from such a law is that objectionable content needs to be consensually defined as such, granting government authority and media platforms the discretion to censor. Though content aiming at mobilizing individuals to commit acts of violence might be easily identified as objectionable, hate speech and "defamation of the state" are matters that are up for interpretation. Germany's Facebook Act could target not just disinformation but also misinformation, including unintentional misstatements of facts or mistakes in reporting, opinion pieces, and political satire—all aspects of journalism that must be protected under the freedom of expression.[48] A YouTube video by a German influencer attacking the governing CDU just days before the party's electoral defeat in state elections in May 2019 triggered an overreaction by the then head of the party.[49] In an interview, Annegret Kramp-Karrenbauer suggested that strong opinions expressed by key influencers online during election periods should face regulation—an idea that did not just cause widespread condemnation about possible censorship but also highlights the difficulties liberal governments face when trying to address the infrastructural vulnerabilities of the information environment.

The EU's legislative proposal for a Digital Services Act might be a compromise that offers a regulatory framework that induces self-regulation and transparency for social media companies. Twitter, Facebook, and others would have to disclose to legislators how their algorithms work and provide moderation tools for the management of content online. Thereby, lawmakers would create an obligation for social media companies to cooperatively work with government to monitor and manage content—obligations most social media giants already fulfill in the EU.[50]

Physical Vulnerabilities

The physical vulnerabilities of the information environment might be equally difficult to address for liberal governments, as subversive operations need to be constrained before the mobilization effect moves from the online to the offline world. This means that this needs to be done before civil-societal, academic, and political institutions move information into the physical realm of policymaking. Though the exploitation of sociopsychological vulnerabilities can mobilize or demobilize civil-societal activity in the virtual domain, which can then easily enter the physical space, it is the spillover into the policy-relevant domain that needs to be prevented. For example, when Russian disinformation campaigns mobilize Americans to protest in a remote locality in the United States, subversion has already had an impact on the physical domain without necessarily being policy relevant. However, when think tanks host conferences sponsored by the UAE in close proximity to or even in cooperation with policymakers, weaponized narratives have a direct impact on policymaking circles.

Therefore, authoritarians generally opt for restrictive measures that either ban think tanks and nongovernmental organizations altogether or place them under the tight political scrutiny of the regime, coercing think tank activities into conforming to the grand strategic narratives of the regime. In Russia, Dugin is convinced that the Kremlin has achieved information resilience by gradually isolating segments of what he refers to as "Atlantic networks," meaning oligarchs, pro-Western liberals, nongovernmental organizations, and think tanks.[51] Russia, like other authoritarian regimes, has neutralized alternative poles of information power that could potentially undermine the authority of the state by assertively enforcing the view that an independent think tank world is in essence subversive.

In liberal countries, banning independent think tanks, nongovernmental organizations, and research centers, regardless of how critical they are of the political status quo and policymaking, is not an option. On the contrary, many governments rely on the work of think tanks for data gathering, consulting, and political decision-making. It is here where liberal governments should develop a more natural skepticism vis-à-vis the information that they are being fed. Though liberal governments have a wide range of in-house sources available, on matters of foreign and security policy, individual policymakers are often relying on a few, often external, sources. The idea that think tanks, especially in Washington, are bastions of independent, scholarly research makes them extremely powerful tools in shaping perception and debate around the heart of American policymaking. At the same time, it is important to highlight that foreign government funding does not always have a direct impact on the research and writing of affiliated experts—although degrees of impact vary from think tank to think tank. Most experts at the leading foreign policy think tanks of the world—such as the Brookings Institution, the Carnegie Endowment for International Peace, Chatham House, and the Royal United Services Institute—would be unlikely to change their positions on an issue to suit a donor's preference (although research agendas might be prioritized over others because of donor funding becoming available). However, because it is difficult to measure the impact of foreign funding on research output, policy engagement, and other activities, it is imperative that funding streams are publicly disclosed to allow consumers of think tank products to pass their own judgment.

In an effort to combat fascist influence in America in the 1930s, the US Justice Department enacted the Foreign Agents Registration Act (FARA) in 1938 with a view to making foreign agents register their activities and publicly disclose their links to foreign powers. Though FARA has long faced an enforcement issue, the Mueller investigation into Russian interference into the 2016 US presidential election brought FARA back to the forefront of political attention—not least because Trump confidant and campaign chairman Paul Manafort as well as the first national security adviser of the administration, Michael Flynn, were charged with failing to register with FARA.[52] The problem with FARA is one of transparency, compliance, and enforcement as well as the very definition of what constitutes a foreign agent. Though public relations firms hired by foreign governments or lobbyists like Manafort working for a Ukrainian pro-Russian party might be fairly straightforward cases, think tanks that accept multimillion-dollar donations from foreign governments fall off the radar.[53] Think tank fellows whose majority of funding depends on foreign governments can engage with policymakers in Washington without having to register for FARA, as their activities are exempt under bona fide, scholastic pursuits.[54] The same goes for academics whose research centers are sponsored by foreign governments. Especially when foreign governments use foreign companies or businesses as intermediaries to channel money to think tanks—as was the case with the UAE channeling money to Trump confidant Elliot Broidy in the US via a Canadian company to host an anti-Qatar conference—here FARA was effectively bypassed.[55]

There are also loopholes when think tankers appear as witnesses in front of the US House of Representatives. Many of the witnesses invited by House committees are nongovernmental witnesses, often from local think tanks, and are required to fill in a truth in testimony form disclosing any foreign funding received that relates to the subject of the hearing. To what extent foreign government funding actually relates to the subject of the hearing is thereby ill defined and provides witnesses with opportunities not to disclose funding. For example, when a think tank such as the Center for Strategic and International Studies receives considerable funding from the UAE, a fellow of the think tank would not have to disclose that his organization receives donations from Abu Dhabi when discussing matters pertaining to Iran and its militias—despite the fact that the UAE has a clear, vested interest in shaping that debate.[56]

Yet think tank funding by foreign governments is far from just an American problem. In Brussels and London, embassies and foreign governments also channel money to think tanks in the hope of at least influencing policy-relevant debate. The FARA model in the United States thereby provides a suitable model to expand the foreign agency debate into academia, requiring lobbyists, think tankers, academics, and other seemingly independent experts to disclose their funding links when engaging policymakers or publishing articles and commentaries. The definition of what constitutes a foreign agent has to be widened, while making sure that relevant agencies are able to enforce the disclosure of professional or funding sources to foreign governments.

In terms of enforcement, the idea of an independent think tank oversight commission as a multistakeholder initiative with government support would be suitable in a liberal context. It could monitor think tank funding, research, and other activities while providing a public register for think tanks listing the information that these organizations already share with tax authorities: donor contributions and funding sources.[57] It could provide an independent source of information for policymakers and media who engage with research outputs, conferences, and individual experts of think tanks in the West, offering a degree of checks and balances without formally operating as an external quality control mechanism.

In Australia, a foreign interference task force was set up in 2019, bringing together academia, security services, and government departments. It was to provide a platform for multistakeholder dialogue on issues of foreign interference, primarily from China, following guidelines that were meant to find a balance between academic freedom and national interest concerns. Concerns over China using its "Thousand Talents Plan" to transfer intellectual property from Australian research centers caused the Australian government to introduce legislation that would allow for bypassing the task force to single-handedly cancel research agreements.[58] This was a step that academia feared would undermine academic freedom.

RESILIENCE THROUGH DETERRENCE?

Although resilience is built around the idea of deterrence by denial, meaning denying the aggressor the potential benefit of subversion, resilience might be strengthened by developing more proactive measures to deter subverting powers through punishment. As outlined above, measures taken in the sociopsychological, infrastructural, and physical domains of the information environment can prepare communities to bounce back from subversive activities. However, these measures do not provide a bulletproof umbrella that shields the information environment, not least because it is unlikely that communities will adopt all measures at the same time. Thus, complete denial is unachievable in the information environment. Left with even a small chance of success compared with the relatively low costs of weaponizing narratives, the aggressor is incentivized to try to probe, unless deterrence by denial is met with a credible regime of punishment.

Therefore, resilience could be supplemented with a degree of deterrence by punishment. Due to the nature of subversion being pervasive and permanent, the offensive form of deterrence, which is built around retaliation, needs to be general and entail the full spectrum of state power. As weaponized narratives can be instrumentalized by aggressors as stand-alone operations or for purposes of force multiplication, deterrers would have to consider a whole spectrum of responses.

However, so far states find it hard to first acknowledge the severity of the threat coming from weaponized narratives, and to institutionalize responses to such operations. Although NATO declared the cyberspace a "domain of operations" alongside conventional air, sea, land, and space environments, definitions of what constitutes "an armed attack" are still vague and mostly apply to cyber-sabotage and not subversion. Beyond general statements made by NATO at the 2016 summit, its response doctrine is still at an early stage in its development, especially when it comes to subversion. To what extent information operations could constitute an equivalent to an armed attack remains ill defined and provides aggressors with sufficient leeway to probe without having to fear an appropriate response.[59] On the national level, most Western states have not developed sophisticated deterrence strategies, with occasional internal papers looking more at resilience rather than proactive countersubversion.

The key issue with countersubversion, as with other malicious activities in the information environment, is attribution. As most subverting powers are operating via highly complex assemblages of virtual and physical surrogates, whose affiliation with a particular subverting power can only seldom be properly established, identifying a surrogate does not always lead to finding the patron. This is particularly true when information users become voluntary or coincidental surrogates of a patron when engaging with weaponized narratives. The gradual network approach to subversion takes a deliberately decentralized route without clear command-and-control structures—as the example of Russia's meddling in the US presidential elections in 2016 and 2020 shows. Though the original source of the operation was in Russia, it was the targeting of susceptible audiences over an extended period of time through a multitude of outlets that eventually created a mobilization effect.

However, the US Cyber Command was able to show first successes against Russian patrons by directly contacting Russians who were linked to specific operations conducted by the Internet Research Agency (IRA) in Saint Petersburg. In the weeks before the midterm elections in 2018, the US Cyber Command had identified and tracked down individuals linked to the IRA, putting them on notice that they were no longer anonymous and that their ability to work and travel freely could be affected if they continued to operate against US interests.[60] The fact that the US authorities were able to connect names, dates, and IP addresses to activities in the information environment, as well as establish links to their electronic networks, meant that at least for those few individuals, their ability to operate in the dark had vanished. More so, an IRA-based accountant, Elena Khusyaynova, was even formally indicted, as the 2018 case *United States of America v. Elena Alekseevna Khusyaynova* shows. The defendant was charged with "conspiracy to defraud the United States," which is further outlined under point 15 of the Criminal Complaint:

> The Conspiracy has a strategic goal, which continues to this day, to sow division and discord in the US political system, including by creating social and political polarization, undermining faith in democratic institutions, and influencing US elections. . . . The Conspiracy has sought to conduct what it called internally "information warfare against the United States of America" through fictitious US personas on social media platforms and other Internet-based media.[61]

Although such moves might have only limited reach in unpacking the full scale of the Russian-backed information network, this case nonetheless demonstrates that states could undermine the idea of anonymity and impunity in the information environment, albeit with an immense commitment of resources. This symbolic action might be a step in the right direction of establishing deterrence by punishment, even if the probability of one's cover being blown is still very low. If states developed more effective, proactive cyber means to detect, isolate, and engage information operatives, deterrence would be more credible.

What is needed in this context is a new infrastructure for information operations in liberal countries that could exclusively focus on both the defense against and instrumentalization of weaponized narratives. Here, especially liberal states need to become bolder in confronting the challenge posed by disinformation and weaponized narratives to take risks in addressing them head-on. Innovation and creativity need to be nurtured in a dedicated institution that deals with information resilience beyond the narrow cyber domain, which is mostly preoccupied with network security, antisabotage, and antiespionage measures. This new institution has to absorb elements of the US Information Agency's public diplomacy agenda and the US Department of Defense's Office of Strategic Influence, which after the September 11, 2001, terrorist attacks on the United States dealt with counterjihadist messaging—both institutions were closed in 1999 and 2016, respectively.[62] In addition, this institution also needs to draw on information operations capability from the military that tend to employ information or psychological operations tactically or operationally rather than strategically. A new institution would become a centralized hub for any government messaging, both defensive and offensive, while actively hunting those who try to target information-psychological stability of communities at home.

In Britain, a new brigade was formed in 2015, the Seventy-Seventh Brigade, with a dedicated task of conducting "white" information operations, while developing a capability of conducting "gray" information operations specifically targeting key audiences at home and overseas.[63] However, though the idea evolved from the challenges NATO faced vis-à-vis Russia's information operations in the Baltics, it did not create an integrated strategic hub for information operations in the United Kingdom. Learning from Russia, Western states need to also externalize more capability to the private sector, building surrogate assemblages between government agencies, hacktivists, and other elements of civil society to foster more extensive coverage of online activities, helping to both unravel hostile information networks and create own information networks that are able to weaponize narratives. As information resilience is a multistakeholder endeavor, states require the support of a vigilant civil society that partners with the state to engage and neutralize potential disruptors—something that would act as a deterrent to some.

The key challenge to instrumentalizing information as a stand-alone lever of power in the Western world remains the aspiration of legitimacy. Empowering information operatives employed directly or indirectly by liberal states to take risks can be effective only if this new infrastructure for information operations has the full support from policymakers and can operate with limited direct public scrutiny. Information operations and counteroperations require flexibility and the space for trial and error as the weaponization of narratives is not an exact science. So, hitting the target cannot always be expected, unlike in kinetic operations. What works in theory might not translate into practice, as human sociopsychology depends as much on chance and coincidence as it depends on understanding cognitive patterns and shortcuts.[64] Facing constant pressure to deliver effectively and legitimately, potentially under public scrutiny, means that information operatives in liberal countries rarely have the freedom to maneuver that their counterparts might enjoy in Russia, the UAE, or China. Especially when launching counternarrative operations that target domestic audiences, the appetite for liberal civil society for such operations would be extremely low. In particular at a time when domestic political and civil-societal polarization undermines trust in government and state, the perception that liberal governments could actively intervene in the public sphere through targeted information operations would further undermine government legitimacy.[65] In competition with authoritarian regimes, liberal states are held to higher standards when it comes to transparency, freedom of speech, and press freedom, which severely limits what liberal states can get away with in the information environment while maintaining the moral high ground.

CONCLUSION

At first glance, liberal societies appear to be more vulnerable to weaponized narratives than communities under authoritarian regime control, where information is often classified as potentially subversive to begin with. Securing a liberal information environment certainly holds far more challenges than securing an already restricted information environment. Where infrastructural and physical vulnerabilities are already minimized, the authoritarian state finds it easier to manipulate the processing, dissemination, and use of information. More important, authoritarians actively engage in countering what they consider to be subversive information with information that conforms more with often clearly outlined strategic narratives, giving sociopsychological vulnerabilities less of a chance to be exploited remotely.

In a liberal context, the benefit of an open information environment where civil society holds the monopoly over the processing, dissemination, and usage of information outweighs the potential risks of being more vulnerable to external exploitation. As the COVID-19 crisis has shown, transparency and open dialogue within civil society and between civil society and policymaking has ensured that an informed public could take precautionary measures before governments assume an assertive, often belated, role. Thus, while few liberal states have introduced legislation to curtail freedom of speech, it remains to be seen to what extent societies are willing to sustain these measures.

Hence, resilience in a liberal information environment should primarily be based on measures borne by civil society and not the state, meaning those that are founded on raised awareness, education, and self-regulation. Any true information resilience requires a transparent, multistakeholder debate across the whole of government and across all institutions of civil society, in an unrestricted public sphere to define the boundaries of what should and what should not be legitimate forms of communication. The sociopolitical debate that underlies any measures taken inclusively between state and civil society has to address the legitimacy of any interference in the information environment, defining an equilibrium between freedom of speech and information resilience. Because the state's monopolization of the processing, dissemination, and usage of information would corrupt the liberal public sphere, measures to increase the resilience of the information environment should come from within civil society through an inclusive, multistakeholder process. Though the state can function as an arbitrator in this process, it is the public, the media, and social media companies, as well as users and consumers, who need to step up to increase the resilience of the information environment. Although sociopsychological vulnerabilities cannot be eradicated, the particular algorithm-curated social media environment, which caters to the worst in human cognition, could be altered.

For that, social media companies need to understand that their subversive business model is a potential threat to national security.

If—in the long chain of information processing, dissemination, and usage—each node would act consciously of the danger of weaponized narratives, the chain of virality could be broken. That is to say that if audiences were more aware of their sociopsychological barriers to objectivity, if social media companies and journalists handled information more responsibly, if algorithms deliberately exposed information consumers with counterintuitive information outside the echo chamber, if think tanks and academia became less partisan and more clearly separated research from activism, and if subject matter experts were more scrutinized in their funding streams, then information environments would less likely succumb to weaponized narratives, subversion, or disinformation.

Information resilience, then, is about the ability to sustain weaponized narratives without civil-societal mobilization generating a critical mass online or offline that could generate its own truth effect. That is to say, critical mass in the information environment is one that can either directly affect authoritative sources in media, academia, and policymaking or create a civil-societal momentum through sufficient engagements on social media that a significant number in the audience perceives the narratives as truthful and acts on them. When weaponized narratives fail to change the will of a significant number of genuine information consumers, an audience has proven to be resilient.

NOTES

1. Rid, *Cyber War*, 134.
2. Jamieson, *Cyberwar*, 11.
3. Revel, "Can the Democracies Survive?" 4.
4. DCDC, *JDP02*, 3.
5. Giles, Sherr, and Seaboyer, *Russian Reflexive Control*, 43.
6. Steward, "Russian Election Interference."
7. Mazzetti, Kirkpatrick, and Goldman, "Adviser to Emirates."
8. Sheline, "Oman's Smooth Transition."
9. Keltner and Robinson, "Extremism."
10. Lamond and Dessel, "Democratic Resilience."
11. McGeehan, "Countering Russian Disinformation."
12. Omand, "Threats," 21.
13. Cockburn, "Schools."
14. Mackintosh, "Finland."
15. Jones and Kovacich, *Global Information Warfare*, 36.
16. Alhussein, "Saudi First," 5.
17. Schneier, "Toward an Information Operations Kill Chain."
18. Pesenti and Pomerantsev, *How to Stop Disinformation*, 10.
19. Pesenti and Pomerantsev.

20. Bell, "Zelensky Myth."
21. Rugge, "Mind Hacking," 7.
22. Braddock and Horgan, "Towards a Guide," 397.
23. UK Ministry of Defence, "Information Advantage," 14.
24. Lamond and Dessel, "Democratic Resilience."
25. Pesenti and Pomerantsev, *How to Stop Disinformation*, 11.
26. Omand, "Threats," 21.
27. Pomerantsev and Weiss, "Menace," 7.
28. UN Special Rapporteur, "Report," section IV, pars. 44–63.
29. European Commission, "Code of Practice."
30. European Commission, "Last Intermediate Results."
31. Paul, "Zuckerberg Defends Facebook."
32. Paul and Chee, "Twitter Suspends Saudi Royal Adviser."
33. Cook, "Understanding and Countering Misinformation," 290.
34. McGuire and Papageorgis, "Relative Efficacy."
35. Agence France Presse, "Fact Checking."
36. Pennycook, Cannon, and Rand, "Prior Exposure," 34.
37. Nyhan, "Why the Fact-Checking at Facebook Needs to Be Checked."
38. Conger, "Twitter Has Labeled 38% of Trump's Tweets."
39. Ball, "Big Tech Didn't Show Its Strength."
40. Frenkel, "QAnon Is Still Spreading."
41. Sputnik News, "Sputnik Latvia Traffic Surges."
42. Gaouette and Hansler, "US to Treat Chinese State Media Like an Arm of Beijing's Government."
43. Darcy, "RT America Ceases Productions."
44. Young, "French Parliament Passes Law against 'Fake News.'"
45. BBC News, "Twitter Blocks French Government."
46. Mchangama and Fiss, "Germany's Online Crackdowns."
47. Eddy and Scott, "Delete Hate Speech."
48. West, "How to Combat Fake News."
49. Chazan, "Blue-Haired Vlogger Takes Aim."
50. Perrigio, "How the EU's Sweeping New Regulations against Big Tech Could Have an Impact."
51. Dugin, "Teoreticheskiye osnovy setevykh voyn," 3.
52. Robinson, "Foreign Agents Registration Act Is Broken."
53. Dennet, "'Foreign Agents' Law."
54. Freeman, "US Foreign Policy Is for Sale."
55. Abramson, *Proof of Conspiracy*, 344.
56. Dennett, "Foreign Influence?"
57. Freeman, *Foreign Funding of Think Tanks*.
58. Hurst, "Australian Universities 'Blindsided.'"
59. Omand, "Threats," 17.
60. Ignatius, "US Military."
61. *United States of America v. Elena Alekseevna Khusyaynova*.
62. Robinson et al., *Modern Political Warfare*, 258.
63. Miller, "Inside the British Army's Secret Information Warfare Machine."
64. Robinson et al., *Modern Political Warfare*, 260.
65. Rugge, "Mind Hacking," 7.

Conclusion

As much as the COVID-19 pandemic was a public health and economic crisis, it was also a crisis in the information space, laying bare a multitude of vulnerabilities in the sociopsychological, infrastructural, and physical domains. Conspiracy theories went just as viral as the virus itself, affecting the media landscape, civil-societal activism, and policy discourse. Although humans have always sought clarity and certainty in times of crisis and uncertainty, the nature of the twenty-first-century information environment has created the perfect context for narratives to distort and manipulate our perception of "truth" and "fact"—at times coincidentally and at other times deliberately through subversion.

Subversion in the context of this book is about the instrumentalization of information to gradually alter the existing sociopolitical consensus and status quo. This gradual assault on the consensus, which is what truth is essentially about, has ramifications for the integrity of civil-societal stability and ultimately can shape sociopolitical order once policymaking is affected. Subversion is about the transformation of narratives that constitute the foundation of how communities make sense of the world around them. In the context of existing societal polarization, narratives have a mobilizing effect that undermines information-psychological stability within a community. Subversion can instrumentalize information in a way that makes it a tool of political power projection that not only manipulates peoples' perceptions but potentially alters their decisions and behaviors. Especially in liberal democracies where social cohesion rests on a shared sense of "truth" and "fact," subversion can undermine the effective functioning of civil society and ultimately disrupt liberal sociopolitical discourse.

As highlighted in chapter 1, the quest for objective truth is often a metaphysical and philosophical one that in its relativist sense can be exploited to call into doubt any form of scientific or factual consensus. And here it is important to highlight that although we live in a world of mediated perception, we accept that facts nonetheless exist. Facts can be scientifically established, even if at times only in a suboptimal manner. Facts are a necessary ingredient of civil-societal and political discourse. Thus, though the philosophical debate about truth should revolve around questions of metaphysics and not scientific fact, truth and fact are not two sides of the same coin. That is to say, though truth is a far more complex metaphysical construct running deeper than mere facts and involving more than just facts, facts are pieces of data that can be scientifically proven.

Hence, a society might exist with multiple versions of the truth but not with multiple versions of fact, which is where the weaponization of narratives comes in. Though narratives do not necessarily try to alter facts, they rearrange facts in constructed storylines that make facts more palatable to specific audiences. While everyone might be entitled to their opinion and narrative, not everyone is entitled to their own facts, as Daniel Patrick Moynihan famously stated.[1] Narratives are versions of the truth compounded by beliefs, emotions, and norms and are often selectively built around established facts. In the realm of narratives, facts are being spun and interpreted to give them meaning. As highlighted in chapter 6, the narrative of political Islam as a "gateway drug to terrorism," as propagated by the United Arab Emirates' (UAE's) information network, might be simplistic and defy the majority scientific consensus on the matter today. But it arranges facts in such a way as to create a story that for many audiences sounds plausible at first—especially when it is tied to existing beliefs and emotions. In the same way, the often-unnuanced debate about the simplistic dichotomy of public health versus economic health during the COVID-19 crisis revolved around narratives about moral judgment calls that were rarely in denial of facts.[2] Instead, the narratives presented two versions of the truth about how COVID-19 affects society, where neither side was entirely right nor wrong.

Both terrorism and the virus display characteristics of a typical twenty-first-century challenge: an omnipresent and invisible threat cloaked in uncertainty that exists in the midst of society, with the state and its law enforcement organizations unable to fully contain it. In this context, fear-based narratives first create a bogeyman against which simplistic responses are deployed. This in turn opens the door to more competing narratives that undermine the consensus and create more confusion. The narratives are deliberately instrumentalized to undermine the ability of targeted audiences to come to grips with uncertainty. Narratives can mobilize people to question government authority or become active within civil society. Through a gradual process of polarization, this mobilization can spill into the physical domain, where weaponized narratives trigger political violence.

At the height of the COVID-19 pandemic, a variety of disinformation and conspiracy theories emerged that exploited the uncertainty and the frustration that came with widely belated and insufficient government responses. A multitude of conspiracy theories emerged ranging from a complete denial of the virus's existence to downplaying its effects on human health. Combined with the narratives of the antivaccine movement, it fueled further outrage in this community, claiming that the government had created COVID-19 in an attempt to curtail constitutional rights, mobilizing people to protest against social distancing rules and vaccine requirements.[3] Meanwhile, during the early stages of the pandemic in the United Kingdom, narratives emerged that claimed the symptoms of COVID-19 were caused by exposure to radio emissions from 5G antennas, triggering people to burn them down.[4] On the other side of the world, the Chinese state directly disseminated narratives about the outbreak of COVID-19 coinciding with a visit from an American sports team in the Wuhan area—a narrative that was aggressively pushed in Arabic by the state-run China Global Television Network targeting audiences in the Arab world that were already susceptible to anti-American rhetoric.[5]

These narratives merge disinformation into storylines in which correlations are confused with causal relations between factual events. And although the emergence of the COVID-19 pandemic occurred as the 5G network in the United Kingdom was rolled out, the fact that Iran also displayed high numbers of symptomatic patients despite not having a single 5G mast was widely disregarded by those who wanted to believe this disinformation-based narrative. The same is true for China's narrative combining two widely unrelated facts to create a subversive storyline that could potentially both cover up Beijing's initial mismanagement of the crisis as well as undermine the reputation of its global rival—an episode that shows similarities with the KGB subversion campaign code-named DENVER amid the AIDS crisis in the 1980s.

SUBVERSION EXPLOITS VULNERABILITIES

Subversion through weaponized narratives is developing into a powerful means of full-spectrum conflict below the threshold of war that bypasses conventional defenses and directly hits the center of gravity for information-psychological stability (e.g., intracommunal relations as well as civil society's relationship with political authority). In an effort to mobilize or demobilize target audiences, both collectively and individually, subversion is an effort that tries to incline the subject to change attitudes, decisions, and ultimately behaviors voluntarily in line with the will of the initiator.

If warfare is reduced to a mere contest of wills, the instrumentalization of information and narratives provides attackers with the ultimate strategic depth, either preparing the ground for military exploitation or precluding the need for conventional kinetic war altogether. Weaponized narratives can bypass conventional defenses and strike the heart of the enemy's will and morale—of civilians and military personnel alike.⁶ Information, when strategically deployed, affects people's cognition directly, delivered subtly and discreetly below the conventional threshold of war without involving conventional defenses. The infrastructural vulnerabilities of the twenty-first-century information environment leave the human mind exposed, providing malicious actors with direct, low-cost entry points to target their biases and fears while mobilizing their anger and hatred. With unmediated interaction between information producer and consumer, traditional defenses for national security are rendered widely useless to shield citizens from the subversive actions of external actors. Subversion's cumulative effect, delivered gradually over time, can generate death by a thousand cuts when parallel operations converge to trigger political violence.

Looking at the various case studies in this book, narratives can be instrumentalized to become a means of strategic power, at times going beyond mere influence to alter how civil society and policymakers behave. Although effects can rarely be precisely predicted, the effect of Russian narratives on civil-societal behavior during the US presidential elections in 2016 and 2020 has been measurable in the same way that the effect of UAE narratives on Egyptian audiences during the early summer of 2013 were measurable. Just as the strategic effect of a destroyed military target cannot always be precisely predicted, the low cost of probing makes it easy to test a variety of avenues until vulnerabilities are exploited. That is, if one narrative does not work, another one might—and all that while any such information operation might either go unnoticed or at least unpunished.

Moreover, the cumulative effect of subversion does not just remain in the virtual world. Weaponized narratives do more than merely accumulate data of trolling and botting online: they spill into the real world. In the same way that weaponized code needs a computer network to interact with it to unleash its full potential, weaponized narratives require a susceptible audience to bring about a change of attitude or behavior. Existing civil-societal polarization, individual grievances, and related sociopsychological vulnerabilities are now widely exposed and provide anyone with access to social media a means to exploit them. Cyberspace-induced emotions such as fear, anger, and hatred are real and can be channeled into outrage that rarely stays on social media. Revelations from a Facebook whistleblower reveal how the social media giant deliberately fueled anger and hatred that do not only intoxicate interactions online but spill into the offline world.⁷

This physical effect that weaponized narratives can have in the analogue world is often underestimated. Just because we cannot be sure exactly how many American voters changed their voting behavior as a result of Russian narratives during the 2016 and 2020 US presidential elections, the fact that it mobilized some while demobilizing others is an effect that had a severe impact on information-psychological stability. More important than the mere mobilizing effect might have been the demobilizing effect emerging from the hyperpolarization of discourse that was fueled by Russian trolls and bots. Creating more uncertainty and revealing the vulnerability of the sociopolitical system of the United States for exploitation in itself has had a demobilizing effect of undermining public confidence and trust in the integrity of the country's sociopolitical relations. The effort to question the integrity of the electoral process by the Trump White House after its electoral defeat in 2020 helped the Russian subversion campaign. The UAE's targeting of policymaking elites in the Trump White House with weaponized narratives on Qatar before the blockade of the emirate by its neighbors was instrumental as well. This triggered the then–US president in June 2017 to endorse the actions taken by Abu Dhabi and Riyadh against a key US ally. This episode shows how effective weaponized narratives can be at shaping complex policy decisions.

Although weaponized narratives are not self-sufficient levers of power, the indirectness of effect does not mean that subversion is nonviolent. Though information itself cannot be violent, the ripple effects of information interacting with existing sociopsychological vulnerabilities can very well be. Where effects spill from the virtual to the physical space, subversion can show its mobilizing power. Mobilization in the societal domain might only come in the form of civil-societal activity, such as a protest; political mobilization only in the form of voting behavior; and policy mobilization in the form of shaping policy decisions; but societal mobilization eventually can lead to political violence, when protests turn violent, and resistance grows into riots or insurgency. As Stephan and Chenoweth demonstrate, the transformational power of nonviolent civil-societal activity might actually be far greater than violent means of resistance.[8] Mobilizing dissidence over time can in fact be a far more effective instrument of power than military conflict in achieving the outcomes of those mobilizing against the state. The erosive and disruptive impact of societal mobilization, albeit an indirect instrument of power, must not be underestimated.

So far, weaponized narratives have already caused violence in the form of clashes between protesters and law enforcement in the United States. The insurrection on Capitol Hill on January 6, 2021, provided a grim glimpse of the cumulative effect that weaponized narratives can have on political violence.[9] The potential in the future for malicious actors to exploit civil-societal and sociopolitical tensions and direct them toward mass protest and revolt is real. The more grievances in liberal societies become widespread, the more sociopsychological and infrastructural vulnerabilities there are for exploitation. Especially as the divide between the public and political authority widens, subversive operations find more susceptible audiences to manipulate. The images of armed vigilantes storming state capitals in the United States at the height of the COVID-19 pandemic in 2020 was just the beginning of a trend illustrating how weaponized narratives can mobilize individuals who are ready to use violence to act on their cyberspace-induced emotions.[10]

Nonetheless, violence should not be the primary test to determine whether a subversive operation can be considered a means of warfare. After all, subversion is a means of subthreshold conflict, which war purists would always object to as qualifying as warfare. Subversion can be strategic and instrumental; it affects the will of people, spills into the physical domain, and can be a precursor to physical violence. Thus, though it does not strictly comply with the narrow metrics of conventional war, it nonetheless shows the most important ingredients of warfare, allowing actors to engage in conflict more readily and to achieve political ends with the necessary strategic patience.

Strategic ends today are more often defined in terms of "disrupt" rather than "seize, hold, and build," meaning information and influence networks can sometimes be more instrumental than a 22,000-pound "Mother-of-All-Bombs," like the one dropped on a small ISIS-offshoot in Afghanistan in April 2017.[11] Killing less than one hundred militiamen and costing $16 million apiece, the greatest nonnuclear ordnance of the US Air Force appears to be a relic of a bygone era, at a time when competitors such as China, Russia, and the UAE are able to sway large audiences globally to endorse predetermined objectives. Subversive narratives can undermine the legitimacy and credibility of established authorities at home, from the sciences to political decision-makers. Narratives can undermine the civil-societal consensus, making governance ever more difficult. They can undermine societal cohesion, pitting neighbors and families against each other. They can undermine civil society as a whole and reinforce authoritarian control in the developing world. And ultimately, subversion can turn the infrastructural liberalization of the information environment against itself, creating political apathy that undermines the very essence of a vibrant sociopolitical discourse. Subversion then succeeds in breaking our will entirely without involving sophisticated kinetic military technology.

STRENGTHEN INFORMATION RESILIENCE

It is therefore imperative that the subversive potential of weaponized narratives is appreciated by those who still believe that information operations are mere adjuncts to conventional modes of warfare and are at best appreciated as a means to prevent war. In reality, as Moscow's phobia of the "Color Revolutions" illustrates, weaponized narratives should not be seen as a means to prevent war but as a means of warfare due to their disruptive and destructive potential, albeit below the conventional threshold of international armed conflict. The realization that Western information environments display inherent vulnerabilities that must be adequately protected is the first step in building information resilience.

The weaponization of narratives relies on a variety of nodes and networks linking a highly diverse range of surrogates together in direct, indirect, or coincidental pursuit of a patron's objectives. Consequently, any response to these complex information and influence networks needs to be multifaceted and multidimensional. It needs to address sociopsychological vulnerabilities of information consumers. It requires cooperation between government, civil society, and those who curate the social media environment. It needs to bring together experts and academia as well as those directly involved in policymaking. Blaming the information warriors in Moscow, Beijing, Riyadh, or Abu Dhabi does not even address half the problem. It is armies of indirect and coincidental surrogates who become the pawns that enable narratives to go viral and affect how we think about certain issues. All elements of subversion campaigns—direct, indirect, or coincidental—need to be included in order to strengthen information resilience. Those who are drawn to narratives based on their cognitive predispositions play as much of a role in information resilience as those social media giants whose business models are built around algorithmically exploiting these predispositions.

Our sociopsychological vulnerabilities might thereby be our Achilles' heel, as the nature of our cognitive wiring is unlikely to change. Though education and counternarratives can play their part in bringing slightly more certainty to the infocalypse, it is only the filling of political say/do gaps through a thorough and inclusive implementation of the social contract that can help do away with those grievances that often function as entry points for disinformation strategies. Ultimately, as in an insurgency environment, if hearts and minds are supportive of government and the sociopolitical status quo, weaponized narratives will not find the fertile ground to create virality and a mobilization effect. However, in the face of the intangible risks and threats of the twenty-first century, a socioeconomic revolution through automation and digitalization, and the globalized character of most issues, certainties will be increasingly hard to come by. This will make it difficult for governments anywhere to fill say/do gaps effectively, given that some public grievances are becoming permanent.

Instead, it is the multistakeholder approach to addressing the infrastructural and physical vulnerabilities of the information environment that will be critical in achieving more information resilience. Conspiracy theories and disinformation have always existed and will continue to exist. But they must not be provided with an incubation space where they can create moral equivalents to facts, peer-reviewed expert judgment, and scientific argument. Though self-regulation should be prioritized over government regulation, there needs to be a realization that freedom of speech cannot be freedom of reach. That is to say, freedom of speech cannot become a thought-terminating cliché that enables disinformation and weaponized narratives to spin into virality, outperforming reason, fact, civil-societal consensus, and cohesion. Social media companies should not necessarily be asked to constrain what can and cannot be said. They should live up to their newly acquired responsibility to act as gatekeepers of "truth" by ensuring that all information has the ability to reach audiences based on veracity and not virality. Already, their algorithms are filtering, selecting, and prioritizing information. Yet this is not based on their veracity but rather on their virality or novelty. The very business model of social media companies thereby provides a constraint of the honest freedom of speech, as anger and hatred-induced narratives travel faster on social media than offline. Hence, the social media environment is already heavily mediated, putting into perspective the remarks of Facebook CEO Mark Zuckerberg about the platform as a "bastion of free expression."[12]

Social media companies can become the great moral equalizer when the democratization of the means of information is not just driven by "a swarm or herd of millions of dopamine-driven smartphone-users swiping through clickbait news on porcelain thrones" but by consumers and providers whose dopamine is not triggered by an overly algorithm-curated information environment.[13] Veracity should not be measured by "shares," "likes," or "engagements" but by a communal consensus that emerges from a truly balanced discourse where information should have a better chance than mis- and disinformation to reach the audience and where the scientific findings of a Nobel Prize laureate appear more credible than the rant of a conspiracy theorist. Actions taken by Twitter, Facebook, and YouTube during COVID-19 to label "disputed" information on the virus or cancel accounts of conspiracy theorists was a step in the right direction of ensuring that disinformation does not get the semblance of veracity.[14]

Social media can be and has been used for noble purposes, giving a voice to the voiceless, as during the Arab Spring. It has become a platform for mobilization in support of virtuous causes where reach was essential, as during the COVID-19 pandemic, when government needed to reach millions of people instantly. It has diversified discourse where nuance was absent and mobilized those to engage in politics who might have been otherwise left stranded by the reporting of traditional media outlets. Thus, the opportunities that come with the social media revolution are essential to protect but must not become an excuse to allow the exploitation of these platforms for nefarious ends.

The same is true for the ivory towers of research and knowledge centers, which play an integral part in informing policymakers and policy but have become subject to weaponized narrative campaigns as well. Both universities and think tanks need to exercise more vigilance when accepting donations or funding, ensuring that neither programs nor individual experts become potential surrogates of the agendas of external patrons. The integrity and trust in the sciences is essential as a critical authority in building information resilience and providing the necessary caveat and critical thinking to problems that might otherwise be polarized and politicized. Accepting that the sciences might not always be able to provide certainty in uncertain times and that a balanced argument is often more tentative than definite, the norms of reasoned scientific inquiry must not be sold out on the basis of pure relativism between facts and so-called alternative facts.

Finally, information resilience also needs to take into account the work of lobbyists and public relations firms, which often function as interlocutors between foreign governments and those who domestically spin narratives across media, academia, and policymaking. Especially when foreign governments are considered friendly, their outreach via public relations companies and lobbyists is often not regarded as problematic—allowing especially the Arab Gulf states to mobilize senior members of the policymaking nexus in Western capitals. The precedent set by the UAE's rather successful lobbying in Washington has now made it imperative for Saudi Arabia and Qatar to engage as heavily in public diplomacy in the United States so as not to lose ground. Though public diplomacy is not problematic at all, it becomes so when defensive messaging turns offensive and attacks individuals, foreign rivals, and policies. It is here that oversight mechanisms are required to ensure that public relations agents do not gain more influence on making foreign policy than the state's very own in-house advisers.

Information resilience then means limiting the reach and depth of the effect weaponized narratives can generate on attitudes, decisions, and behaviors of people on- and offline and both inside and outside policymaking circles. Communities are resilient when narratives bounce off by going through civil-societal discourse without creating a critical mass and momentum able to mobilize people to act. Therefore, it might be easier to create resilience to disinformation that is entirely nonfactual than it is to create resilience against weaponized narratives that hang on a thread of factuality—spinning storylines that are oversimplified and unnuanced, confuse correlations with causality, or lack any balance and critical reflection. In a contested information environment, a good narrative can transport disinformation effectively behind "enemy lines," giving the appearance of credibility if delivered via an authoritative outlet. Though distinguishing between fact and lie might be relatively simple, it is when a lie is wrapped in a palatable story that it can attract the critical mass required to generate a truth effect. Consequently, information resilience is achieved when weaponized narratives are unable to generate a critical mass beyond which their spread and reach as well as their mobilizing effect on- and offline can no longer be easily contained. That is, in resilient communities, weaponized narratives cannot consume a sufficiently great share of the public sphere to be accepted as a version of the truth. Because once a consensus builds, even if just in an echo chamber, narratives can be difficult to challenge, contest, and remove, which leads to polarization.

Hence, with infrastructural vulnerabilities directly affecting our sociopsychological vulnerabilities, communities need to respond collectively, particularly in liberal civil societies, to ensure that the public sphere retains its important mediating role in sociopolitics. The reason is that without a resilient information environment, civil society will take too long to rebound from weaponized narratives, undermining societal cohesion and discourse while breaking a common sense of "truth," which ultimately will take away our ability to speak truth to power.

NOTES

1. Moynihan, *Daniel Patrick Moynihan*, 2.
2. Bourne, "Time to Move."
3. Szabo, "Anti-Vaccine and Anti-Lockdown Movements."
4. Martin, "Coronavirus."
5. Wong, Rosenberg, and Barnes, "Chinese Agents."
6. Douhet, *Command*, 50.
7. Timberg, Dwoskin, and Albergotti, "Inside Facebook."
8. Stephan and Chenoweth, "Why Civil Resistance Works."
9. Levenson, "Today's Rampage."
10. Becket, "Armed Protesters."
11. Wright, "Trump Drops the Mother of All Bombs."
12. Paul, "Zuckerberg Defends Facebook."
13. Carr, *Shallows*, 2.
14. Seitz, "Twitter."

BIBLIOGRAPHY

Abouzeid, Rania. "Bouazizi: The Man Who Set Himself and Tunisia on Fire." *Time*, January 21, 2011.

Abrams, Steve. "Beyond Propaganda: Soviet Active Measures in Putin's Russia." *Connections: The Quarterly Journal* 15, no. 1 (2016).

Abramson, Seth. *Proof of Conspiracy*. New York: Simon & Schuster, 2019.

Agence France Presse. "Fact Checking: How We Work." April 2020. https://factcheck.afp.com/fact-checking-how-we-work.

Agnew, Harriet. "French 'Gilets Jaunes' Protests Have Stoked 'Fake News' Surge, Says Study." *Financial Times*, March 13, 2019.

Ainslie, Donald, and Annemarie Butler. *The Cambridge Companion to Hume's Treatise*. Cambridge: Cambridge University Press, 2015.

Akkad, Dania. "Revealed: UAE-Linked Donors Gave $3m to Democrats and Republicans after Trump Won." *Middle East Eye*, December 24, 2019. www.middleeasteye.net/news/revealed-uae-linked-donors-democrats-republicans.

Akrap, Doris. "Germany's Response to the Refugee Crisis Is Admirable. But I Fear It Cannot Last." *The Guardian*, September 6, 2015.

Al Asoomi, Mohammad. "Qatar Has a Lot to Answer for the Arab Spring." *Gulf News*. August, 23, 2017.

Al-Atrush, Samer, Benjamin Parkin, and Joseph Cotterill. "Ukraine Conflict: Social Media Campaigns in Africa and Asia Tap into Distrust of West." *Financial Times*, April 3, 2022.

Al-Azami, Usaama. *Islam and the Arab Revolutions*. London: Hurst, 2021.

Aldroubi, Mina. "UAE to Take International Lead on Soft Power." *The National*, December 27, 2018.

Alhussein, Eman. "Saudi First: How Hyper-Nationalism Is Transforming Saudi Arabia." *ECFR Policy Brief*, June 2019.

Ali, Lorraine. "How the US, Ukraine, and the Media Have Thrown a Wrench into Russia's Disinformation Machine." *Los Angeles Times*, March 10, 2022.

Al Jazeera. "Egypt Tightens Restrictions on Media, Social Networks." *Al Jazeera*, March 19, 2019.

Allenby, Braden R. "The Age of Weaponized Narrative, or, Where Have You Gone, Walter Cronkite?" *Issues* 33, no. 4 (Summer 2017).

Allenby, Bradley R., and Joel Garreau. "Weaponized Narrative Is the New Battlespace." *DefenceOne*, January 3, 2017. www.defenseone.com/ideas/2017/01/weaponized-narrative-new-battlespace/134284/.

Al Saeedi, Ahmad. سياسي ليبي: قطر وتركيا تواصلان دعم الإرهاب.. والإخوان تعرقل الانتخابات. *Al Ain*, January 26, 2019.

Al-Serori, Leila. "Wie die FPÖ Russland lieben lernte." *Basler Zeitung*, May 20, 2019.

Altemeyer, Richard. "The Other "Authoritarian Personality." *Advances in Experimental Social Psychology* 30 (1998): 47–91.

Alterman, Jon. "The Information Revolution and the Middle East." In *The Future Security Environment in the Middle East: Conflict, Stability, and Political Change*, edited by N. Bensahel and D. L. Byman. Santa Monica, CA: RAND, 2004.

———. "Mid-Tech Revolution." *Middle East Insight* 16, no. 3 (June–July 2001).

Amnesty International. "UAE: Global Call for Release of Prominent Human Rights Defender Ahmed Mansoor." *Amnesty International*, October 16, 2019.

Anderson, Lisa. "Fulfilling Prophecies: State Policy and Islamist Radicalism." In *Political Islam, Revolution, Radicalism or Reform?*, edited by John L. Esposito. Boulder, CO: Lynne Rienner, 1997.

Anonymous. "How to Spot a State-Funded Chinese Internet Troll." *Foreign Policy*, June 17, 2015.

Ansani, Andrea, and Daniele Vittorio. "About a Revolution: The Economic Motivations of the Arab Spring." *International Journal of Development and Conflict* 2, no. 3 (2012).

Archer, Bimpe. "Exiled Palestinian Politician Mohammed Dahlan Issues Libel Proceedings against Social Media Giants Facebook and Twitter in Dublin." *Irish Times*, September 26, 2017.

ARD. "Fake Science." *Das Erste*, July 23, 2018. www.daserste.de/information/reportage-dokumentation/dokus/exclusiv-im-ersten-fake-science-die-luegenmacher-102.html.

Arendt, Hannah. "Truth and Politics." In *Truth: Engagements across Philosophical Traditions*, edited by David Wood and Jose Medina. London: John Wiley & Sons, 2008.

Aristotle. *On Rhetoric*. Translated by George A. Kennedy. Oxford: Oxford University Press, 1991.

Asher-Schapiro, Avi, and Alex Emmons. "At Neocon Think Tank, Steve Bannon Bashes Qatar and Praises Saudi Arabia." *Intercept*, October 25, 2017.

Associated Press. "How the UAE's Effort to Turn Trump against Qatar Became a Focus of Mueller's Investigation." March 26, 2018.

Atlantic Council. *Chinese Discourse Power*. Washington, DC: Atlantic Council, 2020.

Austin, Lloyd James. "Psychological Operations." Joint Publication 3-13.2. Joint Doctrine Development Community, US Joint Forces Command, Chairman of the Joint Chiefs of Staff, Washington, DC, 2010.

Averill, James. "Emotions as Related to Systems of Behavior." In *Psychological and Biological Approaches to Emotion*, edited by Nancy L. Stein, Bennett Leventhal, and Tom Trabasso. Hove, UK: Psychology Press, 1990.

———. "Studies on Anger and Aggression." *American Psychologist*, November 1983.

Awan, Imran. "Cyber-Extremism: Isis and the Power of Social Media." *Social Science & Public Policy*, 2017.

Bacon, Francis. *Novum Organum: Or, True Suggestions for the Interpretation of Nature*. London: Pickering, 1844.

Baker, Peter. "Trump Now Sees Qatar as an Ally against Terrorism." *New York Times*, April 10, 2018.

Baldwin, Bird. T. "John Locke's Contributions to Education." *Sewanee Review* 21, no. 2 (April 1913).

Ball, James. "Big Tech Didn't Show Its Strength by Banning Trump from Social Media; It Showed Its Cowardice." *Independent*, January 11, 2021.

Bandurski, David. "China and Russia Are Joining Forces to Spread Disinformation." Brookings Tech Stream, March 11, 2022. www.brookings.edu/techstream/china-and -russia-are-joining-forces-to-spread-disinformation/.

Banse, Dirk, Florian Flader, and Uwe Müller. "Deutscher Putin-Unterstützer gibt den Russland-Experten." *Die Welt*, April 20, 2014.

Barnard, Anne. "A Man of God and Technology, Trying to Steady Libya." *New York Times*, September 16, 2011.

Barno, David, and Nora Bensahel. "Fighting and Winning in the 'Gray Zone.'" *War on the Rocks*, May 19, 2015.

Barrons, Genevieve. "Suleiman: Mubarak Decided to Step Down #egypt #jan25 OH MY GOD: Examining the Use of Social Media in the 2011 Egyptian Revolution." In *The Arab Spring: Critical Analyses*, edited by Khair El-Din Hasseb. London: Routledge, 2013.

Bar-Tal, Daniel. "Sociopsychological Foundations of Intractable Conflicts." *American Behavioral Scientist* 50, no. 11 (July 2007).

———. "Why Does Fear Override Hope in Societies Engulfed by Intractable Conflict, as It Does in the Israeli Society?" *Political Psychology* 22, no. 3 (2001).

Bartles, Charles. "Getting Gerasimov Right." *Military Review*, January–February 2016.

Bastos, Marco, and Dan Mercea. "The Brexit Botnet and Hyperpartisan Twitter." *Open-AIRE*, October 1, 2017.

Batchelor, Tom. "Marine Le Pen Insists Russian Annexation of Crimea Is Totally Legitimate." *Independent*, January 3, 2017.

Baumeister, Roy, and Brad Bushman. *Social Psychology and Human Nature, Comprehensive Edition*. Boston: Cengage, 2016.

Bayoumi, Yara. "UAE Islamist Group Had No Desire to Topple Government: Families." Reuters, July 2, 2013.

BBC News. "'Russian Meeting with Italy Populists' Investigated." July 11, 2019.

———. "Twitter Blocks French Government with Its Own Fake News Law." April 3, 2018.

BBC Three. "Do You Have a Gender Bias?" March 9, 2017. https://twitter.com/bbcthree /status/839883748514512896.

BBC Trending. "#BBCtrending: Are #GazaUnderAttack Images Accurate?" July 8, 2014. www.bbc.co.uk/news/blogs-trending-28198622.

———. "Syria War: The Online Activists Pushing Conspiracy Theories." April 19, 2018. www.bbc.co.uk/news/blogs-trending-43745629.

Beauchamp, Zack. "Meet the Shady Putin Crony Funding Russia's Troll Farm and Mercenary Army." Vox, February 26, 2018.

Beaumont, Peter. "Morsi 'Power Grab' Angers Egypt Opposition Groups." *Guardian*, November 23, 2012.

Beck, Ulrich. "Living in the Risk Society." *Economy and Society* 35, no. 3 (August 2006).

Becket, Lois. "Armed Protesters Demonstrate against COVID-19 Lockdown at Michigan Capitol." *Guardian*, April 30, 2020.

Bell, Daniel. *The End of Ideology*. Cambridge, MA: Harvard UP, 1960.

Bell, David A. "The Zelensky Myth: Why We Should Resist Hero-Worshipping Ukraine's President." *New Statesman*, March 24, 2022.

Bellin, Eva. "Reconsidering the Robustness of Authoritarianism in the Middle East. Lessons from the Arab Spring." *Comparative Politics* 44, no. 2 (2012).

Bendassolli, Pedro F. "Theory Building in Qualitative Research: Reconsidering the Problem of Induction." *Forum Qualitative Social Research* 14, no. 1, art. 25 (January 2013).

Benner, Katie, Marc Mazzetti, Ben Hubbard, and Mike Isaac. "Saudis' Image Makers: A Troll Army and a Twitter Insider." *New York Times*, October 20, 2018.

Bennett, L., and Steven Livingston. "The Disinformation Order: Disruptive Communication and the Decline of Democratic Institutions." *European Journal of Communication* 33, no. 2 (2018).

Berger, Jonah, and Katherine Milkman. "What Makes Online Content Viral?" *Journal of Marketing Research* 49, no. 2 (2011).

Bergman, Ronan, and Declan Walsh. "Egypt Is Using Apps to Track and Target Its Citizens, Report Says." *New York Times*, October 3, 2019.

Berkowitz, Dan. "Who Sets the Media Agenda? The Ability of Policymakers to Determine News Decisions." In *Public Opinion, the Press, and Public Policy*, edited by David Kennamer. Westport, CT: Praeger, 2018.

Bessi, Alessandro, Fabiana Zollo, Michela Del Vicario, Antonio Scala, Guido Caldarelli, and Walter Quattrociocchi. "Trend of Narratives in the Age of Misinformation." *Plos One* 10, no. 8 (2015).

Bezmenov, Yuri. "Psychological Warfare Subversion & Control of Western Society: Lecture Given in Los Angeles 1983." YouTube, www.youtube.com/watch?v=5gnpCqsXE 8g&t=1s.

Bhattacharjee, Yudhijit. "The Mind of a Con Man." *New York Times*, April 26, 2013.

Bigg, Claire. "Crimea Visit Spotlights Kremlin Sympathies beyond French Fringes." Radio Free Europe / Radio Liberty, July 29, 2015.

Bing, Christopher, and Joel Schectman. "Inside the UAE's Secret Hacking Team of American Mercenaries." Reuters, January 30, 2019.

Bloghardt, Lori P. "The Muslim Brotherhood on Trial in the UAE." *Policywatch* 2064, April 12, 2013.

Boot, Max, and Michael Doran. "Political Warfare." Policy Innovation Memorandum 33, June 2013.

Bourne, Ryan. "Time to Move on the Economy vs. Public Health Debate." CATO Institute Blog, March 27, 2020. www.cato.org/blog/time-move-economy-vs-public -health-debate.

Boyd, Danah. *Streams of Content, Limited Attention: The Flow of Information through Social Media*. New York: Web2.0 Expo, 2009. www.danah.org/papers/talks/Web2 Expo.html.

Boyd-Barrett, Oliver. "Understanding: The Second Casualty." In *Reporting War: Journalism in Wartime*, edited by Stuart Allan and Barbie Zelizer. London: Routledge, 2004.

Braddock, Kurt, and John Horgan. "Towards a Guide for Constructing and Disseminating Counternarratives to Reduce Support for Terrorism." *Studies in Conflict & Terrorism* 39, no. 5 (2016).

Bradshaw, Samantha, and Philip Howard. "Troops, Trolls and Troublemakers: A Global Inventory of Organized Social Media Manipulation." Working Paper 2017.12. Computational Propaganda Research Project, Oxford, 2017.

Bradley, John R. *After the Arab Spring: How the Islamists Hijacked the Middle East Revolts*. London: Palgrave Macmillan, 2012.

Brand, Alice G. "Hot Cognition: Emotions and Writing Behavior." *Journal of Advanced Composition* 6 (1985): 5–15.

Broockman, David, and Joshua Kalla. "The Manifold Effects of Patrisan Media on Viewers' Beliefs and Attitudes: A Field Experiment with Fox News Viewers." *OSF Preprints*, April 1, 2022.

Brüggemann, Michael. "Die Medien und die Klimalüge." In *Lügenpresse: Anatomie eines politischen Kampfbegriffs*, edited by Volker Lilienthal and Irene Nervala. Cologne: Kiepenheuer–Witsch, 2017.

Buchan, Glenn. *Information War and the Air Force: Wave of the Future? Current Fad?* Project Air Force Issue Paper. Santa Monica, CA: RAND, 1996.

Buckner, Elisabeth, and Lina Khatib. "The Martyrs' Revolutions: The Role of Martyrs in the Arab Spring." *British Journal of Middle Eastern Studies* 41, no. 4 (2014).

Bumer, Herbert. *Symbolic Interactionism*. Berkeley: University of California Press, 1969.

Burge, Tyler. *Origins of Objectivity*. Oxford: Oxford University Press, 2010.

Burke, Edmund. *A Philosophical Inquiry into the Origin of Our Ideas of the Sublime and Beautiful*. London: N. Hailes, 1824.

Bussola Institute. "Bussola Institute Honorary Board." July 7, 2020. www.bussolainstitute .org/people/bussola-institute-honorary-board/.

Butler, Desmond, and Tom LoBianco. "The Princes, the President and the Fortune Seekers." Associated Press, May 22, 2018.

Butter, David. "Sisi's Debt to His Gulf Arab Backers." Chatham House Research Paper, April 20, 2020. www.chathamhouse.org/2020/04/egypt-and-gulf/sisis-debt-his-gulf -arab-backers.

Buzan, Barry, Ole Wæver, and Jaap de Wilde. *Security: A New Framework for Analysis*. Boulder, CO: Lynne Rienner, 1998.

Cadwalladr, Carole. "Arron Banks, Brexit and the Russia Connection." *Guardian*, June 16, 2018.

Calabrese, Andrew. "Privatization of the Media." In *The International Encyclopedia of Communication*, edited by Wolfgang Donsbach. London: John Wiley, 2008.

Campbell, Bradley, and Jason Manning. *The Rise of Victimhood Culture*. New York: Palgrave, 2018.

Carlyle, Thomas. *On Heroes, Hero-Worship, and the Heroic in History*. London: Chapman & Hall, 1852.

Carr, Nicholas. *The Shallows: What the Internet Is Doing to Our Brains*. New York: W. W. Norton, 2011.

Casey, James. "The Mass Media and Democracy: Between the Modern and the Postmodern." *Journal of International Affairs* 47, no. 1 (1993).

Castells, Manuell. *Communication Power*. Oxford: Oxford University Press, 2013.

Cavatorta, Francesco, and Vincent Durac. *Civil Society and Democratization in the Arab World: The Dynamics of Activism*. London: Routledge, 2010.

CBS. "Richard A. Clarke: Warnings." *Real Time with Bill Maher*. June 30, 2017. www.you tube.com/watch?v=OCBJSmWY6nE.

Chalif, Rebecca. "Political Media Fragmentation: Echo Chambers in Cable News." *Electronic Media & Politics* 1, no. 3 (2011).

Chase, Michael, and James Mulvenon. *You've Got Dissent! Chinese Dissident Use of the Internet and Beijing's Counter-Strategies*. Santa Monica, CA: RAND, 2002.

Chazan, Guy. "Blue-Haired Vlogger Takes Aim at Angela Merkel's CDU." *Financial Times*, May 25, 2019.

Chekinov, Sergey G., and Sergey Bogdanov. "The Nature and Content of a New-Generation War." *Military Thought* 22, no. 4 (2013).

Cheng, Dean. "Winning without Fighting: The Chinese Psychological Warfare Challenge." Heritage Foundation Backgrounder 2821, July 11, 2013.

Chotiner, Isaac. "Why John Mearsheimer Blames the US for the Crisis in Ukraine." *New Yorker*, March 1, 2022.

Cialdini, Robert B., and Noah J. Goldstein. "Social Influence: Compliance and Conformity." *Annual Review of Psychology* 55 (2004).

Clyde & Co. *Defamation and Social Media in the UAE*. London: Clyde & Co., 2019. www.clydeco.com/insight/article/defamation-and-social-media-in-the-uae.

CNN. "Inside the KGB: An Interview with Retired KGB Maj. Gen. Oleg Kalugin—Cold War Experience." January 1998.

Cockburn, Harry. "Schools to Teach Children about Fake News and 'Confirmation Bias', Government Announces." *Independent*, July 15, 2019.

Cohen, Bernard. *Press and Foreign Policy*. Princeton, NJ: Princeton University Press, 2015.

Cohen, Florette, Daniel Ogilvie, Sheldon Solomon, Jeff Greenberg, and Tom Pyszczynski. "American Roulette: The Effect of Reminders of Death on Support for George W. Bush in the 2004 Presidential Election." *Analyses of Social Issues and Public Policy* 5, no. 1 (2005).

Colquhoun, David. "Publish-or-Perish: Peer Review and the Corruption of Science." *Guardian*, September 5, 2011.

Comey, James. *A Higher Loyalty*. New York: Macmillan, 2018.

Conger, Kate. "Twitter Has Labeled 38% of Trump's Tweets Since Tuesday." *New York Times*, November 5, 2020.

Connable, Ben, Jason H. Campbell, and Dan Madden. *Stretching and Exploiting Thresholds for High-Order War*. Santa Monica, CA: RAND, 2016.

Cook, John. "Understanding and Countering Misinformation about Climate Change." In *Deception, Fake News, and Misinformation Online*, edited by Innocent Chiluwa and Sergei Samoilenko. Hershey, PA: IGI Global, 2019.

Cook, Steven. "Sisi Isn't Mubarak—He's Much Worse." *Foreign Policy*, December 19, 2018.

Cornwell, Alexander. "Emerging Gulf State Cyber Security Powerhouse Growing Rapidly in Size, Revenue." Reuters, February 1, 2018.

Crano, Ricky d'Andrea. "Neoliberal Epistemology and the Truth in Fake News." *Angelaki* 23, no. 5 (2018).

Darcy, Oliver. "RT America Ceases Productions and Lays Off Most of Its Staff." CNN, March 4, 2022.

Davidson, Christopher. "Arab Nationalism and British Opposition in Dubai." *Middle Eastern Studies* 43, no. 6 (2007).

———. "A Tale of Two Desert Dynasties." *The Telegraph*, November 29, 2009.

———. "The UAE, Qatar and the Question of Political Islam." In *Divided Gulf: The Anatomy of a Crisis*, edited by Andreas Krieg. London: Palgrave, 2019.

Davidson, Michael. "Vaccination as a Cause for Autism: Myths and Controversies." *Dialogues in Clinical Neuroscience* 19, no. 4 (December 2017).

Day, Louis A. *Ethics in Media Communications: Cases and Controversies*. Boston: Cengage, 2005.

DCDC (Development, Concepts, and Doctrine Centre). *JDP02: UK Operations—The Defence Contribution to Resilience and Security*. 3rd ed. Shrivenham, UK: DCDC, 2017.

Dearing, James W., and Everett M. Rogers. "Agenda-Setting Research: Where Has It Been, Where Is It Going?" *Annals of the International Communication Association* 11, no. 1 (1988).

Dechene, Alice, Christoph Stahl, Joichim Hansen, and Michaela Wanke. "The Truth about the Truth: A Meta-Analytic Review of the Truth Effect." *Personality and Social Psychology Review* 14, no. 2 (2010).

Defty, Andrew. *Britain, American and Anti-Communist Propaganda, 1945–53*. London: Routledge, 2004.

Della Porta, Donatella. *Social Movements, Political Violence, and the State: A Comparative Analysis of Italy and Germany*. Cambridge: Cambridge University Press, 1995.

Delmar-Morgan, Alex, and David Miller. *The UAE Lobby: Subverting British Democracy?* London: Spinwatch, 2018.

Del Vicarioa, Michela, Alessandro Bessi, Fabiana Zollo, Fabio Petroni, Antonio Scala, Guido Caldarelli, H. Eugene Stanley, and Walter Quattrociocchi. "The Spreading of Misinformation Online." *PNAS* 113, no. 3 (January 19, 2016).

Dennett, Lydia. "The 'Foreign Agents' Law Paul Manafort Is Charged with Breaking Is Wildly Underenforced." *Vox*, November 3, 2017.

———. "Foreign Influence at the Witness Table?" www.pogo.org/investigation/2018/09 /foreign-influence-at-the-witness-table.

Denzau, Arthur, and Douglas North. "Shared Mental Models: Ideologies and Institutions." *Kyklos*, no. 1 (1994).

Descartes, Rene. *Discourse on the Method of Rightly Conducting the Reason, and Seeking Truth in the Sciences*, translated by John Veitch. London: Sutherland and Knox, 1850.

De Telegraaf. "Wilders verrast met Rusland-reis." November 22, 2017.

DeYoung, Karen. "How Thomas Barrack's Alleged Illegal Lobbying Shaped Trump's Policies in the Gulf." *Washington Post*, July 21, 2021.

DeYoung, Karen, and Ellen Nakashima. "UAE Orchestrated Hacking of Qatari Government Sites." *Washington Post*, July 16, 2017.

Deutsch, Karl, and Dieter Senghaas. "A Framework for a Theory of War and Peace." In *The Search for World Order*, edited by Quincy Wright, Albert Lepawsky, Edward Henry Buehrig, and Harold Dwight Lasswell. New York: Appleton-Century-Crofts, 1971.

DFRLab. "Libyan Hashtag Campaign Has Broader Designs: Trolling Qatar." *Medium*, July 31, 2019. https://medium.com/dfrlab/libyan-hashtag-campaign-has-broader -designs-trolling-qatar-8b2ba69c7334.

Diamond, Larry. "Liberation Technology." *Journal of Democracy* 21, no. 3 (July 2010).

Diamond, Larry, and Marc Plattner, eds. *Liberation Technology: Social Media and the Struggle for Democracy*. Baltimore: Johns Hopkins University Press, 2012.

Dickey, Lauren. "Confronting the Challenge of Online Disinformation in Taiwan." In *Taiwan*, edited by Pamela Kennedy and Jason Li. Washington, DC: Stimson Center, 2019.

Dilanian, Ken, and Kit Ramgopal. "Facebook Blocks Russia-Backed Accounts, but Other Sites Keep Churning Out Content Aimed at America." NBC News, October 9, 2020.

Diwan, Kirstin. "Who Is Sunni? Chechnya Islamic Conference Opens Window on Intra-Faith Rivalry." Arab Gulf State Institute, blog post, September 16, 2016.

Dogantekin, Vakkas. "Twitter Shuts Down Troll Armies of Saudi Arabia." United Arab Emirates, Anadolu Agency, September 20, 2019.

Douhet, Giulio. *The Command of the Air*, translated by Dino Ferrari. Washington, DC: Air Force History and Museums Program, 1998.

Dubov, Dimitry. *Active Measures of the USSR against the United States.* Kyiv: National Institute for Strategic Studies Ukraine, 2017.

Dugin, Aleksandr. "Network-Centric Wars: The New Theory of War—Theoretical Foundations of Network Wars." In *Network Wars: The Threat of a New Generation*, edited by Aleksandr Dugin. Moscow: International Eurasian Movement, 2009.

———. "Teoreticheskiye osnovy setevykh voyn." *Informatsionnye voyny* 1, no. 5 (2008).

Dweck, Carol S., and Joyce Ehrlinger. "Implicit Theories and Conflict Resolution." In *The Handbook of Conflict Resolution*, edited by M. Deutsch, P. Coleman, and E. Marcus. San Francisco: Jossey-Bass, 2006.

Economist. "The Gulf's Little Sparta." April 6, 2017.

Economy, Elisabeth. "The Great Firewall of China: Xi Jinping's Internet Shutdown." *Guardian*, June 29, 2018.

Eddy, Melissa, and Mark Scott. "Delete Hate Speech or Pay Up, Germany Tells Social Media Companies." *New York Times*, June 30, 2017.

Eickelman, Dale F., and Jon W. Anderson. "Preface to the Second Edition." In *New Media in the Muslim World: The Emerging Public Sphere*, edited by D. F. Eickelman and Jon W. Anderson. Bloomington: Indiana University Press, 2003.

———. "Redefining Muslim Publics." In *New Media in the Muslim World: The Emerging Public Sphere*, edited by D. F. Eickelman and Jon W. Anderson. Bloomington: Indiana University Press, 2003.

Eidelson, Roy, and Judy Eidelson. "Dangerous Ideas: Five Beliefs That Propel Groups toward Conflict." *American Psychologist* 58, no. 3 (2003).

El Errian, Essam. "What the Muslim Brothers Want." *New York Times*, February 9, 2011.

El Gomati, Anas. "The Libyan Revolution Undone: The Conversation Will Not Be Televised." In *Divided Gulf*, edited by Andreas Krieg. London: Palgrave, 2019.

Ellis, Emma. "Coronavirus Conspiracy Theories Are a Public Health Hazard." *Wired*, March 27, 2020.

Ellison, Sarah, and Elahe Izadi. "'Definitely Not the Results We Want': Facebook Staff Lamented 'Perverse Incentives' for Media." *Washington Post*, October 26, 2021.

Ellul, Jacques. *Propaganda: The Formation of Men's Attitudes.* New York: Vintage, 1973.

Elmasry, Mohamad. "Unpacking Anti-Muslim Brotherhood Discourse." *Jadaliyya*, June 28, 2013.

Encyclopaedia Britannica. *The Ideas That Made the Modern World.* London: Encyclopaedia Britannica, 2008.

Ennis, Stephen. "Dmitry Kiselyov: Russia's Chief Spin Doctor." BBC Monitoring, April 2, 2014.

Entman, Robert N. "Framing: toward Clarification of a Fractured Paradigm." *Journal of Communication* 43, no. 4 (1993).

Erickson, Amanda. "If Russia Today Is Moscow's Propaganda Arm, It's Not Very Good at Its Job." *Washington Post*, January 12, 2017.

Erikson, Robert, Norman R. Luttbeg, and Ken Tedin. *American Public Opinion*. New York: Macmillan, 1988.

European Commission. "Code of Practice on Disinformation." 2018. https://ec.europa.eu/digital-single-market/en/news/code-practice-disinformation.

———. "Last Intermediate Results of the EU Code of Practice against Disinformation." 2019. https://ec.europa.eu/digital-single-market/en/news/last-intermediate-results-eu-code-practice-against-disinformation,

Exoo, Calvin. *The Pen and the Sword: Press War and Terror in the 21st Century*. London: Sage, 2010.

Eysenck, Hans, J. *The Psychology of Politics*. London: Routledge, 1999.

Fabiani, Riccardo. "Tunisia's Leap into the Unknown." International Crisis Group, July 28, 2021. www.crisisgroup.org/middle-east-north-africa/north-africa/tunisia/tunisias -leap-unknown.

Fan, Rui, Jichang Zhao, Yen Chen, and Ke Xu. "Anger Is More Influential Than Joy: Sentiment Correlation in Weibo." *Plos One* 9, no. 10 (October 2014).

Farhad, Amin. "Has Iran's Presence in Iraq Marginalized Sunnis?" *Jerusalem Post*, February 29, 2020, www.jpost.com/opinion/has-irans-presence-in-iraq-marginalized -sunnis-619313.

Farrel, Theo. *The Norms of War*. London: Lynne Rienner, 2005.

Fazio, Lisa K. "Knowledge Does Not Protect against Illusory Truth." *Journal of Experimental Psychology: General* 144, no. 5 (2015).

Ferguson, A. "Plato's Simile of Light, Part II: The Allegory of the Cave (Continued)." *Classical Quarterly* 16, no. 1 (1922).

Ferrara, Emilio, Onur Varol, Clayton Davis, Filippo Menczer, and Allessandro Flammini. "The Rise of Social Bots." *Communications of the ACM* 59, no. 7 (2016).

Festinger, Leon. *A Theory of Cognitive Dissonance*. Stanford, CA: Stanford University Press, 1957.

Fiedler, Maria. "Russlands Spiel mit den Rechten." *Tagesspiegel*, April 9, 2019.

Filkins, Dexter. "A Saudi Prince's Quest to Remake the Middle East." *New Yorker*, April 9, 2018.

Fiske, Susan T., and Shelley E. Taylor. *Social Cognition*. New York: McGraw-Hill, 1984.

Fitzgerald, Chad W., and Aaron Brantly. "Subverting Reality: The Role of Propaganda in 21st-Century Intelligence." *International Journal of Intelligence and Counter-Intelligence* 30, no. 2 (2017).

Floridi, Luciano. *Information: A Very Short Introduction*. Oxford: Oxford University Press, 2010.

Foucault, Michel. "Truth and Power." In *Contemporary Sociological Theory*, edited by Craig J. Calhoun. New York: Blackwell, 2007.

FPC. "How the People's Republic of China Amplifies Russian Disinformation." US Department of State, April 27, 2022. www.state.gov/briefings-foreign-press-centers /how-the-prc-amplifies-russian-disinformation.

FPPMS (Forum for Promoting Peace in Muslim Societies). *Pursuit of Peace*. Translated by Tarek El Gawhary. Edited by Krista Bremer. Abu Dhabi: FPPMS, 2014.

France24. "Egypt's Rival Camps Wage Online Battle over Sisi." September 26, 2019.

Frankfurter Allgemeine Zeitung. "Schröder: Putin weiter lupenreiner Demokrat." March 7, 2012.

Freedman, Lawrence. "Defining War." In *The Oxford Handbook of War*, edited by Julian Lindely-French and Yves Boyer. Oxford: Oxford University Press, 2011.

———. "Strategic Studies and the Problem of Power." In *Strategy and International Politics: Essays in Honour of Sir Michael Howard*, edited by Lawrence Freedman, Paul Hayes, and Robert O'Neill. Oxford: Oxford University Press, 1992.

Freedman, Lawrence, and Srinath Raghavan. "Coercion." In *Security Studies: An Introduction*, edited by Paul D. Williams. Abingdon, UK: Routledge, 2018.

Freedom House. *Freedom on the Net 2018: The United Arab Emirates*. Washington, DC: Freedom House, 2018. https://freedomhouse.org/report/freedom-net/2018/united -arab-emirates.

Freeman, Ben. *Foreign Funding of Think Tanks in America*. Washington, DC: Center of International Policy, 2020.

———. "US Foreign Policy Is for Sale." *Nation*, February 21, 2019.

Frenkel, Sheera. "QAnon Is Still Spreading on Facebook, Despite a Ban." *New York Times*, December 18, 2020.

Fridman, Ofer. "Hybrid Warfare or Gibridnaya Voyna? Similar, but Different." *RUSI Journal*, April 3, 2017.

———. *Russian "Hybrid Warfare": Resurgence and Politicization*. Oxford: Oxford University Press, 2018.

Friedman, Thomas. "Saudi Arabia's Arab Spring, at Last." *New York Times*, November 23, 2017.

Fukuyama, Francis. "Against Identity Politics." *Foreign Affairs*, September/October 2018.

———. *Identity: The Demand for Dignity and the Politics of Resentment*. New York: Farrar, Straus & Giroux, 2018.

Fuller, John F. C. *Tanks in the Great Wars, 1914–1918*. London: Murray, 1920.

Galeotti, Mark. "Hybrid, Ambiguous, and Non-Linear? How New Is Russia's 'New Way of War'?" *Small Wars & Insurgencies* 27, no. 2 (2015).

———. "I'm Sorry for Creating the 'Gerasimov Doctrine.'" *Foreign Policy*, March 5, 2018.

Galtung, Johan. "Violence, Peace, and Peace Research." *Journal of Peace Research* 6, no 3 (1969).

Gaouette, Nicole, and Jennifer Hansler. "US to Treat Chinese State Media like an Arm of Beijing's Government." CNN, February 19, 2020.

Garret, Don. *Hume*. London: Routledge, 2015.

Gaub, Florence. "The Cult of ISIS." *Survival* 58, no. 1 (2016).

Gayer, Corinna, Shiri Landman, Eran Halperin, and Daniel Bar-Tal. "Overcoming Psychological Barriers to Peaceful Conflict Resolution: The Role of Arguments about Losses." *Journal of Conflict Resolution* 53, no. 6 (2009).

Gearty, Conor. *Terror*. London: Faber & Faber, 1992.

Gebauer, Mathias. "Aufklärung unerwünscht!" *Der Spiegel*, April 12, 2019.

Gerasimov, Valery. "The Value of Science in Foresight." *Voyenno-Promyshlennyy Kuryer* 8, no. 476 (February 27, 2013). www.vpk-news.ru/articles/14632.

Gerges, Farwaz. "The Irresistible Rise of the Muslim Brothers." *New Statesman*, November 28, 2011.

Gertz, Bill. "Security Fears about Infiltration by Terrorists." *Washington Times*, February 22, 2006.

Ghonim, Wael. *Revolution 2.0: The Power of the People Is Greater Than the People in Power*. Boston: Houghton Mifflin Harcourt, 2012.

Giles, Keir. *Handbook of Russian Information Warfare*. Rome: NATO Defence College, 2016.

Giles, Keir, and W. Hagestad. "Divided by a Common Language: Cyber Definitions in Chinese, Russian and English." Cyber Conflict (CyCon), 5th International Conference, 2013.

Giles, Keir, James Sherr, and Anthony Seaboyer. *Russian Reflexive Control*. Kingston, Canada: Royal Military College of Canada, 2018.

Godeo, Robert. "Troubled Tunisia: What Should We Do?" Cable EO 12958 from US Embassy in Tunis, July 17, 2009.

Gorodnichenko, Yuriy, Tho Pham, and Oleksandr Talavera. *Social Media, Sentiment, and Public Opinions: Evidence from #Brexit and #USElection*. NBER Working Paper 24631. Cambridge, MA: National Bureau of Economic Research, 2018.

Graham, David A. "Putin's Useful Idiots." *Atlantic*, February 24, 2022.

Grey, Colin. *The Strategy Bridge: Theory for Practice*. Oxford: Oxford University Press, 2010.

Griffin, Em. *A First Look at Communication Theory*. New York: McGraw-Hill, 2003.

Grim, Ryan. "Diplomatic Underground: The Sordid Double Life of Washington's Most Powerful Ambassador." *Intercept*, August 30, 2017.

———. "Gulf Government Gave Secret $20 Million Gift to DC Think Tank." *Intercept*, August 10, 2017.

Grim, Ryan, and Akbar Shahid Ahmed. "His Town." *Huffington Post*, September 2, 2015.

Grim, Ryan, and Jilani Zaid. "Hacked Emails Show Top UAE Diplomat Coordinating with Pro-Israel Think Tank against Iran." *Intercept*, June 3, 2017.

Grossmann, Shelby, Renee Di Nesta, Tara Keradpir, and Carly Miller. "Blame It on Iran, Qatar, and Turkey: An Analysis of a Twitter and Facebook Operation Linked to Egypt, the UAE, and Saudi Arabia." *Stanford Internet Observatory*, April 2, 2020.

Gunitsky, Seva. "Corrupting the Cyber-Commons: Social Media as a Tool of Autocratic Stability." *Perspectives on Politics* 13, no. 1 (March 2015).

Haaretz. "The Arab Spring Turned into Arab Winter." December 19, 2011.

Habermas, Jürgen. "The Public Sphere: An Encyclopaedia Article." Translated by Sara Lennox and Frank Lennox. *New German Critique* 3 (1974).

———. *The Structural Transformation of the Public Sphere*. Translated by Thomas Burger. Cambridge, MA: MIT Press, 1991.

———. "Wahrheitstheorien." In *Wirklichkeit und Reflexion*, edited by H. Fahrenbach. Pfüllingen: Neske, 1973.

Haller, Michael. "Transparenz schafft Vertrauen." In *Lügenpresse: Anatomie eines politischen Kampfbegriffs*, edited by Volker Lilienthal and Irene Nervala. Cologne: Kiepenheuer–Witsch, 2017.

Hamid, Shadi. "The Rise of Anti-Liberalism." *Atlantic*, February 20, 2018.

Hamid, Shadi, William McCants, and Rashid Dar. *Islamism after the Arab Spring: Between the Islamic State and the Nation-State*. Washington, DC: Brookings Institution Press, 2017.

Hamzawy, Amr. "Egyptian Liberals and Their Anti-Democratic Deceptions." In *Egypt and the Contradictions of Liberalism*, edited by Dalia Fahmy and Daanish Faruqi. London: Oneworld, 2016.

———. *Legislating Authoritarianism: Egypt's New Era of Repression*. Washington, DC: Carnegie Endowment for International Peace, 2017.

Hanafi, Safi. "The Arab Revolutions: The Emergence of a New Political Subjectivity." In *The Arab Spring: Critical Analyses*, edited by Khair El Din Hasseb. London: Routledge, 2013.

Hancock, Jeffrey T. "Psychological Principles for Public Diplomacy in an Evolving Information Ecosystem." In *Can Public Diplomacy Survive the Internet? Bots, Echochambers, and Disinformation*, edited by Shawn Powers and Markos Kounalakis. Washington, DC: Advisory Commission on Public Diplomacy, 2017.

Harris, Shane, Greg Miller, and Josh Dawley. "CIA Concludes Saudi Crown Prince Ordered Jamal Khashoggi's Assassination." *Washington Post*, October 15, 2019.

Hearst, David. "Exclusive: Dahlan Investigated by ICC for Links with Saif al-Islam Gaddafi." *Middle East Eye*, October 14, 2017.

Hedges, Matthew. *Reinventing the Sheikhdom: Clan, Power, and Patronage in Mohammad bin Zayed's UAE*. London: Hurst, 2021.

Hegel, Georg Wilhelm Friedrich. *The Phenomenology of Mind*, translated by James Black Baillie. Mineola, NY: Dover, 2003.

Helft, Miguel, and David Barboza. "Google Shuts China Site in Dispute over Censorship." *New York Times*, March 22, 2010.

Helmus, Todd, Elizabeth Bodine-Baron, Andrew Radin, Madeline Magnuson, Joshua Mendelsohn, William Marcellino, Andriy Bega, and Zev Winkelman. *Russian Social Media Influence*. Santa Monica, CA: RAND, 2018.

Hendricks, Vincent, and Mads Vestergaard. "Verlorene Wirklichkeit? An der Schwelle zur postfaktischen Demokratie." *Aus Politik und Zeitgeschichte: Warheit* 67, no. 13 (2017).

Herb, Michael. "Kuwait and the United Arab Emirates." In *Politics and Society in the Contemporary Middle East*, edited by Michele Penner Angrist. Boulder, CO: Lynne Rienner, 2010.

Hermida, Alfred. "Nothing but the Truth: Redrafting the Journalistic Boundary of Verification." In *Boundaries of Journalism*, edited by Matt Carlson and Seth C. Lewis. London: Routledge, 2015.

Herrman, John. "In the Trenches of the Facebook Election." *Awl*, November 21, 2014. www.theawl.com/2014/11/in-the-trenches-of-the-facebook-election/.

Hoffman, Frank G. "Examining Complex Forms of Conflict: Gray Zone and Hybrid Challenges." *Prism* 7, no. 4 (2018).

———. "Hybrid Warfare and Challenges." *Joint Forces Quarterly*, no. 52 (1st quarter of 2009).

Holmes, Amy. *Coups and Revolutions: Mass Mobilization, the Egyptian Military, and the United States from Mubarak to Sisi*. Oxford: Oxford University Press, 2019.

Holmes, Oliver, and Alexander Dziadosz. "Special Report: How Syria's Islamists Govern with Guile and Guns." Reuters, June 20, 2013.

Holpuch, Amanda. "Jimmy Carter: 'Illegitimate' Trump Only President Because of Russian Meddling." *Guardian*, June 28, 2019.

Howard, Philip, Bharath Ganesh, and Dimitra Liotsiou. *The IRA, Social Media, and Political Polarization in the United States, 2012–2018*. Oxford: Computational Propaganda Research Project, 2018.

Huang, Eustance. "Facebook Removes 'Coordinated' Fake Accounts in UAE, Egypt, Nigeria, and Indonesia." CNBC, October 3, 2019.

Hudson Institute. "Countering Violent Extremism: Qatar, Iran, and the Muslim Brotherhood." October 23, 2017. www.hudson.org/events/1475-countering-violent-extremism-qatar-iran-and-the-muslim-brotherhood102017.

Hughes, Adam. "Highly Ideological Members of Congress Have More Facebook Followers Than Moderates Do." Pew Research Center, 2017. www.pewresearch.org/fact-tank/2017/08/21/highly-ideological-members-of-congress-have-more-facebook-followers-than-moderates-do/.

Human Rights Watch. "Egypt: Rab'a Killings Likely Crimes against Humanity." August 12, 2014.

Hurst, Daniel. "Australian Universities 'Blindsided' by Government Seeking Powers to Cancel Global Agreements." *Guardian*, September 1, 2020.

Hussain, Murtaza. "How the UAE Tried to Silence a Popular Arab Spring Activist." *Intercept*, October 21, 2014.

Ignatius, David. "The US Military Is Quietly Launching Efforts to Deter Russian Meddling." *Washington Post*, February 7, 2019.

Intelligence and Security Committee of Parliament. "Russia." House of Commons, HC 632, July 21, 2020.

International Crisis Group. "Rebels without a Cause: Russia's Proxies in Eastern Ukraine." *Europe Report* 254, July 16, 2019.

International Telecommunications Union. "Estimated Internet Users 2000 to 2009." June 24, 2014. www.itu.int/ITUD/ict/statistics/material/excel/EstimatedInternet Users00-09.xls.

Jamieson, Kathleen H. *Cyberwar: How Russian Hackers and Trolls Helped Elect a President*. Oxford: Oxford University Press, 2020.

Joint Publication 3-13. "Information Operations." US Joint Forces Command, Chairman of the Joint Chiefs of Staff, Washington, DC, 2012.

Jones, Andrew, and Gerald Kovacich. *Global Information Warfare: The New Digital Battlefield*. London: CRC Press, 2016.

Jonsson, Oscar. *The Russian Understanding of War*. Washington, DC: Georgetown University Press, 2019.

Jonsson, Oscar, and Robert Seely. "Russian Full-Spectrum Conflict: An Appraisal after Ukraine." *Journal of Slavic Military Studies* 28 (2015).

Joscelyn, Thomas. "Osama Bin Laden's Files: The Arab Revolutions." *Long War Journal*, March 3, 2015. www.longwarjournal.org/archives/2015/03/osama-bin-ladens-files -the-arab-revolutions.php.

Jost, John. "The End of the End of Ideology." *American Psychologist* 61, no. 7 (October 2006).

Jost, John, Christopher Federico, and Jaime Napier. "Political Ideology: Its Structure, Functions, and Elective Affinities." *Annual Review of Psychology* 60 (2009).

Jost, John, Brian Nosek, and Samuel Gosling. "Ideology: Its Resurgence in Social, Personality, and Political Psychology. *Perspectives on Psychological Science* 3, no. 2 (2008).

Kader, Binsal. "Internet Penetration in Middle East Tripled in 8 Years." *Gulf News*, October 28, 2017.

Kahneman, Daniel, Paul Slovic, and Amos Tversky. *Judgment under Uncertainty: Heuristics and Biases*. Cambridge: Cambridge University Press, 1982.

Kaiman, Jonathan. "China Cracks Down on Social Media with Threat of Jail for 'Online Rumours.'" *Guardian*, September 10, 2013.

Kakutani, Michiko. "The Death of Truth: How We Gave Up on Facts and Ended Up with Trump." *Guardian*, July 14, 2018.

Kane, Sean. "Barqa Reborn? Eastern Regionalism and Libya's Political Transition." In *The Libyan Revolution and Its Aftermath*, edited by Peter Cole and Brian McQuinn. Oxford: Oxford University Press, 2015.

Kant, Immanuel. *Critique of Pure Reason*, translated by J. M. D. Meiklejohn. London: Henry Bohn, 1855.

Kaphle, Anup. "The Foreign Desk in Transition." In *The New Global Journalism: Foreign Correspondence in Transition*, edited by Ann Cooper and Taylor Owen. New York: Tow Center for Digital Journalism, 2015.

Karlsen, Geir Hågen. *Divide and Rule: Ten Lessons about Russian Political Influence Activities in Europe*. New York: Palgrave, 2019.

Karnitschnig, Matthew. "Putin's Useful German Idiots." *Politico*, March 28, 2022.

Kassir, Sami. *Being Arab*. London: Verso Books, 2013.

Kazarin, Pavel. "The Nature of War as a Scientific Category." *Military Thought* 11, no. 4 (2002).

Kello, Lucas. *The Virtual Weapon and International Order*. New Haven, CT: Yale University Press, 2018.

Keltner, Dacher, and Robert J. Robinson. "Extremism, Power, and the Imagined Basis of Social Conflict." *Current Directions in Psychological Science* 5 (1996).

Kennan, George F. *The Inauguration of Organized Political Warfare*. Redacted version, April 30, 1948. Washington, DC: History and Public Policy Program Digital Archive, Woodrow Wilson International Center for Scholars, 1948.

———. *Measures Short of War: The George F. Kennan Lectures at the National War College, 1946–1947*, edited by Giles D. Harlow and George C. Maerz. Washington, DC: National Defense University Press, 1991.

Kerr, Simeon. "UAE Blacklists 83 Groups as Terrorists." *Financial Times*, November 16, 2014.

Ketchley, Neil. *Egypt in a Time of Revolution*. Cambridge: Cambridge University Press, 2017.

Khashoggi, Jamal. "Saudi Arabia Wasn't Always This Repressive. Now It's Unbearable." *Washington Post*, September 18, 2017.

Khatib, Dania. *The Arab Lobby and the US: Factors for Success and Failure*. London: Routledge, 2015.

Kianpour, Suzanne. "Emails Show UAE-Linked Effort against Tillerson." BBC News, March 5, 2018.

Kinzer, Stephen. *All the Shah's Men: An American Coup and the Roots of Middle East Terror*. New York: Wiley, 2008.

Kirby, Jen. "Yes, Russia Is Interfering in the 2020 Election." Vox, September 21, 2020.

Kirchherr, Julian. "Why We Can't Trust Academic Journals to Tell the Scientific Truth." *Guardian*, June 6, 2017.

Kirkpatrick, David. "The Most Powerful Arab Ruler Isn't MBS. It's MBZ." *New York Times*, June 2, 2019.

———. "Recordings Suggest Emirates and Egyptian Military Pushed Ousting of Morsi." *New York Times*, March 2, 2015.

———. "Saudi Arabia Arrests 11 Princes, including Billionaire Alwaleed bin Talal." *New York Times*, November 4, 2017.

———. "The White House and the Strongman." *New York Times*, July 27, 2019.

Kirkpatrick, David, and Mark Mazzetti. "How 2 Gulf Monarchies Sought to Influence the White House." *New York Times*, March 21, 2018.

Kissinger, Henry. "How the Enlightenment Ends." *Atlantic*, June 2018.

Kitson, Frank. *Low-Intensity Operations: Subversion, Insurgency and Peacekeeping*. London: Faber & Faber, 2010.

Klus, Adam. "Myatezh Voina: The Russian Grandfather of Western Hybrid Warfare." *Small Wars Journal*, November 2016.

Kraidy, Marwan, and Marina Krikorian. "The Revolutionary Public Sphere: The Case of the Arab Uprisings." *Communication and the Public* 2, no. 2 (2017).

Kramer, Andrew. "To Battle Fake News, Ukrainian Show Features Nothing but Lies." *New York Times*, February 26, 2017.

Kramer, Xenia, Tim Kaiser, Stefan Schmidt, Jim Davidson, and Vladimir Lefebvre. "From Prediction to Reflexive Control." *International Interdisciplinary Scientific and Practical Journal, Reflexive Processes and Control* 2, no. 1 (2003).

Krieg, Andreas. "Divided over Narratives: The New Fault Line in the Arab World." Middle East Institute, July 24, 2019.

———. "Gulf Security Policy after the Arab Spring: Considering Changing Security Dynamics." In *The Small Gulf States*, edited by Khalid Almezaini and Jean Marc Rickli. London: Routledge: 2016.

———. "How Saudi Arabia and the UAE Are Silencing Dissent." *Middle East Eye*, February 11, 2019.

———. "Laying the 'Islamist' Bogeyman to Rest." *LobeLog*, October 10, 2019.

———. "Macron's 'Crusade' against Islam Reveals a Dangerous Double Standard." *Middle East Eye*, November 3, 2020.

———. "Never Mind Russia, the UAE Has United with AIPAC to Capture Washington." *Middle East Eye*, March 13, 2018.

———. "On the Sinister Objectives of Abu Dhabi's 'Crusade' against Political Islam." *Middle East Eye*, January 21, 2020.

———. *Sociopolitical Order and Security in the Arab World*. London: Palgrave, 2017.

———. "Trump and the Middle East: 'Barking Dogs Seldom Bite.'" *Insight Turkey* 19, no. 3 (2017).

———. "The UAE's War over Narratives in Brussels." *LobeLog*, April 12, 2019.

———. "The Weaponization of Narratives amid the Gulf Crisis." In *Divided Gulf: The Anatomy of a Crisis*, edited by Andreas Krieg. London: Palgrave, 2019.

Krieg, Andreas, and Jean-Marc Rickli. "Surrogate Warfare: The Art of War in the 21st Century?" *Defence Studies* 18, no. 2 (2018).

———. *Surrogate Warfare: The Transformation of War in the 21st Century*. Washington, DC: Georgetown University Press, 2019.

Kristol, Irving. *Neoconservatism: The Autobiography of an Idea*. New York: Simon & Schuster, 1995.

Krüger, Uwe. "Medien Mainstream." In *Lügenpresse: Anatomie eines politischen Kampfbegriffs*, edited by Volker Lilienthal and Irene Nervala. Cologne: Kiepenheuer–Witsch, 2017.

Kurbjuweit, Dirk. "Der Wutbürger." *Der Spiegel*, October 11, 2010.

Kuypers, Jim. *Press Bias and Politics: How the Media Frame Controversial Issues*. Westport, CT: Greenwood, 2002.

Lakatos, Imre. "Science and Pseudoscience." *Methodology of Scientific Research Programmes: Philosophical Papers* 1 (1980).

Lamb-Sinclair, Ashley. "When Narrative Matters More Than Fact." *Atlantic*, January 9, 2017.

Lamond, James, and Talia Dessel. "Democratic Resilience." Center for American Progress, September 3, 2019. www.americanprogress.org/issues/security/reports/2019/09/03/473770/democratic-resilience/.

Lamore, Charles. "Descartes and Skepticism." In *The Blackwell Guide to Descartes' Meditations*, edited by Stephen Gaukroger. London: John Wiley & Sons, 1999.

Lange-Ionatamišvili, Elina. *Analysis of Russia's Information Campaign against Ukraine*. Riga: NATO StratCom Centre of Excellence, 2015.

Le Bon, Gustave. "The Leaders of Crowds and Their Means of Persuasion." In *The Crowd: A Study of the Popular Mind*. 2nd ed. Dunwoody, GA: Norman S. Berg, 1897.

Lerner, Jennifer, Ye Li, Piercarlo Valdesolo, and Karim Kassam. "Emotion and Decision Making." *Annual Review of Psychology* 66 (2015).

Levenson, Michael. "Today's Rampage at the Capitol, as It Happened." *New York Times*, January 6, 2021.

Lewandowsky, Stephan, Werner Stritzke, Alexander Freund, Klaus Oberauer, and Joachim Krueger. "Misinformation, Disinformation, and Violent Conflict." *American Psychologist* 68, no. 7 (October 2013).

Lewis, Michael, and Carolyn Saarni. "Culture and Emotions." In *The Socialization of Emotions*, edited by Michael Lewis and Carolyn Saarni. New York: Plenum, 1985.

LIAS (Leuven Institute for Advanced Study). "Dr. Aref Nayed, Chairman of LIAS, Speaks at 2015 WEF." 2015. www.liasinstitute.com/en/news-read/Aref_Nayed_at_WEF.

Libicki, Martin C. "The Convergence of Information Warfare." *Strategic Studies Quarterly* 11, no. 1 (Spring 2017).

———. *What Is Information Warfare?* Washington, DC: National Defense University Press, 1995.

Lichter, Robert, Stanley Rothman, and Linda Lichter. *The Media Elite: America's New Power-Brokers.* Bethesda, MD: Adler & Adler, 1986.

Liddell Hart, Basil Henry. *Strategy.* Santa Barbara, CA: Praeger, 1967.

Linebarger, Paul. *Psychological Warfare.* New York: Duell, Sloan & Pearce, 1954.

Lister, Charles. "Dynamic Stalemate: Surveying Syria's Military Landscape." Policy Brief, Brookings Institution, Doha, 2014.

Lord, Carnes. "Public Diplomacy and Soft Power." In *Strategic Influence: Public Diplomacy, Counterpropaganda, and Political Warfare*, edited by Michael Waller. Washington, DC: Institute of World Politics Press, 2008.

Lynch, Cecelia. "A Neo-Weberian Approach to Studying Religion and Violence." *Millennium: Journal of International Studies* 43, no. 1 (2014).

Lynch, Marc. *Voices of a New Arab Public: Iraq, Al Jazeera, and Middle East Politics Today.* New York: Columbia University Press, 2006.

MacFarquhar, Neil. "Inside the Russian Troll Factory: Zombies and a Breakneck Pace." *New York Times*, February 18, 2018.

———. "Yevgeny Prigozhin, Russian Oligarch Indicted by US, Is Known as 'Putin's Cook.'" *New York Times*, February 16, 2018.

Mackintosh, Eliza. "Finland Is Winning the War on Fake News; What It's Learned May Be Crucial to Western Democracy." CNN, May 2019. https://edition.cnn.com/interactive/2019/05/europe/finland-fake-news-intl/.

Malinova, Olga. "Constructing the 'Usable Past': The Evolution of the Official Historical Narrative in Post-Soviet Russia." In *Cultural and Political Imaginaries in Putin's Russia*, edited by Niklas Bernsand and Barbara Törnquist-Plewa. London: Brill, 2019.

Maliukevičius, Nerijus. "Tools of Destabilization: Kremlin's Media Offensive in Lithuania." *Journal on Baltic Security* 1, no. 1 (2015).

Mandaville, Peter. *Global Political Islam.* London: Routledge, 2007.

Manheim, Jarol B. *Strategic Public Diplomacy and American Foreign Policy: The Evolution of Influence.* Oxford: Oxford University Press, 1994.

Manson, Katrina, Henry Foy, and Hannah Murphy. "Biden, Putin and the New Era of Information Warfare." *Financial Times*, June 15, 2021.

Marczak, Bill, and Nicholas Weaver. "China's Great Cannon." Citizen Lab, Research Brief, April 2015.

Marschall, Stefan. "Lügen und Politik im Postfaktischen Zeitalter." *Aus Politik und Zeitgeschichte: Wahrheit* 67, no. 13 (2017).

Marshall, Joshua. "Remaking the World: Bush and the Neoconservatives." *New York Times*, October 21, 2003.

Martin, Alexander. "Coronavirus: The 5G Conspiracy Theory Just Won't Go Away— Here's Why It's Nonsense." Skynews, April 21, 2020.

Marwa, Morgan. "How Surveillance, Trolls, and Fear of Arrest Affect Egypt's Journalists." Committee to Protect Journalists, June 12, 2017.

Mason, Rowena. "Egypt Crisis: UK Will Not Take Sides, Says William Hague." *Guardian*, August 19, 2013.

Mazzetti, Mark, Adam Goldman, Ronen Bergman, and Nicole Perlroth. "A New Age of Warfare: How Internet Mercenaries Do Battle for Authoritarian Governments." *New York Times*, March 21, 2019.

Mazzetti, Mark, David Kirkpatrick, and David Goldman. "Adviser to Emirates with Ties to Trump Aides Is Cooperating with Special Counsel." *New York Times*, March 6, 2018.

Mazzetti, Mark, Nicole Perlroth, and Ronen Bergman. "It Seemed like a Popular Chat App; It's Secretly a Spy Tool." *New York Times*, December 22, 2019.

McAdam, Doug, and Dieter Rucht. "The Cross-National Diffusion of Movement Ideas." *Annals of the American Academy of Political and Social Science* 528 (July 1993).

McCarthy, Niall. "China Now Boasts More Than 800 Million Internet Users and 98% of Them Are Mobile." *Forbes*, August 23, 2018.

McClosky, Herbert, and John Zaller. *The American Ethos: Public Attitudes toward Capitalism and Democracy*. Cambridge, MA: Harvard University Press, 1984.

McCornack, Steven, and Malcom Parks. "Deception Detection and Relationship Development: The Other Side of Trust." *Annals of the International Communication Association* 9, no. 1 (1986).

McGeehan, Nicholas. "The Men behind Man City: A Documentary Not Coming Soon to a Cinema Near You." *Medium*, December 18, 2017. https://medium.com/@NcGeehan /the-men-behind-man-city-a-documentary-not-coming-to-a-cinema-near -you-14bc8e393e06.

McGeehan, Timothy, P. "Countering Russian Disinformation." *Parameters* 48, no. 1 (Spring 2018).

McGuire, William J., and Demetrios Papageorgis. "The Relative Efficacy of Various Types of Prior Belief-Defense in Producing Immunity against Persuasion." *Journal of Abnormal and Social Psychology* 62, no. 2 (1961).

Mchangama, Jacob, and Joelle Fiss. "Germany's Online Crackdowns Inspire the World's Dictators." *Foreign Policy*, November 6, 2019.

McKernan, Bethan. "Saudi Police Arrest Three More Women's Rights Activists." *Independent*, May 23, 2019.

Merill, Jamie. "A Qatari Exile, a Spin War, and a 'Cack-Handed' Push for a Coup." *Middle East Eye*, September 13, 2017.

Merill, Jeremy B., and Will Oremus. "Five Points for Anger, One for a 'Like': How Facebook's Formula Fostered Range and Misinformation." *Washington Post*, October 26, 2021.

Merton, Robert K. "The Normative Structure of Science." In *The Sociology of Science: Theoretical and Empirical Investigations*, edited by Robert K. Merton. Chicago: University of Chicago Press, 1973.

———. "A Note on Science and Democracy." *Journal of Legal and Political Sociology* 1 (1942).

Messner, Evgeny. *Myatezh: Imya Tret'yey Vsemirnoy*. Buenos Aires: Institute for the Study of the Problems of War and Peace Named after Prof. General N. N. Golovin, 1960.

———. *Vseminaya Myatezhevoyna*. Buenos Aires: Institute for the Study of the Problems of War and Peace Named after Prof. General N. N. Golovin, 1971.

Michaelson, Ruth. "Egypt: Children Swept Up in Crackdown on Anti-Sisi Protests." *Guardian*, October 8, 2019.

Michaelson, Ruth, and Michael Safi. "#Disinformation: The Online Threat to Protest in the Middle East." *Guardian*, December 15, 2019.

Middle East Eye. "Pro-Saudi Think Tank in Washington Shuts Down." July 30, 2019.

———. "'A Surprise Trip': UAE Royal Adviser Resurfaces 10 Days after Reported Arrest." January 27, 2017.

Miller, Carl. "Inside the British Army's Secret Information Warfare Machine." *Wired*, November 14, 2018.

Milliken, Jennifer. "The Study of Discourse in International Relations." *European Journal of International Relations* 5, no. 2 (1999).

Milyo, Jeffrey, and Tim Groseclose. "A Measure of Media Bias." *Quarterly Journal of Economics* 120, no. 5 (November 2005).

Ministry of Communication and Information Technology. "Saudi Arabia Is the Most Twitter-Crazy Country in the World: *Business Insider*." October 15, 2019. www.mcit .gov.sa/en/media-center/news/91426.

Mishra, Pankaj. *Age of Anger: A History of the Present*. New York: Farrar, Straus & Giroux, 2017.

Mittermaier, Amira. "Death and Martyrdom in the Arab Uprisings: An Introduction." *Ethnos: Journal of Anthropology*, 2014.

Mocanu, Delia, Luca Rossi, Qian Zhang, Marton Karsai, and Walter Quattrociocchi. "Collective Attention in the Age of (Mis)information." *Computers in Human Behavior* 51 (2015).

Montague, James, and Tariq Panja. "Ahead of Qatar World Cup, a Gulf Feud Plays Out in the Shadows." *New York Times*, February 1, 2019.

Morozov, Evgeny. *The Net Delusion: How Not to Liberate the World*. New York: Penguin Books, 2011.

Moscovici, Serge. "Notes towards a Description of Social Representations." *European Journal of Social Psychology* 18 (1988).

Mosebach, Bernd. "Klimastiftung und Nord Stream 2–Neue Dokumente: Schwesig in Erklärungsnot." *ZDF*, April 15, 2022. www.zdf.de/nachrichten/politik/schwesig -nordstream2-klimastiftung-ukraine-krieg-russland-100.html.

Moynihan, Daniel Patrick. *Daniel Patrick Moynihan: A Portrait in Letters of an American Visionary*, edited by Steve Weisman. New York: PublicAffairs, 2010.

Mueller, Robert S., III. *Report on the Investigation into Russian Interference in the 2016 Presidential Election*. Vol. I of II. Washington, DC: US Department of Justice, 2019.

Myers, Steven Lee, and Paul Mozur. "China Is Waging a Disinformation War against Hong Kong Protesters." *New York Times*, August 13, 2019.

Na'eem, Jeenah. "The Egyptian Crisis: Two Coups Later the Military Is Still in Control." In *Promoting Progressive African Thought Leadership*, edited by Aziz Pahad and Garth le Pere. Pretoria: Africa Institute of South Africa, 2015.

Nardelli, Alberto. "Revealed: The Explosive Secret Recording That Shows How Russia Tried to Funnel Millions to the 'European Trump.'" *Buzzfeed*, July 10, 2019.

Narula, Sunil. "Psychological Operations (PSYOPs): A Conceptual Overview." *Strategic Analysis* 28, no. 1 (2004).

NBC News. "Confronting Russian President Vladimir Putin." Megyn Kelly, March 9, 2018.

Nelson, Elisabeth, Robert Orttung, and Anthony Livshen. "Measuring RT's Impact on YouTube." *Russian Analytical Digest* 177, December 8, 2015.

Nemtsova, Anna. "A Chill in the Moscow Air." *Newsweek*, February 5, 2006.

Nervala, Irene. "Lügenpresse: Begriff ohne jede Vernunft?" In *Lügenpresse: Anatomie eines politischen Kampfbegriffs*, edited by Volker Lilienthal and Irene Nervala. Cologne: Kiepenheuer–Witsch, 2017.

Nicander, Lars. "The Role of Think Tanks in the US Security Policy Environment." *International Journal of Intelligence and CounterIntelligence* 28, no. 3 (2015).

Nietzsche, Friederich. "Truth and Lies in a Non-Moral Sense." In *Philosophy and Truth: Selection from Nietzsche's Notebooks of the Early 1870s*. Edited and translated by Daniel Breazeale. Atlantic Highlands, NJ: Humanities Press, 1979; orig. pub. 1873.

Nissen, Thomas E. "Terror.com: ISS's Social Media Warfare in Syria and Iraq." *Contemporary Conflicts: Military Studies Magazine* 2 (2014).

Noueihed, Lin, and Alex Warren. *The Battle for the Arab Spring: Revolution, Counter-Revolution, and the Making of a New Era*. New Haven, CT: Yale University Press, 2013.

Nuseibah, Ghanem. "Fighting Jew Hate and Muslim Hate Together." *Times of Israel Blog*, October 31, 2019. https://blogs.timesofisrael.com/fighting-jew-hate-and-muslim -hate-together/.

Nye, Joseph S. "The Information Revolution and Soft Power." *Current History* 113, no. 759 (2014).

Nyhan, Brendan. "Why the Fact-Checking at Facebook Needs to Be Checked." *New York Times*, October 23, 2017.

Oliphant, James. "Trump Offers to Mediate Talks on Qatar Crisis." Reuters, September 7, 2017.

Olsson, Eva-Karin. "Public Diplomacy as a Crisis Communication Tool." *Journal of International Communication* 19, no. 2 (2013).

Omand, Sir David. "The Threats from Modern Digital Subversion and Sedition." *Journal of Cyber Policy* 3, no. 1 (2018).

Oppenheim, Lawrence. *International Law: A Treatise*. Vol. 2: *War and Neutrality*. London: Longmans, Green & Co., 1906.

Orgad, Liav. *The Cultural Defense of Nations*. Oxford: Oxford University Press, 2015.

Orwell, George. *1984*. Boston: Houghton Mifflin Harcourt, 1983.

Ott, Brian. "The Age of Twitter: Donald J. Trump and the Politics of Debasement." *Critical Studies in Media Communication* 34, no. 1 (2017).

Owen, Roger. *State Power and Politics in Making of Modern Middle East*. London: Routledge, 2000.

Owen-Jones, Marc. *Digital Authoritarianism in the Middle East: Deception, Disinformation, and Social Media*. London: Hurst, 2022.

———. "Hacking, Bots and Information Wars in the Qatar Spat." *Washington Post*, June 7, 2017.

———. "Propaganda, Fake News, and Fake Trends: The Weaponization of Twitter Bots in the Gulf Crisis." *International Journal of Communication* 13 (2019).

Oxford Dictionary. "Post Truth." https://en.oxforddictionaries.com/definition/post-truth.

Pacepa, Ion Mihai, and Ronald J. Rychlak. *Disinformation*. Washington, DC: WND Books, 2013.

Paret, Peter. *Understanding War*. Princeton, NJ: Princeton University Press, 1992.

Parker, Claire. "Influential Voices in Egypt, Saudi Arabia and UAE Celebrate Tunisia Turmoil as Blow to Political Islam." *Washington Post*, July 27, 2021.

Parry, Ryan. "Top Arab Spy and Prince's Conduit to the Kremlin Were at the Seychelles Meeting between Trump Donor Erik Prince and Russian Oligarch." *Daily Mail*, December 3, 2018.

Paul, Christopher, and Miriam Matthews. "The Russian 'Firehose of Falsehood' Propaganda Model." *RAND Perspective*, 2016.

Paul, Kari. "Zuckerberg Defends Facebook as Bastion of 'Free Expression' in Speech." *Guardian*, October 18, 2019.

Paul, Katie, and, Foo Yun Chee. "Twitter Suspends Saudi Royal Adviser Qahtani, Fake Gulf Accounts." Reuters, September 20, 2019.

PBS Frontline. "Putin's Revenge." October 25, 2017. www.pbs.org/wgbh/frontline/film /putins-revenge/.

Pennycook, Gordon, Tyrone Cannon, and David G. Rand. "Prior Exposure Increases Perceived Accuracy of Fake News." *Journal of Experimental Psychology: General* 147, no. 12 (2018).

Perrigio, Billy. "How the EU's Sweeping New Regulations against Big Tech Could Have an Impact beyond Europe." *Time*, December 30, 2020.

Pesenti, Marina, and Peter Pomerantsev. *How to Stop Disinformation Lessons from Ukraine for the Wider World*. London: Legatum Institute, 2016.

Peters, Michael A., and Tina Besley. "The Royal Society, the Making of 'Science,' and the Social History of Truth." *Educational Philosophy and Theory* 51, no. 3 (2019).

Piatov, Philip. "Moskaus Propaganda gibt's jetzt auch auf Deutsch." *Die Welt*, November 27, 2017.

Pincus, Walter. "Neutron Killer Warhead Buried in ERDA Budget." *Washington Post*, June 6, 1977.

Plato. *Republic*. Translated by Robin Waterfield. Oxford: Oxford University Press, 1994.

Plous, Scott. *The Psychology of Judgment and Decision Making*. New York: McGraw-Hill, 1993.

Polyakova, Alina. "Strange Bedfellows: Putin and Europe's Far Right." *World Affairs* 177, no. 3 (October 2014).

Pomerantsev, Peter. "Russia: A Postmodern Dictatorship?" *Global Transitions*, October 2013.

Pomerantsev, Peter, and Michael Weiss. "The Menace of Unreality: How the Kremlin Weaponizes Information, Culture and Money." *Interpreter*, November 2014.

Popper, Karl. *Conjectures and Refutations: The Growth of Scientific Knowledge*. London: Routledge, 2014.

Postman, Neil. "The Information Environment." *Review of General Semantics* 36, no. 3 (Fall 1979).

Pöttker, Horst. "Die Aufgabe Öffentlichkeit respektieren." In *Lügenpresse: Anatomie eines politischen Kampfbegriffs*, edited by Volker Lilienthal and Irene Nervala. Cologne: Kiepenheuer–Witsch, 2017.

Powell, Lauren. "Counter-Productive Counterterrorism: How Is the Dysfunctional Discourse of Prevent Failing to Restrain Radicalisation?" *Journal of Deradicalization*, Fall 2016.

Pryor, Lisa. "How to Counter the Circus of Pseudoscience." *New York Times*, January 5, 2018.

Qassemi, Sultan. "UAE's Reformed Foreign Ministry a Pioneer in the Region." Middle East Institute, April 11, 2017.

Qiu, Linda. "Fingerprints of Russian Disinformation: From AIDS to Fake News." *New York Times*, December 12, 2017.

Radvanyi, Jarol. "Introduction to Psyops." In *Psychological Operations and Political Warfare in Long-Term Strategic Planning*, edited by Janos Radvanyi. New York: Praeger, 1990.

Ramesh, Randeep. "UAE Told UK: Crack Down on Muslim Brotherhood or Lose Arms Deals." *Guardian*, November 6, 2015.

Rawnsley, Adam. "Right-Wing Media Outlets Duped by a Middle East Propaganda Campaign." *Daily Beast*, July 7, 2020. www.thedailybeast.com/right-wing-media-outlets -duped-by-a-middle-east-propaganda-campaign.

Reilley, Robert. "Conducting a War of Ideas with Public Diplomacy: An Insider's View." In *Strategic Influence: Public Diplomacy, Counterpropaganda, and Political Warfare*, edited by Michael Waller. Washington, DC: Institute of World Politics Press, 2008.

Reinemann, Carten. "Die Vertrauenskrise der Medien: Fakt oder Fiktion?" In *Lügenpresse: Anatomie eines politischen Kampfbegriffs*, edited by Volker Lilienthal and Irene Nervala. Cologne: Kiepenheuer–Witsch, 2017.

Rettig, Jessica. "Death Toll of 'Arab Spring.'" *US News & World Report*, November 8, 2011.

Reuter, Christoph. "Russlands perfider Feldzug gegen die Wahrheit." *Der Spiegel*, December 21, 2017.

Reuters. "Addiction and Intrigue: Inside the Saudi Palace Coup." July 19, 2017.

———. "Saudi Arabia Arrests Prominent Cleric Safar al-Hawali: Activists." July 21, 2018.

———. "Turkey Adds Former Palestinian Politician Dahlan to Most Wanted List." December 13, 2019.

———. "UAE Bans Expressions of Sympathy towards Qatar—Media." June 7, 2017.

Revel, Jean-François. "Can the Democracies Survive?" *Commentary*, June 1984.

Rheingold, Howard. *Smart Mobs: The Next Social Revolution*. New York: Basic Books, 2002.

Richey, Mason. "Contemporary Russian Revisionism: Understanding the Kremlin's Hybrid Warfare and the Strategic and Tactical Deployment of Disinformation." *Asia Europe Journal* 16 (2018).

Rid, Thomas. *Active Measures: The Secret History of Disinformation and Political Warfare*. London: Profile Books, 2020.

———. *Cyber War Will Not Take Place*. Oxford: Oxford University Press, 2013.

Risen, James. "Secrets of History: The CIA in Iran: A Special Report—How a Plot Convulsed Iran in '53 (and in '79)." *New York Times*, April 16, 2000.

Roberts, David. "Mosque and State." *Foreign Affairs*, March 18, 2016.

Roberts, Dexter. *China's Disinformation Strategy*. Washington, DC: Atlantic Council, 2020.

Robinson, Linda, Todd C. Helmus, Raphael Cohen, Alireza Nader, Andrew Radin, Madeline Magnuson, and Katya Migacheva. *Modern Political Warfare: Current Practices and Possible Responses*. Santa Monica, CA: RAND, 2018.

Robinson, Nick. "The Foreign Agents Registration Act Is Broken." *Foreign Policy*, July 22, 2019.

Robinson, Piers. "Researching US Media State Relations and Twenty-First-Century Wars." In *Reporting War: Journalism in Wartime*, edited by Stuart Allan and Barbie Zelizer. London: Routledge, 2004.

Rolfe, Brooke. "Sydney University Professor Slammed as an 'Embarrassment to Academia.'" *Daily Mail*, September 4, 2017.

Romanoff, Larry. "China's Coronavirus: A Shocking Update—Did the Virus Originate in the US?" Center for Research on Globalization, March 4, 2020. www.globalresearch.ca/china-coronavirus-shocking-update/5705196.

Romerstein, Herbert. "Disinformation as a KGB Weapon in the Cold War." *Journal of Intelligence History* 1, no. 1 (2001).

Ronfeldt, Daniel, and John Arquilla. *Whose Story Wins?* Santa Monica, CA: RAND, 2020.

Rosen, James. "Arab Spring Optimism Gives Way to Fear of Islamic Rise." Fox News, October 28, 2011. www.foxnews.com/politics/2011/10/28/arab-spring-optimism-gives-way-to-fear-islamic-rise.html.

Rosenau, Jon N. *States, Sovereignty, and Diplomacy in the Information Age.* Washington, DC: US Institute of Peace, 1999.

Rosenau, William. *Subversion and Insurgency.* Santa Monica, CA: RAND, 2007.

Ross, Thomas. "Honduras Wins Secret CIA Base." *Sun Times*, November 21, 1971.

Roy, Jo. "'Polis' and 'Oikos' in Classical Athens." *Greece & Rome* 46, no. 1 (April 1999).

Rousseau, Jean Jacques. *The Social Contract or Principles of Political Right*, translated by G. D. H. Cole. Mineola, NY: Courier Dover, 2003; orig. pub. 1762.

RT. "RT Weekly TV Audience Grows by More Than a Third over 2 Years." *Russia Today*, April 3, 2018. www.rt.com/about-us/press-releases/ipsos-market-research-rt/.

Rugge, Fabio. "Mind Hacking: Information Warfare in the Cyber Age." Instituto per GLI Studi di Politica Internazionale, January 11, 2018. www.ispionline.it/it/pubblicazione/mind-hacking-information-warfare-cyber-age-19414.

Rugh, William A. *The Arab Press: News Media and Political Process in the Arab World.* Syracuse: Syracuse University Press, 1987.

Rui Fan, Jichang Zhao, Yan Chen, and Ke Xu. "Anger Is More Influential Than Joy: Sentiment Correlation in Weibo." *Plos One* 9, no. 10 (2014).

Russian Presidency. *Указ Президента Российской Федерации от 10.01.2000 г. № 24.* Moscow: Kremlin, 2000.

Ryan, Maria. *Full-Spectrum Dominance: Irregular Warfare and the War on Terror.* Stanford, CA: Stanford University Press, 2020.

Sachsman, David B., and David W. Bulla. *Sensationalism: Murder, Mayhem, Mudslinging, Scandals, and Disasters in 19th-Century Reporting.* London: Transaction, 2013.

Salem, Ola, and Hassan Hassan. "Arab Regimes Are the World's Most Powerful Islamophobes." *Foreign Policy*, March 29, 2019.

Sampson, Wallace. "Antiscience Trends in the Rise of the 'Alternative Medicine' Movement." *Annals of the New York Academy of Science*, June 24, 1996.

Satariano, Adam, and Alba Davey. "Burning Cell Towers, Out of Baseless Fear They Spread the Virus." *New York Times*, April 10, 2020.

Scales, Robert H. "Clausewitz and World War IV." *Military Psychology* 21, no. 1 (2009): S23–S35.

Schadlow, Nadia. "Peace and War, the Space Between." *War on the Rocks*, August 18, 2014.

Schantzer, Jonathan. *The Muslim Brotherhood's Global Threat.* Washington, DC: FDD, 2017.

Schantzer, Jonathan, and Kate Havard. "By Hosting Hamas, Qatar Is Whitewashing Terror." *Newsweek*, May 11, 2017.

Schmidt, Brian C., and Michael C. Williams. "The Bush Doctrine and the Iraq War: Neoconservatives versus Realists." *Security Studies* 17, no. 2 (2008).

Schneider, Norbert. "Zwei mal drei macht vier." In *Lügenpresse: Anatomie eines politischen Kampfbegriffs*, edited by Volker Lilienthal and Irene Nervala. Cologne: Kiepenheuer–Witsch, 2017.

Schneier, Bruce. "Toward an Information Operations Kill Chain." *Lawfare Blog*, April 24, 2019. www.lawfareblog.com/toward-information-operations-kill-chain.

Schoultz, Lars. *That Infernal Little Cuban Republic: The United States and the Cuban Revolution*. Chapel Hill: University of North Carolina Press, 2009.

Schwartz, Oscar. "You Thought Fake News Was Bad? Deep Fakes Are Where Truth Goes to Die." *Guardian*, November 12, 2018.

Scott-Geddes, Arthur. "UAE Embassy Appoints Former British Envoy Alistair Burt as Emirates Society Chairman." *The National*, December 18, 2019.

Seddon, Max. "Documents Show How Russia's Troll Army Hit America." *BuzzFeed*, June 2, 2014. www.buzzfeed.com/maxseddon/documents-show-how-russias-troll-army-hit-america#31fidzl.

Seib, Philip. *The Al Jazeera Effect: How the New Global Media Are Reshaping World Politics*. Lincoln, NE: Potomac Books, 2008.

Seitz, Amanda. "Twitter to Label Disputed COVID-19 Tweets." Associated Press, May 11, 2020.

Selliaas, Andreas, and Pal Ødegård. "Mr Fuller Goes to Washington." *Josimar Football*, February 6, 2019. http://josimarfootball.com/mr-fuller-goes-to-washington/.

Serani, Deborah. "If It Bleeds, It Leads: The Clinical Implications of Fear-Based Programming in News Media." *Psychoanalysis & Psychotherapy* 24, no. 4 (Winter 2008).

Sest, Natalie, and Evita March. "Constructing the Cyber-Troll: Psychopathy, Sadism, and Empathy." *Personality and Individual Differences* 119 (2017).

Shapin, Steven. *The Social History of Truth: Civility and Science in Seventeenth-Century England*. Chicago: University of Chicago Press, 2014.

Shapiro, Samantha. "Revolution, Facebook-Style." *New York Times Magazine*, January 22, 2009.

Shaw, Martin. "Conceptual and Theoretical Frameworks for Organised Violence." *International Journal of Conflict and Violence* 3, no. 1 (2009).

Sheline, Annelle. "Oman's Smooth Transition Doesn't Mean Its Neighbors Won't Stir Up Trouble." *Foreign Policy*, January 23, 2020.

Shih, Gerry, Emily Rauhala, and Lena H. Sun. "Early Missteps and State Secrecy in China Probably Allowed the Coronavirus to Spread Farther and Faster." *Washington Post*, February 1, 2020.

Shoemaker, Pamela, Martin Eichholz, Kim Euyni, and Branda Wrigley. "Individual and Routine Forces in Gatekeeping." *Journalism and Mass Communication Quarterly* 78, no. 2 (2001).

Shoemaker, Pamela, and Timothy Voss. *Gatekeeping Theory*. New York: Routledge, 2009.

Shuster, Simon. "Why Russia Can Claim Victory as Trump Casts Doubt on the US Presidential Vote." *TIME*, November 6, 2020.

Simon, Herbert. "Motivational and Emotional Controls of Cognition." *Psychological Review* 74, no. 1 (January 1967).

Singer, Peter W., and Emerson T. Brooking. *Like War: The Weaponization of Social Media*. New York: Houghton Mifflin Harcourt, 2018.

Smith, David, and Sabrina Siddiqui. "Gulf Crisis: Trump Escalates Row by Accusing Qatar of Sponsoring Terror." *Guardian*, June 9, 2017.

Smith, Jordan. "Is This Professor 'Putin's American Apologist'?" *Chronicle of Higher Education*, November 15, 2017.

Smith, Lee. "A Coming Arab Winter?" Hudson Institute. *Weekly Standard*, June 6, 2011.

Smith, Paul A. *On Political War*. Washington, DC: National Defense University Press, 1989.

Soage, Ana N., and Jorge F. Granganillo. "The Muslim Brothers in Egypt." In *The Muslim Brotherhood: The Organization and Policies of a Global Islamist Movement*, edited by Barry Rubin. New York: Palgrave, 2010.

Sonwalkar, Prasun. "Out of Sight, Out of Mind?" In *Reporting War: Journalism in Wartime*, edited by Stuart Allan and Barbie Zelizer. London: Routledge, 2004.

Spencer, Richard. "UAE Was behind Tunisian Power Grab, Claims Speaker." *The Times*, July 31, 2021.

Spjut, R. J. "Defining Subversion." *British Journal of Law and Society* 6, no. 2 (Winter 1979).

Sputnik News. "Sputnik Latvia Traffic Surges after .lv Domain Ban." April 7, 2016. www .sputniknews.com/russia/20160407/1037629017/sputnik-latvia-traffic-domain.html.

Stanley, Jason. "In Defence of Truth, and the Threat of Disinformation." In *Can Public Diplomacy Survive the Internet? Bots, Echochambers, and Disinformation*, edited by Shawn Powers and Markos Kounalakis. Washington, DC: Advisory Commission on Public Diplomacy, 2017.

Stephan, Maria J., and Erica Chenoweth. "Why Civil Resistance Works." *International Security* 33, no. 1 (Summer 2008).

Stephens, Mitchell. *A History of News*. Oxford: Oxford University Press, 2007.

Steward, Emily. "Russian Election Interference Is Far from Over." Vox, February 19, 2018.

Stockmann, Daniela, and Ting Luo. "Which Social Media Facilitate Online Public Opinion in China?" *Problems of Post-Communism* 64 (2017).

Stone, Jon. "Nigel Farage and Brexit Party Vote against EU Resolution to Stop Russian Election Meddling." *Independent*, October 10, 2019.

Strachan, Hew, and Sibylle Scheipers. "Introduction." In *The Changing Character of War*, edited by Hew Strachan and Sibylle Scheipers. Oxford: Oxford University Press, 2010.

Stroud, Barry. "The Goal of Transcendental Arguments." In *Transcendental Arguments: Problems and Prospects*, edited by Robert Stern. Oxford: Oxford University Press, 1999.

Sunstein, Cass R. "The Daily We: Is the Internet Really a Blessing for Democracy?" *Boston Review*, 2001. http://bostonreview.net/forum/cass-sunstein-internet-bad-democracy.

Sun Tzu. *The Art of War*. New York: Penguin Books, 2008.

SWR. "Kritik an Mainzer Nahost-Experte Prof. Günter Meyer." October 8, 2018.

Szabo, Liz. "The Anti-Vaccine and Anti-Lockdown Movements Are Converging, Refusing to Be 'Enslaved.'" *Los Angeles Times*, April 24, 2020.

Taylor, Philip M. *Global Communications, International Affairs and the Media since 1945*. London: Routledge, 1997.

———. *Munitions of the Mind*. Manchester: Manchester University Press, 2003.

Ter Veer, Ben. "The Struggle against the Deployment of Cruise Missiles: The Learning Process of the Dutch Peace Movement." *Bulletin of Peace Proposals* 19, no. 2 (1988).

Tetlock, Philip E., and Ariel Levi. "Attribution Bias: On the Inconclusiveness of the Cognition-Motivation Debate." *Journal of Experimental Social Psychology* 18, no. 1 (1982): 68–88.

Thomas, Elise. "As the Coronavirus Spreads, Conspiracy Theories Are Going Viral Too." *Foreign Policy*, April 14, 2020.

Thomas, Timothy. "Information Security Thinking: A Comparison of US, Russian, and Chinese Concepts.'" Nuclear Strategy and Peace Technology International Seminar on Nuclear War and Planetary Emergencies, August 2001.

———. "Russia's Reflexive Control Theory and the Military." *Journal of Slavic Military Studies* 17, no. 2 (2004).

Thöne, Eva. "Der Weiß-Schwarz-Denker." *Der Spiegel*, April 24, 2017.

Timberg, Craig. "New Report on Russian Disinformation, Prepared for the Senate, Shows the Operation's Scale and Sweep." *Washington Post*, December 17, 2018.

———. "Spreading Fake News Becomes Standard Practice for Governments across the World." *Washington Post*, July 17, 2017.

Timberg, Craig, Elizabeth Dwoskin, and Reed Albergotti. "Inside Facebook, Jan. 6 Violence Fueled Anger, Regret over Missed Warning Signs." *Washington Post*, October 22, 2021.

Toler, Aric. "Details on Newly Uncovered GRU Online Personas." *Bellingcat*, December 26, 2017. https://www.bellingcat.com/news/uk-and-europe/2017/12/26/details -newly-uncovered-gru-online-personas.

Torbakov, Igor. "'Middle Continent' or 'Island Russia': Eurasianist Legacy and Vadim-Tsymburskii's Revisionist Geopolitics." In *Cultural and Political Imaginaries in Putin's Russia*, edited by Niklas Bernsand and Barbara Törnquist-Plewa. London: Brill, 2019.

Törnberg, Petter. "Echo Chambers and Viral Misinformation: Modeling Fake News as Complex Contagion." *Plos One* 13, no. 9 (2018).

Trager, Eric. *Arab Fall: How the Muslim Brotherhood Won and Lost Egypt in 891 Days.* Washington, DC: Georgetown University Press, 2016.

———. "The Muslim Brotherhood Is the Root of the Qatar Crisis." *Atlantic*, July 2, 2017.

Trew, Bell. "Bee Stung: Was Jamal Khashoggi the First Casualty in a Saudi Cyberwar?" *Independent*, October 20, 2019.

Tromblay, Darren. "Intelligence and the Intelligentsia: Exploitation of US Think Tanks by Foreign Powers." *International Journal of Intelligence and CounterIntelligence* 31, no. 1 (2018).

Tuch, Hans N. *Communicating with the World: US Public Diplomacy Overseas.* New York: St. Martin's Press, 1990.

UK Ministry of Defence. "Allied Joint Doctrine for Psychological Operations." *AJP-3.10.1,* 2014.

———. "Information Advantage." *Joint Concept Note* 2/18. London: UK Ministry of Defence, 2018.

Ulrichsen, Kristian. "Perceptions and Divisions in Security and Defense Structures in Arab Gulf States." In *Divided Gulf: The Anatomy of a Crisis*, edited by Andreas Krieg. London: Palgrave, 2019.

Unger, Craig. *American Kompromat.* New York: Penguin Books. 2021.

United States Senate. "Putin's Asymmetric Assault on Democracy in Russia and Europe: Implications for US National Security." *Committee on Foreign Relations of the US Senate Report,* January 18, 2018.

United States of America v. Elena Alekseevna Khusyaynova. AO 91 (Rev. I 1/1 I) Criminal Complaint. 2018. www.justice.gov/opa/press-release/file/1102316/download.

United States of America v. Al Malik Alshahhi et al. 1:21-cr-00371, US District Court for the Eastern District of New York (Brooklyn). 2021. www.justice.gov/opa/press -release/file/1413381/download/.

Unkelbach, Christian, and Sarah C. Rom. "A Referential Theory of the Repetition-Induced Truth Effect." *Cognition* 160 (2017).

UN Special Rapporteur on the Promotion and Protection of the Right to Freedom of Opinion and Expression. "Report to the United Nations Human Rights Council on a Human Rights Approach to Platform Content Regulation" (A/HRC/38/35). 2018. https://freedex.org/wp-content/blogs.dir/2015/files/2018/05/G1809672.pdf.

US Department of Defense. *DOD Dictionary of Military and Associated Terms*. Washington, DC: US Department of Defense, 2019.

US Department of State. "Pillars of Russia's Disinformation and Propaganda Ecosystem." Global Engagement Center, August 2020.

US Government Publication Office. *The Muslim Brotherhood's Global Threat: Hearing before the Subcommittee on National Security of the Committee on Oversight and Government Reform of the House of Representatives*. Washington, DC: US Government Publication Office, 2018.

Van der Linden. "The Conspiracy-Effect: Exposure to Conspiracy Theories (about Global Warming) Decreases Pro-Social Behavior and Science Acceptance." *Personality and Individual Differences* 87 (2015).

Van Herpen, Marcel. *Putin's Propaganda Machine: Soft Power and Russian Foreign Policy*. Lanham, MD: Rowman & Littlefield, 2015.

Van Inwagen, Peter. "It Is Wrong Everywhere, Always and for Anyone to Believe Anything upon Insufficient Evidence." In *The Possibility of Resurrection and Other Essays in Christian Apologetics*, edited by Peter van Inwagen. Boulder, CO: Westview Press, 1997.

Vasara, Antti. *Theory of Reflexive Control: Origins, Evolution and Application in the Framework of Contemporary Russian Military Strategy*. Helsinki: National Defence University, 2020.

Vickers, Andrew. "Alternative Cancer Cures: 'Unproven' or 'Disproven'?" *Cancer Journal for Clinicians* 54, no. 2 (March–April 2004).

Von Clausewitz, Carl. *On War*, translated by Michael Howard and Peter Paret. Oxford: Oxford University Press, 2007.

Vosoughi, Soroush, Deb Roy, and Sinan Aral. "The Spread of True and False News Online." *Science* 359 (2018): 1146–51.

Walden, Max. "Coronavirus Began in US, Not China, Chinese Official Suggests." ABC News, March 13, 2020. www.abc.net.au/news/2020-03-13/coronavirus-originated-in-united-states-china-official-says/12055278.

Waldman, Paul. "How Trump and Republicans Wield the Politics of Victimhood." *Washington Post*, October 29, 2018.

Walker, Shaun. "'We Can Find You Anywhere': The Chechen Death Squads Stalking Europe." *Guardian*, September 21, 2019.

Walker, Tim. "Mandrake: Remainers Are Put on Hold by the BBC." *New European*, February 6, 2019. www.theneweuropean.co.uk/top-stories/mandrake-on-the-remain-campaigners-dropped-last-minute-by-bbc-1-5881776.

Waller, Michael. "The American Way of Propaganda: Lessons from the Founding Fathers." In *Strategic Influence: Public Diplomacy, Counterpropaganda, and Political Warfare*, edited by Michael Waller. Washington, DC: Institute of World Politics Press, 2008.

Walsh, Declan, and Nada Rashwan. "'We're at War': A Covert Social Media Campaign Boosts Military Rulers." *New York Times*, September 6, 2019.

Wang, Cindy, and Samson Ellis. "Taiwan Shuts Pro-China TV Channel in Battle Over Press Freedom." *Bloomberg*, November 18, 2020.

Ward, Lee R. A. "Psychological Barriers to Dispute Resolution." *Advances in Experimental Social Psychology* 27 (1995).

Warzel, Charlie. "He Predicted the 2016 Fake News Crisis; Now He's Worried about an Information Apocalypse." *BuzzFeed*, February 11, 2018.

Waterson, Jim, and Saeed Deghan. "Independent's Deal with Saudi Publisher Back under Spotlight." *Guardian*, October 19, 2018.

Wei-Chun Wang, Nadia M. Brashier, Erik A. Wing, Elizabeth J. Marsh, and Roberto Cabeza. "On Known Unknowns: Fluency and the Neural Mechanisms of Illusory Truth." *Journal of Cognitive Neuroscience* 28, no. 5 (2016).

Weigel, Moira. "Political Correctness: How the Right Invented a Phantom Enemy." *Guardian*, November 30, 2016.

Weinberg, David. *Qatar and Terror Finance*. Washington, DC: FDD, 2017.

Wesslau, Frederik. "Putin's Friends in Europe." European Council on Foreign Relations, *Commentary*, October 19, 2016. www.ecfr.eu/article/commentary_putins_friends_in_europe7153.

West, Darrel. "How to Combat Fake News and Disinformation." Brookings Institution, December 18, 2017.

———. *Internet Shutdowns Cost Countries $2.4 Billion Last Year*. Washington, DC: Brookings Center for Technology Innovation, 2016.

Wharton, Bruce. "Remarks on 'Public Diplomacy in a Post-Truth Society.'" In *Can Public Diplomacy Survive the Internet? Bots, Echochambers, and Disinformation*, edited by Shawn Powers and Markos Kounalakis. Washington, DC: Advisory Commission on Public Diplomacy, 2017.

White, Gordon. "Civil Society, Democratization and Development (II): Two Country Cases." *Democratization* 2, no. 2 (1995).

White, Jon. "Dismiss, Distort, Distract, and Dismay: Continuity and Change in Russian Disinformation." Free University Brussels, Institute for European Studies Policy Brief, 2016.

———. "Russian Disinformation." Free University Brussels, Institute for European Studies Policy Brief, 2016.

Wickham, David. *The Muslim Brotherhood: Evolution of an Islamist Movement*. Princeton, NJ: Princeton University Press, 2013.

William & Associates. *Egyptian Public Opinion Survey, April 14–27, 2011*. Salem, MA: International Republican Institute, 2011.

Wilson, Glenn D., ed. *The Psychology of Conservatism*. London: Academic Press, 1973.

Wilson Center. "How Egypt Unraveled: Two Wild Weeks." Woodrow Wilson International Center for Scholars. July 8, 2013. www.wilsoncenter.org/article/how-egypt-unraveled-two-wild-weeks.

Winter, Richard. "Truth or Fiction: Problems of Validity and Authenticity in Narratives of Action Research." *Educational Action Research* 10, no. 1 (2002).

Wintour, Patrick. "Donald Trump Tweets Support for Blockade Imposed on Qatar." *Guardian*, June 6, 2017.

Wired. "Inside the British Army's Secret Information Warfare Machine." November 14, 2018. www.wired.co.uk/article/inside-the-77th-brigade-britains-information-warfare-military.

Wong, Edward, Matthew Rosenberg, and Julien Barnes. "Chinese Agents Helped Spread Messages That Sowed Virus Panic in US, Officials Say." *New York Times*, April 22, 2020.

Woolley, Samuel. "Computational Propaganda and Political Bots: An Overview." In *Can Public Diplomacy Survive the Internet? Bots, Echochambers, and Disinformation*, edited by Shawn Powers and Markos Kounalakis. Washington, DC: Advisory Commission on Public Diplomacy, 2017.

Worth, Robert F. "How a Single Match Can Ignite a Revolution." *New York Times*, January 21, 2011.

———. "Mohammed bin Zayed's Dark Vision of the Middle East's Future." *New York Times*, January 9, 2020.

Wright, Quincy. *A Study of War*. Chicago: University of Chicago Press, 1942.

Wright, Robin. "Trump Drops the Mother of All Bombs on Afghanistan." *New Yorker*, April 14, 2017.

Young, Karen. *The Political Economy of Energy, Finance and Security in the United Arab Emirates*. London: Palgrave, 2014.

Young, Zachary. "French Parliament Passes Law against 'Fake News.'" *Politico*, April 7, 2018.

Youssef, Adham, and Ruth Michaelson. "Egypt Sentences 75 Muslim Brotherhood Supporters to Death." *Guardian*, September 8, 2018.

Zayani, Mohammad. *Arab Satellite Television and Politics in the Middle East*. Abu Dhabi: Emirates Center for Strategic Studies and Research, 2004.

Zetter, Lionel. *Lobbying: The Art of Political Persuasion*. 3rd ed. Bedford, UK: Harriman House, 2014.

Ziv, Amitai. "Mysterious UAE Cyber Firm Luring Ex-Israeli Intel Officers with Astronomical Salaries." *Haaretz*, October 16, 2019.

Zollner, Barbara. "Surviving Repression: How Egypt's Muslim Brotherhood Has Carried On." Carnegie Middle East Center, March 11, 2019.

INDEX

ABOUT THE AUTHOR

Andreas Krieg is an associate professor of security studies at King's College London and is currently temporarily assigned to the Royal College of Defence Studies, where he applies his subject matter expertise to professional military and diplomatic education. In his research, he has focused on a range of different subjects relating to the academic discipline of security studies within a geostrategic context of the Middle East and North Africa. In particular, he is currently interested in the evolution of statecraft and strategic affairs in the twenty-first century as states increasingly delegate governmental functions to nonstate actors to achieve political ends. His 2019 coauthored book, *Surrogate Warfare: The Transformation of War in the Twenty-First Century* (Georgetown University Press, 2019), explores security assemblages between state and nonstate actors on the military and digital battlefields. Outside academia, he works as a geostrategic consultant through his London-based political risk firm, MENA analytica Ltd.